Engineering Manhood

RACE AND THE ANTEBELLUM VIRGINIA MILITARY INSTITUTE

Jonson Miller

LEVER PRESS

Lever Press (leverpress.org) is a publisher of pathbreaking scholarship. Supported by a consortium of liberal arts institutions focused on, and renowned for, excellence in both research and teaching, our press is grounded on three essential commitments: to be a digitally native press, to be a peer-reviewed, open access press that charges no fees to either authors or their institutions, and to be a press aligned with the ethos and mission of liberal arts colleges.

The complete manuscript of this work was subjected to a partly closed ("single blind") review process. For more information, please see our Peer Review Commitments and Guidelines at https://www.leverpress.org/peerreview

DOI: https://doi.org/10.3998/mpub.11675767
Print ISBN: 978-1-64315-017-8
Open access ISBN: 978-1-64315-018-5

Library of Congress Control Number: 2019954613

Published in the United States of America by Lever Press, in partnership with Amherst College Press and Michigan Publishing

Contents

Member Institution Acknowledgments

Lever Press is a joint venture. This work was made possible by the generous support of Lever Press member libraries from the following institutions:

Adrian College

Agnes Scott College

Allegheny College

Amherst College

Bard College

Berea College

Bowdoin College

Carleton College

Claremont Graduate
    University

Claremont McKenna College

Clark Atlanta University

Coe College

College of Saint Benedict /
    Saint John's University

The College of Wooster

Denison University

DePauw University

Earlham College

Furman University

Grinnell College

Hamilton College

Harvey Mudd College

Haverford College

Hollins University

Keck Graduate Institute

Kenyon College

Knox College

Lafayette College Library

Lake Forest College

Macalester College

Middlebury College

Morehouse College
Oberlin College
Pitzer College
Pomona College
Rollins College
Santa Clara University
Scripps College
Sewanee: The University of the
    South
Skidmore College
Smith College
Spelman College
St. Lawrence University

St. Olaf College
Susquehanna University
Swarthmore College
Trinity University
Union College
University of Puget Sound
Ursinus College
Vassar College
Washington and Lee
    University
Whitman College
Willamette University
Williams College

List of Figures

INTRODUCTION

On September 2, 1856, more than one hundred young, white Virginia men, mostly in their late teens, gathered at the Virginia Military Institute (VMI). Some of them were sons of prosperous farmers, merchants, and tradesmen. Others were sons of professionals and perhaps even of state legislators. New students, some with hardly any formal education whatsoever, had just arrived in Lexington to join the school. Other students had drilled and studied there nearly every day for up to three years and, in the process, acquired one of the strongest math and science educations available in the United States. All of them gathered that day to hear one of the most dominant figures in their lives address them as they prepared to enter their classrooms for the new academic year.

Superintendent Francis Henney Smith spoke to these cadets to impart the importance of their mission and his high expectations, just as he had done in one form or another every year for the previous sixteen years. Having already described the successes of several graduates, Smith provided an example of a graduate who overcame economic and educational disadvantages to become a successful engineer.

Another youth with scarcely better early opportunities and whose associations at home were little calculated to favor the development of mental or moral worth, enters the Institution shortly after. A boy in age, his deficiencies, in even academic education, well nigh arrested him in his first year's course. He struggles against them. He graduates with distinction in his studies. He teaches for several years with satisfaction to his patrons. He commences the profession of Engineering, and now, after a service of less than 10 years in a public life, is the chief engineer on one of the most important rail-roads of Virginia, exercising an influence and commanding a confidence, inferior to few men in the service of the state.[1]

Smith sought to inspire the new students, to assure them that their merit, not their background, would lead them to success through service to Virginia. They, moreover, could become the equal of any man. Despite the clues and available records, I cannot determine to whom Smith refers; too many graduates fit the description. Regardless, we face more important questions than the identity of this engineer.

How did VMI, a southern educational institution, come to provide education for the sons of white farmers and tradesmen? What does it mean that Smith placed importance on the story of a young man struggling against his station to attain a high status? Why did Smith uphold this man and others, whose accomplishments lay entirely within the realm of civilian work, as successes of a military school? How could Smith consider working as the chief engineer of a private railroad as service to Virginia rather than to personal ambition? The answers to these questions live in the social and political struggles out of which VMI itself emerged. It is there that the identities Smith called upon in his speech and the meaning of engineering at VMI make sense.

Social struggles and the intersecting identities (class, ethnic, gender, professional, racial, etc.) of their participants are inescapably linked. Participants deploy, reshape, and claim or disclaim legitimacy for various identities as part of their struggles. This is true even when the identities are embedded in technical fields, such as engineering, whose members base their professional legitimacy partly on claims to objective knowledge and technical merit. To reveal these processes, I examine the history of VMI from its founding in the 1830s until the eve of the Civil War.

VMI provided one of the earliest and most thorough engineering educations available in antebellum America. It, along with West Point, served as a model for subsequent schools that spread throughout the South before the Civil War. It was, in all of the United States, the single most influential site of school training for engineers outside of West Point. The officers of the school created a particular sense of what an engineer knew, what an engineer did, and who an engineer was. They created a curriculum, a disciplinary system, and an academic culture for the students, all of which contributed to an engineering identity, but there was nothing straightforward about the academic decisions the officers made. The creation of any identity is an ongoing process that requires effort and occurs in intersecting fields of struggle with several groups of actors.

At VMI, identity formation occurred in the context of struggles for economic gain and political power between overlapping class, ethnic, and regional constituencies across Virginia. The founders and advocates of the school used it as a means of gaining political power in Virginia through the enfranchisement of all white men. With this power, Virginia's emerging middle class and the largely Scots-Irish men of western Virginia would create state-supported infrastructure projects to expand the market economy in western Virginia and to diversify the economy of Virginia in general. The role of VMI would be to create a new objective, disinterested, universal servant-leader to reshape Virginia's politics and economy. Although the founders and advocates largely failed to achieve their political goals, the actors deployed identities, including competing white manhoods, as tools in these struggles. Inescapably, by deploying identity the way they did, they also legitimized some expressions of identity within engineering while delegitimizing others. One consequence was that the actors made it impossible for themselves to see women, black men, and even many white men as potential engineers. We cannot separate identity from broader cultural, economic, political, or social struggles. It is only in the context of those struggles that identities, technical or otherwise, make sense. The identities and the struggles were one.

To understand the political struggles of the officers of VMI, I find myself necessarily dealing with intersecting identities of the participants, including class, ethnic, gender, racial, and regional identities. Intersectional theory, especially as it emerged out of critical race theory, feminist theory, and political movements, helps us to understand the relations between these seemingly distinct identities that come together in individuals. Intersectional theorists debate whether intersectionality is about the identities of individuals or structures of power or whether there is no distinction between the two.[2] Regardless, for understanding how both identity and power operated at antebellum VMI, psychologist Stephanie Shields's definition is useful. She argues that intersectionality claims that identities, "which serve as organizing features of social relations," are not distinct and separate; they "mutually constitute, reinforce, and naturalize one another." We practice, rather than receive, "each aspect of identity as informed by other identities we claim." Moreover, "identities in one category come to be seen as self-evident or 'basic' through the lens of another category."[3]

An examination of racial categories and the way people talked about gender categories in the past reveals that these categories are not self-evident or natural even on their own, let alone in relation to other categories of identity. I do not employ the terms *white* or *manhood* in a way that assumes any single meaning. In fact, I focus much attention on conflicting senses of white manhood that provided an important context for the founding of VMI and that directly contributed to the meaning and purpose of an engineer held by the school's officers. I reject *white* and *white manhood* as a priori terms of analysis and employ them instead as concepts and identities that require historical explanation.

Sociologist Michael Kimmel acknowledges that most of the history written about the United States has been about men and their activities, but, he argues, "such works do not explore how the experience of being a man, of *manhood*, structured the lives of the men who are their subjects, the organizations and institutions they created and staffed, the events in which they participated. American men have no history of themselves *as men*."[4] The latter part is no longer true; there has been much research by historians and sociologists on American men *as men*.[5] What all of this research makes clear is that there is no single experience of manhood. At any given time, a man's class, race, sexuality, and the region in which he was born or lived shapes his experience of his manhood. Consequently, social theorists speak not of masculinity but of plural masculinities in recognition of the fact that no single meaning or experience of manhood exists.[6]

This is not to say that men from differing backgrounds are not often confronted by a common dominant expression of masculinity, to which they may or may not measure up. But even when this is the case, that dominant meaning of American manhood changes over time. Illustrating this point, historian Anthony Rotundo maps out the transformation of a dominant masculinity among the middle or middling classes of the North. It began with what he calls "communal manhood" in New England up through the early eighteenth century. In this masculinity, one's manhood was defined by duty to the community and control over one's passions. From the late eighteenth to the early nineteenth centuries, a "self-made manhood" developed in response to the growth of the market economy. Men then defined themselves by their individual accomplishments, rather than their duty to the community, and valued their passions as the driver for their accomplishments. This self-made manhood was succeeded by a "passionate manhood" that valued aggression, toughness, virility, consumption, and leisure.[7] Variation in experiences with and meanings of masculinity between men and across time reveals that we cannot take masculinity for granted.

Just as gender and masculinity in America have a history and constantly change, so too do race as a taxonomical system and whiteness as a particular category in that system. Americans established basic racial categories, especially black, Indian, and white, before the 1830s, with whiteness constructed primarily in opposition to blackness and Indianness. White Americans, however, continued to maintain fluid boundaries for those categories and had no fixed conceptualization of race itself as a category. Nonetheless, prior to the 1840s, white appears to have included largely the same peoples included under white today, given its construction in relation to American Indians and black people. For example, Jews, often excluded from whiteness later, counted as white for purposes of obtaining citizenship. However, they still generally experienced discrimination and limitations because of their Jewish identity. English, French, Scots-Irish, and Welsh people counted as white. By the 1840s, Irish people, at least in the urban North, often lived outside or at least uncomfortably with whiteness, living side-by-side with black Americans and, along with them, experienced violence at the hands of white rioters, as well as engaging in their own violence against black people.[8]

At antebellum VMI, the identities of engineer, Virginian, white, and man reinforced and gave meaning to one another. For example, by challenging one practice of manhood, they sought to change the meaning of whiteness and to do so in ways that supported their attempts to gain political power. These differing aspects of identity also naturalized one another in order to produce a universal and disinterested identity–no longer ethnic or regional—for the new servant-leaders who were to wield power in Virginia.

Historian Nikhil Singh provides powerful insight about universalizing identities. He analyzes claims about American exceptionalism and how a universal American identity based on civic values, such as a commitment to our constitutional order rather than ethnicity, can supposedly "overcome racial division and racism." However, such universalism is, historically, actually "implicated in creating and sustaining racial division" because American claims to universalism always and necessarily excluded some people. Most significantly, "The ability to leave oneself behind and enter into the national abstraction was to be the property of particular subjects and unavailable to others." The supposedly universal American identity that welcomed anyone was actually "depending on a prior order of ascription."[9] In other words, you had to already be a particular kind of person to participate in this supposed universal American identity. Although the types of Europeans seen as capable of or participating in American identity varied over time, black people were always excluded. Likewise, at VMI, the disinterested and universal engineer and servant-leader presupposed being a particular kind of white man and to necessarily be neither a woman nor black nor Indian. So, the officers of VMI simultaneously advocated a new egalitarianism of white men competing with one another on the basis of merit and reinforced white supremacy. Being an engineer meant being a particular kind of man. It did not just happen to be that cadets at VMI or engineers-to-be were white men; it was necessary that they be so.

ACCESS AND POWER IN ENGINEERING

The structuring of American engineering as the domain of white men is not just something of the past. Just as officers of VMI insisted that engineers be particular kinds of people, so do engineers today. Although post–World War II civil rights and feminist movements transformed higher education and opened up the professions, engineering has been particularly resistant to the inclusion of women and minorities in America and elsewhere. Anthropologists, historians, and sociologists of engineering and technology have increased their efforts in the last twenty years to understand the origins of this exclusion, with most of the effort going toward understanding the exclusion of women. This research has gone beyond the examination of structural (economic and legal) barriers. Identity, including gender and racial identities, are central concerns of the new research. Moreover, scholars have recognized that identity isn't just a stable marker that admits some and excludes others; it is something that participants in the field create, perform, and fight over. These identity struggles occur in the interpersonal dynamics of the classroom and workplace and also in fights over the structural barriers themselves. The result has been the maintenance of a narrow community of practitioners who, along with their employers and government, get to make decisions about what counts as engineering, what engineering is for, what problems it solves, how it defines problems in the first place, and, consequently, who benefits from engineering.

Today women earn 57 percent of bachelor's degrees but constitute only one-third of doctors and lawyers in the United States. However, they do constitute one-half of *new* doctors and lawyers. But, in 2011, women earned just 17 percent of American bachelor's degrees awarded in engineering, and, in 2009, women constituted only 13 percent of the tenured and tenure-track engineering faculty. Moreover, women constituted just 13.3 percent of full-time working engineers between 2012 and 2016. Underrepresented minorities (African Americans, non-white Hispanics, and American Indians), who are 30 percent of the overall American population and 36 percent of the traditional college-aged population, earn 20 percent of bachelor's degrees and constitute fewer than 12 percent of lawyers. Underrepresented minorities earned only 12 percent of bachelor's degrees awarded in engineering in 2011 and, in 2009, constituted just 6 percent of the tenured and tenure-track faculty. Between 2012 and 2016, only 12.7 percent of working engineers were underrepresented minorities. African Americans, who constituted 12 percent of the population, earned just 4 percent of 2011 bachelor's degrees in engineering and constituted just 5.1 percent of working engineers.[10]

Research on the origins of underrepresentation has identified the importance of gendered and racialized interpersonal dynamics and the efforts of engineers to code engineering work as masculine and white. Historian Ruth Oldenziel writes, "[American] engineers built bridges. They also constructed cultural infrastructures and engaged in narrative productions. Strategies of professionalization, the compilation of encyclopedias, the writing of autobiographies, the singing of songs, and the telling of jokes were all part and parcel of the cultural work of maintaining engineering as a male occupation."[11]

The same was true of American engineering schools following World War II. Historian Amy Sue Bix documents men's harassment of women and questioning of their place in those institutions that "often made women feel like uninvited intruders in classrooms, laboratories, and residence halls." Men's behavior and a "chain of gender stereotypes" tried to place women into one of two roles, either as "normal" women, for whom engineering was not a proper course and were therefore just looking for husbands, or as "not 'proper'" women, whom men could insult as unattractive. In either case, men could see engineering education as "wasted on women" and not have to take women seriously as either engineering students or as future professional engineers.[12] The particular traits of white manhood are performed as part of the interpersonal dynamics of engineers in both classrooms and the workplace. Unsurprisingly, white male engineers may not see women and minorities as potential engineers and may exclude them from the informal networks that are often important for educational and professional advancement.[13]

Science and technology studies scholar Wendy Faulkner argues that we must "find out more about the men and masculinities of engineering" if we are to understand the exclusion of women and minorities.[14] Notice her use of the plural *masculinities*, reminding us that masculinity, as well as femininity, is heterogeneous. She reveals in her ethnographic work that different masculinities are performed in different contexts, such as different stages of one's career or in different companies or fields. Moreover, not all men are comfortable or successful with all or any of these masculinities. By using a simple masculine/feminine binary when studying the gendered dynamics of engineering, we may hide important dynamics that exist between men. Male engineers respond to and participate in gender identities even in all-male environments.[15]

Oldenziel and Lisa Frehill point out that when examining the question of the participation of women and minorities in engineering, we must not take for granted who counts as an engineer. During the twentieth century, the definition of who was an engineer in America was deliberately defined in ways that excluded the technical work done by women that still contributed to engineering projects. Such work included "lab assistants, draftsmen, chemists, detailers, checkers, tracers, and testing technicians." Middle-class professional engineers deliberately crafted the definition of engineer to exclude women, as well as lower-class men, in order to increase the professional status of engineering.[16]

Such stratification of technical work has also occurred in the context of making engineering more "democratic." Sally Hacker documents a century of debate about the inclusion of calculus in American engineering education. Engineering educators, as well as students, have recognized, and still do, the role of mathematics and, in particular, mathematics examinations in "weeding out" students from engineering. Some educators expressed hope that an emphasis on mathematics would result in more objective evaluation of students that would not privilege wealthier or more connected students. It didn't work. In the late nineteenth and early twentieth centuries, some engineers expressed concern that the

use of calculus as a filter was unnecessarily excluding less prepared, less elite men from engineering and, by drawing on data
from employers of engineers, argued that grades in engineering
courses did not correspond to the competence and success of engineers at work. Course grades did not capture the qualities that
made a good engineer. Nonetheless, calculus exams became and
remained the primary differentiator between technical workers
and the engineers who managed them. Professional organizations
and engineering programs insisted upon maintaining calculus in
order to maintain the higher professional status of engineering. As
more women trained and went to work as engineers in the 1970s
and 1980s, they were "actively recruited for the lower levels" that
paid less, such as drafting.[17]

Even trying to count the number of men and women in engineering, as I've done above, is not an innocent act; some technical workers were able to define engineering in a way that avoided
counting women, as well as black and lower-class men. The way I
counted engineers above takes for granted the class-, gender-, and
race-laden definition created through the exertion of power by one
segment of technical workers to serve their own interests.

Since the early nineteenth century, white politicians and educators deliberately segregated education in ways that largely excluded
women and minorities from engineering. My own employer
Drexel University is typical of American technical schools.[18]
Although admitting women to the school since its founding in
1891, it excluded women from the engineering program until 1943,
when Drexel responded to wartime needs and the decline of men's
enrollment by admitting women to engineering.[19] The University
of Maryland system provided racially segregated education for
black and white people until its implementation of the 1954 *Brown
vs. Board of Education* decision. The state concentrated engineering education at the white College Park campus, while it focused
the black Eastern Shore campus on agriculture and the trades. This
segregation created a two-tiered system of technical training, with

white people on track to become professionals and black people on track to become technicians and tradesmen.[20]

As historian Amy Slaton shows, even integrated school systems of Chicago in the 1960s served to segregate engineering and technical training through other means. Like other schools in that era, the Illinois Institute of Technology and the University of Illinois in Chicago responded to increased educational opportunities for minorities. But many engineering educators associated that expansion with the lowering of standards, which they saw as a danger to the field of engineering. They argued that the place for working toward greater inclusion was in primary and secondary education, not higher education. Minority students needed to be as fully prepared as their white counterparts before arriving in engineering programs. Early life experiences and education were the problem and where the solutions had to be implemented. The result was that, just like in Jim Crow–era Maryland, Illinois created a vision of a two-tiered system in which, as articulated by a City of Chicago commission, "young minority men would contribute to Chicago industry: as 'competent repairmen and mechanics to service new [aerospace and data-processing] equipment,'" whereas young white men and "a few high-achieving black students would graduate into engineering positions."[21]

Part of what was at stake in American engineering was "rigor." Engineering educators demanded that their programs remain rigorous, defined in a narrow way that emphasized the admission of, as Slaton observes, "qualified, rather than qualifiable, students," thereby exempting engineering programs "from the work of bringing disadvantaged students up to speed academically." Engineering educators and policymakers across America, both during and after the era of educational segregation, viewed merit and the ability to meet rigorous academic standards as a moral capacity of white and perhaps a few black people. In other words, they saw not mere academic qualities but also moral qualities, which were unevenly distributed among white and black people, as markers of potential engineers. Black students remained largely invisible as potential engineers.[22]

Marie Hicks documents the transformation of the labor force in British computing in the 1960s. Like in the United States, women tended to dominate the programming and operation of computers. As part of an effort to modernize British industry and reverse the decline of Britain's global preeminence in computing, the government facilitated the masculinization of the field. The effort at modernization failed, and it failed because of British industry's unwillingness to draw fully on the expertise of women in the industry. Discrimination against women in hiring and promotion wasn't just about gender. The shift to male computers was also about "powerful ideas about women's sexuality. Assumptions that women's lives would be defined by heterosexuality in ways that required them to leave the work force made work outside the home secondary to the dictates of marriage, procreation, and family." She argues, "sexuality, the organization of labor markets, and the functioning of the economy as a whole became inextricably linked." Employers and government also defined female operators and programmers in terms of dis/ability, class, nationality, and race. These categories mutually reinforced one another to impose an identity for workers that then explained the discrimination against them. It defined "women's economic position as lower than men's, and in making women's economic lives secondary for most of the twentieth century."[23]

Engineers have to be people. So, the officers of VMI had, inescapably, to make claims about who their students were and who they were to be as engineers. They had, in other words, to contend with identity. But, in defining engineers as certain types of people, they excluded others. These choices make sense only in the context of the political and social struggles in which the participants were engaged. The identities and struggles mutually constituted one another. This was true in antebellum America; it is true today.

IDENTITY AND KNOWLEDGE IN ENGINEERING

It is not just the identities of engineers that matters; engineering knowledge matters as well. We should not take it for granted that engineers will know certain things. Indeed, the histories and even current practices of engineers of different countries reveal that engineers approach their work in a great variety of ways and with sometimes very different types of knowledge.[24] By denaturalizing the contents of their knowledge and understanding the processes by which a community of engineers recognizes certain types of knowledge as authoritative, we can gain insight into what it means to be an engineer in a particular time and place and in what fields of struggle for authority they were engaged. The identities of engineers, the contents of engineering knowledge, and struggles for political or professional authority are intertwined.

Engineering studies scholars Gary Downey and Juan Lucena argue, "what counts as engineering knowledge and what counts as an engineer are linked tightly together."[25] Downey and Lucena describe efforts of engineers from several countries and at different times to, in response to challenges from outside their field, assert their relevance to their nations by changing what counted as engineering knowledge. Changing the contents of this knowledge, often through reforming engineering education, was a common part of the strategy. For example, in response to the growing acceptance of industrial improvement and expansion as expressions of progress in Germany in the early twentieth century, German engineers created a new tier of engineering schools, the *Fachhochschulen*, or institutes of specialized higher education, that were more focused on making practical contributions to industry than were the older, more theoretical higher technical institutes. Engineers of the new schools accepted the philosopher Hegel's concept of progress as the emancipation of an innate German spirit that was the driving force of history for an idealized German people. As engineers, they were to participate in the emancipation of that spirit through quality production. They were to produce not just locomotives but German locomotives that expressed this spirit. To produce quality goods that represented this spirit, the schools emphasized "gaining a feel" for the materials with which they were to work, thus providing the students with a more intuitive knowledge than the theoretical knowledge of engineers of the higher technical institutes. In this case, a community of German engineers reorganized their educational institutions and changed what counted as engineering knowledge in order to position engineers as the bearers of progress within German society, all in order to elevate their professional status and authority.[26]

American engineers also employed particular types of knowledge in the nineteenth and twentieth centuries to exclude those—women and black people—whose presence in the field would, engineers feared, diminish the status of engineering.[27] Into the early nineteenth century, technical work and "useful knowledge" were the domains of all Americans—men and women, black and white people. The knowledge women and girls applied in the home to, for example, make clothing counted as useful knowledge just as much as the knowledge men applied in metalworking. The white men who were carving out a middle-class space for engineering professionalized their field partly by emphasizing the role of particular forms of knowledge, such as mathematics and science, in their work. They laid claim not to useful knowledge but to "applied science" and "technology," creating a tiered system of technical work. In this system, women and male artisans were in the lower tier, and middle-class white men occupied the upper tier, with its exclusive claim to being "engineering." White, middle-class men had to do what Oldenziel calls the "cultural work" of maintaining these boundaries of engineering, with women and black and lower-class men contesting those boundaries all along.[28] As discussed in the previous section, Slaton shows how twentieth-century institutions of higher education created two-tiered systems in which the one for white men tended to count as professional engineering, while the one for black men tended to count as technical labor, each with distinct and ranked bodies of knowledge.

The work of Downey, Frehill, Lucena, Oldenziel, and Slaton reveals that the contents of knowledge within a field can indicate what it means to be a participant in that field and who gets to participate in the field. Engineering knowledge is used not just to solve what appear to be purely technical engineering problems but also to achieve authority, both within the field of engineering and outside of it. So, in order to understand the fields of struggles in which the officers of VMI were engaged, we must examine what they imparted to their students as authoritative knowledge. Moreover, we must also examine *how* they imparted that knowledge. Engineering educators can use pedagogy and discipline, like the curriculum itself, to claim authority. From both the contents of the knowledge and its means of transmission, we might understand in what fields the officers were trying to claim authority and for what purposes they wanted to wield that authority.

Alice Pawley and Donna Riley direct us to the consequences of these decisions about what counts as engineering as well as intersecting decisions about who counts as an engineer. They document the fuzzy, inconsistent, and context-dependent boundaries that engineers draw around what counts as engineering and what does not in America. Despite the emergence of new fields of engineering and regardless of the variety of work that engineers actually do, engineers tend to define engineering as associated with heavy machinery, large-scale infrastructure and construction, and military technology.[29] Engineers also tend to define their work in terms of problem-solving, but they do so in narrow ways. For example, engineering problem-solving may include "improving the quality of working life" but only when the work done in that life is paid labor, thus excluding the unpaid work that is more often associated with the domestic work of women and the poor.[30] Moreover, engineers tend to define and solve problems in purely technical terms and through expert calculation and quantification.

Perceived in this way, problem-solving tends to exclude all else, including social relations between the people defining or experiencing the problem and "even basic compassion."[31]

Narrow definitions of what counts as engineering, an engineering problem, and an engineer have consequences that "weigh differently on women than men." American engineering tends to define and solve problems in ways that disproportionately benefit men and the wealthy.[32] Moreover, Pawley and Riley consider how narrow conceptions of engineering haven't just historically excluded work done by women and minorities that might otherwise count as engineering but also that what has come to count as engineering problems is itself unattractive to women and minorities. Riley argues that the underrepresentation of women and minorities is the wrong question. Instead, the question of what engineering is for is the real problem. Black people and American Indians, for example, have historically been the targets of science and technology in the contexts of colonialism, slavery, unethical medical experiments, and war. Changing or even broadening the very purpose of engineering might open up the field to presently underrepresented people.[33]

It is not an accident or happenstance that American engineering is so disproportionately male and white; it took much work to create this situation. There have been and are economic, legal, and other structural barriers that have limited the participation of women and minorities. But beyond intersecting with, and constituting those other structural elements, engineers work to maintain professional identities that continually reproduce white manhoods of engineering. To understand ongoing disparities in American engineering we must, therefore, understand the processes by which engineering communities create those identities. I'm not arguing that engineering communities today simply inherited gendered and racialized engineering identities of the past. Instead, I examine how engineers and their communities create and maintain identities in unique contexts that give meaning to those identities.

The officers of VMI deliberately crafted a particular white manhood for their cadets. VMI developed in the context of a struggle to redefine white manhood in order to gain political power. Consequently, it didn't just happen to be that engineers from VMI were white men just because that's how things were back then; if men were to carry out their roles in a broader political struggle, it was necessary that they be particular kinds of white men. Were they not so, their purpose in larger struggles for political power would make no sense. Again, there is no separation between social or political struggles and the identities of the participants. Participants deploy and reshape identities as part of the struggles. They make sense of their identities in the context of the struggles. So, we too must understand their identities if we are to understand their struggles.

NARRATIVE OUTLINE

Before beginning my analysis of identity construction, social struggle, and engineering at VMI, I must first identify the context and significance of the school. Chapter 1 describes the kind of place VMI was and what kind of students went there. It also places VMI in the broader context of antebellum engineering. Most engineers learned on the job, but a minority of them trained in formal engineering programs at institutions of higher education. VMI, along with all other southern military schools, is little discussed in the history of formal engineering education, which is dominated by references to Norwich University, Rennselaer Polytechnic Institute, and West Point. However, VMI was in fact second only to West Point in both the thoroughness of its curriculum and in the number of working engineers it trained in the period.

Chapter 2 identifies the immediate context out of which VMI emerged. The largely English-descended planters east of the Blue Ridge Mountains dominated political power in Virginia. They exerted their control partly by restricting suffrage to land- and slave-owning white men, which disproportionately disenfran-chised the largely Scots-Irish men of western Virginia. The people of western Virginia wanted state investment in internal improve-ments, particularly roads and canals, to facilitate the expansion of the market economy. Eastern planters, living along some of the best navigable waterways in the country, had little need of such invest-ment, which they themselves would pay for through taxes on their land and slaves. Consequently, the planters rejected most efforts at improvements. Western Virginians responded with demands for a new state constitution that included universal enfranchisement of white men, which would enable them to gain the improvements they desired. But the planters dominated the constitutional con-vention of 1829, leaving westerners still largely disenfranchised. Leaders of Rockbridge County, the future home of VMI, responded by calling for a new institution of higher education that would serve white boys of the lower classes who would not typically be able to go to the liberal colleges. Their purpose was to use educa-tion as a means of demonstrating the merit of poorer white men and, thereby, legitimize the equality of white men and challenge the aristocratic republicanism that denied universal white man-hood suffrage. For unclear reasons, the state legislature funded the proposal. This political context established VMI as an institution that cultivated an ethic of meritocratic competition among equal white men.

It was not until after the founding legislation was passed that the school became identified with engineering. Chapter 3 focuses on the intervention of a northern education reform activist, the Virginia state engineer, and the hiring as superintendent of a West Point–trained engineer and educator. Their efforts resulted in VMI adopting not just an engineering curriculum but, more specifically, the math- and science-intensive approach to engineering typical of state engineering schools of France and West Point. VMI's gov-erning board and superintendent also adopted the disciplinary sys-tems of those schools, which emphasized quantitative measuring of both academic and disciplinary merit. This system provided the means for facilitating and demonstrating the meritocratic competition that VMI's officers created for their institution and hoped to scale up to Virginia society as a whole.

Chapter 4 provides a detailed description and analysis of the pedagogical methods and curriculum of VMI. There was nothing neutral or natural about this curriculum. It offered a particular type of engineering knowledge, one grounded in the theoretically oriented curriculum of West Point and French state engineering schools, rather than the empirical, rule-of-thumb approaches of most American engineers. The officers of VMI employed the curriculum to serve their own needs. First, the mathematical and scientific curriculum did not require knowledge of Greek and Latin, which made the school accessible to boys of a class that tended not to have the classical education necessary for admission to liberal colleges. Second, a distinct curriculum and pedagogy provided VMI with an alternative form of authority upon which to compete with established colleges. Some of the school's officers argued not just for the legitimacy of their new form of education but also for its superiority over the colleges that eastern planters sent their boys to.

At VMI, engineers were supposed to know math and science. Chapter 5 then examines what they were to do with that knowledge. The officers of the school promoted engineering, as well as education, as a disinterested profession of service, service to a middle-class articulation of the interests of the state. The graduates were to go on to become servants to, but also leaders of, Virginia. They would do so by using their engineering knowledge not for personal ambition but to contribute to the "physical progress" of Virginia. This meant building transportation infrastructure and cultivating the natural resources of the state to open up its productive potential and diversify the economy beyond cash crops cultivated by slave labor. In so doing, Virginia could once again take its rightful position as an economic and political leader of the country, a position from which the state fell under the leadership of the planters. Graduates of VMI, as engineers and teachers, were to become servant-leaders of the state within a more rational and meritocratic social order for equal white men.

To carry out the disinterested service described above, VMI's officers had to transform their students into particular kinds of white men. Chapter 6 describes that transformation. Not everyone was capable of serving. They had to possess character traits valued by the emerging middle class: industriousness, self-discipline, honor, and obedience to lawful authority. By being capable of submitting to authority and mastering themselves, they would demonstrate the republican quality of public virtue or independence deemed necessary for participation in governance. Class and property ownership were not, they argued, the markers of virtue. Instead, these qualities could be found in white men of any class. They could not, however, be found among black people or women, who were constitutionally incapable of independence and had to remain subordinate to white men. If engineering meant disinterested service to the state, then, for the officers of VMI, engineers had to be white men. Moreover, they had to be particular kinds of white men.

VMI and the intersecting identities the school's officers cultivated emerged out of a particular struggle for political power in Virginia, a struggle that pitted Scots-Irish men of western Virginia against English men of eastern Virginia, the emerging middle class against the planter elite. The 1850 constitutional convention finally provided voting rights for all white men and resolved some of the conflicts out of which VMI emerged. Moreover, the coming of North-South tensions that ultimately led to secession and civil war strained the alliances and identities cultivated at VMI. Chapter 7 describes the changing political context that forced changes in identity and the meaning of VMI. Prior to the 1850s, the discipline of the school served to suppress ethnic differences among students in order to cultivate a supposedly universal Virginia identity. But

North-South tensions provoked conflicts over secession and slavery. The Scots-Irish officers, students, and townspeople had somewhat turned against slavery and opposed secession. Universality was now harder to claim.

The coming of the war and ongoing east-west tensions resulted in the splitting of Virginia, leaving VMI no longer an institution promoting the interests of the middle class and the Scots-Irish, the majority of whom seceded to form West Virginia. Instead, it was now a military training ground for a Virginia populated mostly by English-descended white people and enslaved black people. The old alliance between middle-class English, on the one hand, and Scots-Irish school officers, on the other, broke down. The old identities the school cultivated ceased to make sense in the context of new struggles. Consequently, identities had to change. Following the war and abolition, VMI became an institution promoting the "lost cause" myth. The men of VMI, as well as other southern military schools, became symbols of the ideal man. They were courageous and virtuous white southern men who had tried but failed to defend the independence of the South against a rapacious North.

Historians of engineering have produced a substantial literature on how engineers draw on their national identities to legitimize their field. Fewer historians have examined intersecting identities of engineers. By leaving the national scale and analyzing the cultivation of engineering at a very local level, we can see how engineers and their advocates brought together and transformed multiple, mutually reinforcing identities to create a new type of person, a new type of engineer, a new type of servant-leader for Virginia. The officers of the school deployed these men with their intersecting identities as weapons in a struggle for political power. It is only in the context of that struggle that the particular constellation of identities makes sense. This book does not and cannot make the argument that VMI produced a particular link between white manhood and engineering that then spread and explains the present. Instead, through this case, we see that identities are particular to the struggles in which they are embedded, whether those are struggles for professional authority, political power, or whatever else. As circumstances change, engineers reconstitute their professional identities within the context of their other shifting and intersecting identities. As they engage in these struggles, engineers also reconstitute engineering knowledge, the purpose of engineering, who can be seen as an engineer, and who benefits from engineering.

CHAPTER ONE

VMI

Challenging the Northern Story of Antebellum Engineering

The Virginia Military Institute (VMI) opened in 1839, a time when American men could take one of several paths into professional engineering. Each path brought with it differing expectations of what an engineer was supposed to know, do, and be. Scholars often frame their discussion of these paths in terms of an American inheritance and reshaping of an initially dominant British tradition of on-the-job training and a French tradition of theoretical training in formal schools that began in America with West Point after the War of 1812. VMI and the rest of the southern military school tradition are identified, properly so, with the French tradition.[1] Before the Civil War, every southern state possessed at least one public military school and, including private schools, founded more than eighty schools that trained 11,000 young men by 1861. Most of the public schools recognized VMI as a model.[2]

The size and scope of the southern military school tradition suggests that VMI and its French "inheritance" was a significant contributor to early American engineering. In fact, I argue that it was the second greatest contributor of school-trained, working engineers, second only to West Point. Nonetheless, historians of engineering have overlooked or downplayed the significance of VMI and other southern military schools in favor of northern schools, especially Norwich University, Rensselaer Institute, and West Point. Given the number of engineers it trained and its influence on other military schools, VMI challenges this North-oriented historiographic norm. Moreover, these numbers and VMI's influence make the school a worthy place to begin a study of white manhood in antebellum engineering.

ENGINEERING IN THE EARLY REPUBLIC AND ANTEBELLUM AMERICA

Before the 1850s, engineering meant primarily civil engineering but also mining engineering and military engineering and the rare use of the term *engineer* for men in charge of steam engines, especially on US Navy ships. Civil engineers, or at least those people recognized as such, were primarily transportation project planners, managers, and consultants.

A principal job of an early-nineteenth-century civil engineer was to determine the feasibility of proposals and then plan and manage projects. Community leaders might have formed a corporation to build a turnpike to connect two towns, for example, but then might have hired an engineer for objective oversight, both to determine whether the project was feasible and to ensure against corruption of the project by particular local interests. Historian Daniel Hovey Calhoun describes an idealized work process of an engineer as follows: (1) The chief engineer would determine the best route or location for the project. (2) The chief would report to the governing corporation on how best to proceed and on costs and perhaps even suggest a railroad instead of a canal or a road instead of a canal. (3) The chief would develop detailed plans. (4)

The chief would make recommendations and offer advice on contracting labor for the actual construction. And (5) the chief and possibly assistant engineers would inspect the work to ensure that it was done as specified. Notice that this process kept the chief engineer and the contracting of labor separate, thus limiting the possibility that engineers would cut corners. In other cases, such as the Erie Canal project, engineers engaged in direct management of labor. Either way, engineers saw themselves as independent professionals rather than as employees.[3]

Engineering practice was often not so professional or formal as described above. In Virginia, for example, the only formal engineer involved in a road project was often the state engineer who offered advice and did inspections regarding routes, grades, surfacing, and so forth, but had no actual authority to enforce good engineering practices. Claudius Crozet, the founding president of VMI's Board of Visitors, was one such longtime state engineer. In Virginia, a turnpike company would locate the route, estimate the costs, and then directly contract out to a builder, with all aspects often done poorly. Roads often ended up longer than needed, had grades too steep to allow heavy shipping, or were insufficiently surfaced to allow usage in wet periods. There was little the state engineer could do about it. As historian Robert Hunter said of the state engineer's job, it was "thankless and frustrating." The person responsible for obtaining labor for projects varied. Often it was either the builder or the company.[4] The state engineer, however, could be directly involved when it came to the leasing or purchasing of enslaved laborers, who might be owned directly by the state. Crozet himself made recommendations for the acquisition of enslaved workers.[5]

Historian John Rae analyzed biographical data on possible engineers in the United States up to 1860. He found sufficient information on 1,672 men to draw some conclusions about their social backgrounds. Eighty-five percent of them were born in the United States, with just 15 percent, including French-born Crozet, coming from other countries, all but 2 percent being from Europe. The data is incomplete, but Rae estimates that between one-half and three-fourths of engineers came from the middle or upper classes. The fathers of these men were planters, businessmen, financiers, professionals, military officers, or engineers. The fathers of the others were more likely to be farmers than to be laborers or even craftsmen.[6]

What we might now, looking back, think of as mechanical engineering was carried out in the early nineteenth century by people who generally called themselves mechanics. It was only in the 1850s that a subset of these mechanics created a professional elite that referred to themselves as mechanical engineers.[7] These mechanics primarily came from either the US Navy, where they were needed for boilers in the new steamships, or else worked in machine shops producing the textile machines at the heart of the Industrial Revolution as well as locomotives and steam engines for boats. US Navy steam engine mechanics had the title of assistant engineer by 1837. From the beginning, the navy offered high status to these men. By the 1840s, they were required to pass exams on their knowledge of relevant scientific principles, mathematics, and mechanics as well as asking about prior work experience in machine or naval shops. The engineers could learn these subjects at the US Naval Academy founded in 1842, though cadets could not formally study steam engineering there until 1866. Nonetheless, these higher-status men were already separating themselves from other mechanics by the 1840s.[8]

From that time and up until the Civil War, machine shops grew in size to include within them foundries, specialized milling machines and lathes, drafting rooms, and managerial offices. As the shops grew in size and complexity, so too did the labor within them. By the 1840s, there opened a divide between labor and management, with the latter increasingly filled with salaried men working under the titles of superintendent or sometimes engineer, while the stratification of labor culminated in the position of master mechanic. It was in railroad companies and shops of the

1850s that men supervising railroad shops and machinery began to call themselves mechanical engineers in order to distinguish themselves from civil engineers but also to claim their middle-class professional status.[9] Nonetheless, at the time of the founding of VMI, *engineer*, in the professional sense, referred exclusively to civil and military engineers.

TRAINING AMERICAN ENGINEERS

VMI opened within a heterogeneous professional culture that left the United States with no single national pattern of engineering training. Men entered engineering through a variety of pathways, including on-the-job training and various academic approaches. Nonetheless, in the period prior to the opening of VMI in 1839, the country possessed little capacity to train or otherwise obtain engineers. Although foreign engineers played an important role in the development of American engineering, they did not come to the country in any great numbers, despite attempts to recruit them. The United States had few engineering schools and, except for West Point, which provided comprehensive civil and military engineering training, those few offered minimal training and produced few engineers. Most engineers learned their trade through on-the-job craft training under the guidance of more experienced engineers.[10] John Rae estimates that 31.7 percent of engineers trained in an "institute or college of engineering or science" or a "military academy" between 1790 and 1830, though this number nearly doubled between 1830 and 1860. So, in the years before the opening of VMI, almost 70 percent of engineers learned through apprenticeships or on-the-job training, though perhaps supplemented with self-learning or some relevant formal education.[11]

The scale of the Erie Canal project made it an important training ground for American engineers. The first two engineers, James Geddes and Benjamin Wright, knew how to survey but were not trained as engineers to supervise other workers on the project.

Nonetheless, competent engineers were hard to find, so the two men figured it out as they went and gradually promoted men from lower positions as they too learned the work of engineering. A few men began as "axmen" clearing the canal path or as assistants to surveyors, promoted to surveyor, then to assistant engineer. Some assistant engineers became principal or chief engineers, taking over the management of the construction of individual sections of the canal. According to Calhoun, between the start of construction in 1816 and the canal's completion in 1825, forty-three men acquired the rank of assistant engineer and twenty-four became principal engineers, perhaps doubling the number of competent engineers. Many of these men, actively recruited in some cases, went on to lead their own projects elsewhere. While this sort of on-the-job training remained dominant, other engineers took on formal apprentices.[12]

Professional engineering in America began during the Revolutionary War, when the Continental Congress, with the aid of French military engineers, established the Corps of Engineers. Consequently, French engineering knowledge and practice exerted great influence on American engineering, especially through later training of engineers at French-inspired schools, including West Point and VMI. The state engineering schools of France were military schools with uniformed cadets living under military discipline. Students began their studies at the École Polytechnique before going on to more specialized schools. The École Polytechnique was the most prestigious engineering school in France and the world. It emphasized mathematics and science as the theoretical foundation of engineering practice. For them, theory referred to mathematics and the "calculation" of the movements of bodies and mechanical forces as well as of economic factors. To acquire this theoretical knowledge and ability to calculate, engineering students took courses in calculus, descriptive geometry, analytical geometry, chemistry, mechanics, electrical theory, hydrostatics, drawing, and other sciences. Theory was the foundation of their authority, a mark of their superiority over the "practical" knowledge of mechanics or even doctors. Mathematics was not, however, to remain purely abstract; it was to be applied to provide for the needs of the state and the nation. French engineers promoted mathematics and the exact sciences as general, universal, and impartial, which the engineers argued allowed them to engage in large-scale rational planning of society and to confront novel situations that might confound craft- or on-the-job-trained men. Through calculation, the application of theory, they could ideally exert total control over nature and labor in order to reconstruct landscapes to unleash the productive forces of the nation.[13]

Following the American Revolution, the new United States government made permanent the army's artillery and fortifications engineering corps and eventually stationed it at West Point, New York. Congress later transformed the base of the corps into the US Military Academy, which it established to, in part, continue training military engineers. The academy, however, had no formal classes or curriculum until after the War of 1812, when the superintendent endeavored to more explicitly remodel the school after the École Polytechnique. Crozet, who studied at the École Polytechnique, participated in reconstructing the academy's curriculum, particularly its math courses, in order to make them more rigorous and to better conform to that of the École Polytechnique.[14] By 1833, the year in which future VMI superintendent Francis Henney Smith graduated, the West Point curriculum included, along with the expected military studies, civil and military engineering, architecture, mathematics, drawing, natural philosophy, chemistry and mineralogy, rhetoric, moral and political science, and French.[15]

Independent civil engineering developed at the same time as the West Point reforms with large-scale civilian infrastructural projects, including the Erie Canal, whose construction began in 1816. With so few American engineers available and little capacity for formally training new ones, many men learned engineering on the job by advancing from lower labor to higher engineering positions. West Point graduates provided the one substantial source of formally trained engineers for these projects. The academy trained more officers than the US Army could accommodate with posts, so many graduates left the military to apply their training to new transportation projects.[16]

Other formal engineering programs appeared in the 1820s and 1830s. Alden Partridge, a former superintendent and professor of engineering at West Point, founded the American Literary, Scientific, and Military Academy, now Norwich University, in 1820 in Vermont. Partridge intended to use the school to produce citizen-soldiers who also trained as civil engineers.[17] Although based on the West Point model and employing military discipline, Norwich did not offer the intensive and structured engineering training of West Point. Norwich became more of an academy, rather than a college or institute like VMI, and primarily served boys between twelve and eighteen years old. It subsequently functioned largely as a preparatory school. Rather than a rigorous engineering and military training, it offered a mix of liberal arts, classical, scientific, engineering, and military training, from which cadets and their parents could, to a large extent, choose their own course of study. These studies included surveying, algebra, higher math courses, Latin, Greek, philosophy, Spanish, French, topography, and geography. Because of the less-than-universal enthusiasm for engineering among the cadets and their parents, Partridge soon reduced the school's emphasis on engineering but maintained the sciences as the school's strongest department.[18]

The Rensselaer Institute, now the Rensselaer Polytechnic Institute, offered a different approach to formal engineering training. It offered a civil engineering program after 1835 but had offered some surveying and engineering courses to complement the early agricultural emphasis of the school since 1828.[19] In contrast to West Point and Norwich professors, who followed the mathematically oriented model of the École Polytechnique, Amos Eaton, Rensselaer's engineering instructor, argued against teaching much mathematics beyond arithmetic and limited trigonometry.[20] In his own engineering textbook, he didn't use "algebraic expressions . . . because they are unnecessary" and "[i]n truth, our lives our too short to devote much time to speculative mathematics."[21] This changed sometime after Eaton died in 1842. B. Franklin Greene, who became the school's director in 1846, reorganized the curriculum based on those of European technical schools, especially the École Polytechnique and the École Centrale des Arts et Manufactures of France.[22] By at least 1847, Rensselaer students, like VMI students, studied algebra, trigonometry, descriptive geometry, calculus, and other mathematical subjects.[23]

In addition to technical and military schools, traditional colleges and universities also attempted to provide some engineering training. A few schools, including Columbia University, the University of Vermont, the University of Virginia, and Princeton University, offered courses or lecture series beginning in the late 1820s for students interested in gaining some engineering training but not in earning a degree. Students could, however, obtain a certificate in engineering from the University of Virginia after 1836. These engineering courses sometimes consisted only of mathematics and mechanics. Some colleges and universities, including the College of William and Mary, the University of Alabama, and the University of Georgia, offered some engineering courses as electives in traditional degree programs. Consequently, all of these programs served to supplement the craft knowledge and experience of the students rather than to function as a complete training in engineering. These limited courses declined after 1850.[24]

In contrast to today, Americans entered engineering from a variety of pathways, including on-the-job training, self-teaching, one of several academic approaches, or some combination of the three. In this regard, engineering did not necessarily differ from other professions at that time. Also, as with other occupations, becoming an engineer by no means guaranteed that a man would remain an engineer for his entire career. In fact, most did not.[25]

VMI AS AN ENGINEERING SCHOOL

One might describe the VMI of the 1840s and 1850s several different ways. It was certainly a military school in that it employed uniforms, taught military subjects, and used military discipline, all modeled after that of West Point. It was, however, independent of the US Army, and cadets were under no obligation to serve in even the state militia after graduating, as is still the case today. One might also describe VMI as a school offering a mathematical and scientific education. Indeed, it did offer one of the best such educations available in America in the antebellum period. But, as I demonstrate in chapter 3, the founders of the school crafted that curriculum to primarily support a civil and military engineering curriculum. So, while most graduates did not go on to work as professional engineers, we might also call VMI an engineering school. That appears to be how its first president, Claudius Crozet, and superintendent, Francis Henney Smith, viewed the school.

Virginia's state legislature partly justified establishing this public school on the need for a guard for the state militia arsenal in Lexington in what was then central Virginia (see Figure 1.1). They incorporated the arsenal into the school and replaced the existing guard with the school's cadets. The cadets, between the ages of sixteen and twenty-five, lived under military discipline, including the use of uniforms, marching, and the West Point demerit system for enforcing behavior. They underwent military training and studied military subjects alongside their other studies, which were dominated by engineering, mathematics, and various sciences. Unlike at West Point, the cadets were served by enslaved people, either owned directly or rented by the institution.

Two types of students attended the school: state and pay cadets. Students were admitted as state cadets if they demonstrated financial need and sufficient moral standards. VMI was legally required to reserve spots for young men from throughout the state rather than privileging any single region. They paid fees but did not pay

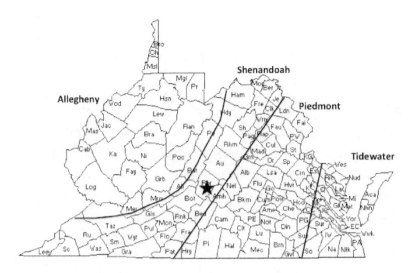

Figure 1.1. Virginia in 1829. County boundaries as they existed at the time of the 1829–1830 constitutional convention. Bold lines show the four constitutional divisions of Virginia. The Blue Ridge Mountains separate the Piedmont and Shenandoah Valley. The star indicates the location of Lexington in Rockbridge County. Note that what is today West Virginia was part of Virginia until 1861.

the more substantial tuition. Pay cadets paid fees and tuition for the privilege of attending. All cadets had to serve as guards of the militia arsenal kept at the school, but state cadets had the additional obligation of teaching for two years in a school in Virginia.

Unlike Norwich, all cadets undertook an identical curriculum. Their courses changed and expanded over the school's first few decades, but the core curriculum consisted of French and Latin, a few liberal arts courses, roughly the same mathematics course available at the École Polytechnique and West Point, chemistry, natural philosophy, statics and dynamics, and civil and military engineering. This was a curriculum that would be roughly familiar to engineering students in the United States today.

The school remained an institution exclusively for white men until 1968, when VMI eliminated race as a formal criterion for admissions and admitted its first black cadet. Even still, it remained an institution for men until 1996, when the US Supreme Court ruled 7-to-1 in favor of a woman who, along with 347 other women, had been rejected by the school on the basis of sex.[26]

SIGNIFICANCE OF VMI AS A SOURCE OF ENGINEERS

VMI was no small school. Even during its first years, its enrollment compared favorably with or even exceeded those of traditional colleges. Around the time VMI opened, Washington College (now Washington and Lee University) had only 3 or 4 students, Hampden-Sydney about 60, the University of Virginia around 191, the University of North Carolina around 89, Princeton 227, and Yale 438 undergraduate students. Many colleges experienced increased enrollments over the following decades. Likewise, VMI grew to 91 cadets in 1845 and 120 in 1850. Meanwhile, Washington College increased rapidly and substantially, with more than 45 in 1849, Hampden-Sydney had around 51, the University of North Carolina grew to 450 by 1861, Princeton grew to probably more than 270, and Yale stayed constant with 432 undergraduates.[27] Throughout the antebellum period, VMI remained larger than Washington College and outpaced Hampden-Sydney. In 1861, almost half of America's colleges had fewer than 100 students and only 16 had more than 200, making VMI larger than average.[28]

Regarding engineering education more specifically, VMI more than matched Rensselaer and Norwich in the number of engineers it trained before the Civil War. Providing a conservative minimum estimate, the *Register of Cadets*, which notes known occupations of former cadets, indicates 47, or 14 percent, of the 338 cadets (graduates or otherwise) from the classes of 1842 to 1851 engaged in some kind of engineering work.[29] Historian Jennifer Green calculates that 10 percent of all southern military school cadets before the Civil War and 14 percent of actual graduates worked as engineers.[30] These numbers, however, underestimate the number given missing data, the number of cadets who taught engineering but are not indicated as having done so, and the number indicated as serving in the military who may have worked as military engineers. VMI superintendent Smith, in an assessment of the work of the 226 graduates up to 1856, noted that at least 59 worked as civil engineers.[31] This amounts to just more than one-quarter of the graduates up through 1856 having worked as civil engineers.

Compared to other antebellum schools, VMI produced a relatively large number of formally trained engineers. By 1837, two years before the first cadets arrived at the VMI, West Point had probably, according to historian Daniel Calhoun, graduated 200 of the civil engineers who worked in America, while Norwich University graduated between 24 and 34, and Rensselaer approximately 24, with another 16 from Norwich and 29 from Rensselaer by 1843.[32] These numbers, however, may overestimate the actual number of students trained in engineering, because Calhoun erroneously identifies Norwich as primarily an engineering school, not recognizing that it served primarily as a boy's academy and that the school did not require the engineering course. Indeed, many parents chose more liberal courses for their sons. Also, graduation from Rensselaer no more indicated that a man went on to work as engineer than did graduation from VMI. However, published lists of Rensselaer graduates and their careers positively identify engineers in roughly the numbers Calhoun gives. By counting, appropriately so, architects, surveyors, teachers of engineering, and those graduates explicitly identified as engineers, I count 29 engineers through the class of 1837 and another 23 through the class of 1843.[33] Considering this, VMI, with its, at a minimum, 47 engineers by 1851 more than matched Rensselaer and Norwich in their contribution of engineers. If we assume Green's conservative calculation that 10 percent of all southern military school cadets worked as engineers and that about 11,000 boys went to these schools before the Civil War, then, collectively, the schools contributed at least 1,100 engineers to America. These 1,100 may account for roughly 10 percent of American engineers at the time.[34]

Calhoun argues that Rensselaer and Norwich graduates did not attain the same high professional status and success of West Point engineers, who provided a disproportionate number of chief engineers on large transportation projects compared to those engineers trained on the job.[35] The Norwich graduates would have received a less thorough engineering training than either West Point or VMI cadets, having had perhaps as much math and science, if they chose to, but little actual engineering training besides surveying, despite Partridge's attempts to employ West Point as a model. Likewise, Rensselaer students likely learned little mathematics until after 1842 and, given the first engineering professor's contempt for book learning, studied little from the books written by West Point engineers. Consequently, having neither the intensive theoretical training of West Point and VMI cadets nor the practical experience of craft-trained engineers, graduates of Norwich and Rensselaer may have been less valued by employers. So, despite the greater historiographic emphasis on Norwich and Rensselaer,[36] VMI likely had a greater impact on the development of professional engineering in America during the antebellum period.

Historians of American engineering education, to the extent that they discuss the antebellum period at all, have minimized or even overlooked the southern military schools. Instead, they emphasize northern schools, especially Norwich, Rensselaer, and West Point. Daniel Calhoun, in his early and important study of the history of American civil engineering, gives a detailed discussion of the roles of northern schools in the development of formal engineering education. However, he reduces VMI to just one in a list of eleven other schools that taught something related to engineering between 1831 and 1841. Moreover, he follows the list with the statement, "Most of these [schools] made engineering no more than a minor part of instruction; in many, the courses offered probably went into a decline with the depression of 1837–1843."[37] By subsuming VMI into his generalizations, he downplays VMI's longevity—students continue to study engineering there today—and the thoroughness of its engineering instruction. Terry Reynolds, however, did note the general lack of recognition of the southern military schools in his 1992 overview of antebellum engineering education. But, given the limitations of a single journal article on a broader topic, he provides no analysis of the schools and their place in the history of engineering education. He does, however, list some of the courses VMI provided, thus giving some impression of the thoroughness of its curriculum.[38]

Despite their minimal historiographic presence, the southern military schools altogether trained at least 1,100 working engineers before the Civil War, far greater than the contributions of Rensselaer and Norwich. After West Point, the first and most prolific trainer of engineers, VMI was the single most significant source of school-trained engineers in antebellum America. Rather than the North being the historiographic norm, it is the South or, to include West Point, military schools in general that should, if anything, be the historiographic norm.

The obscurity of the southern military schools in the history of engineering mirrors these schools' long-standing invisibility within the history of higher education in general. Only recently have historians given significant attention to them as cultural, educational, and political institutions.[39] Green notes, "Exploring military schools thus fills in the neglected history of education in the antebellum South. The northern experience has become the historiographic model, with the South relegated to an exception." She then notes in particular, "Engineering programs were rare nationwide; as a major site of engineering education, military schools merit more historiographic attention."[40] I agree.

CHAPTER TWO

EDUCATION AND WHITE MANHOOD IN
THE STRUGGLE FOR POLITICAL POWER

On December 5, 1834, thirteen men gathered for a weekly meeting of the Franklin Society in Lexington, Virginia.[1] Such men had
done so since at least 1811, when the literary and debating society
adopted its new name in honor of Benjamin Franklin's "usefulness,
seriousness, intellectuality, and patriotism" using "a name that all
the people claimed regardless of creed or class."[2] They raised the
following question: "Would it be politic for the state to establish
a military school at the arsenal near Lexington, in connexion [sic]
with Washington College on the plan of the W. Point Academy"?
Over the next three weeks, the members debated this issue, first
voting unanimously in opposition, then unanimously in favor.[3]

   The Rockbridge County community took seriously any con-
clusion of this society, through which white artisans, mechanics,
farmers, and merchants as well as lawyers and politicians discussed
political and cultural affairs.[4] After both presiding over meetings
during which the members voted to discuss the issue as well as
joining the final unanimous vote in favor of it, one member, Alfred

Leyburn, would join the Virginia House of Delegates during the next legislative session and introduce a petition advocating the establishment of the school.[5] After about fifteen months of debate, the Virginia General Assembly adopted the plan. They authorized the replacement of the guard of the Lexington Arsenal with a corps of cadets, drawn from across the commonwealth, who would take on the guard duty in exchange for an education they could not otherwise afford.[6] It would take, however, three more years before the first cadets arrived and before John Thomas Lewis Preston (see Figure 2.1), a prominent Lexington lawyer and landowner, named the school the Virginia Military Institute (VMI).[7]

Before the Virginia General Assembly considered the establishment of the first of the southern military schools, citizens of Rockbridge County debated other education proposals as well, with at least ten articles promoting different schemes appearing in the *Lexington Gazette*, the weekly paper of Rockbridge County, between mid-July 1835 and mid-January 1836 and with additional articles appearing after the submission of petitions to the House of Delegates. These proposals, despite their sometimes-heated language, shared a common goal of providing an education to poorer white boys, boys who were disenfranchised by property-ownership requirements for suffrage. The presence of this agreement, as well as the disagreement over how to accomplish it, and the perceived importance of the issue suggests that something important happened, something that proponents of the Virginia Military Institute hoped a school could help resolve.

Historian Bradford Wineman provides much insight into the origins of the VMI proposal in its local context of western Virginia. Most white people of Rockbridge County, including Preston, the principal advocate of founding VMI, were of Scots-Irish ancestry. Virginia's Scots-Irish settlers were enthusiastic about education.[8] This does not explain the origins of VMI, but it does help us make sense of the fact that the people of Rockbridge County would

Figure 2.1. John Thomas Lewis Preston (1811–1890). Portrait of John Thomas Lewis Preston, Preston Library, Virginia Military Institute, Lexington, Virginia.

turn to education to solve a problem or that appeals to education would possess power in their political discourse. More important, Wineman points to the fact that most of these Scots-Irish men of Rockbridge County were also supporters of the Whig Party who sought infrastructure development and government promotion of economic prosperity.[9] But how would the proposed school secure those interests? And what have these interests of the men of western Virginia to do with the men of eastern Virginia who dominated the state legislature and ultimately secured legislation to support the school? Wineman is right to turn us away from explanations for the origins of the southern military school tradition in general and toward the local context of VMI itself.[10] But we must also address statewide politics and acknowledge conflicts—not just consensus—within the state and even among the men of Rockbridge County to understand how the school proposal and the school itself functioned in the debates and conflicts.

I argue VMI emerged out of sectional struggles between the elites of eastern and western Virginia. In this struggle, Scots-Irish elites west of the Blue Ridge, ultimately along with their allies in the growing middle class elsewhere in the state, accepted a new concept of innately independent and equal white men that legitimized universal white male suffrage as a means of shifting political power away from the planter elite of the east, who were largely of English descent. This occurred in the context of America's Market Revolution, a rapid expansion of manufacturing and of buying and selling in a market economy that transformed politics and social relations.[11] The men of western Virginia, however, fought for social and political transformations as a means of creating the market expansion in the first place. The failure of western Virginians to achieve this redistribution of power or gain sufficient support for internal improvements during Virginia's 1829–1830 constitutional convention provides the primary context for the movement to establish a military school in Lexington, the first of the southern military school tradition. Although the western elite failed to institutionalize the new white manhood in universal suffrage in 1830, they continued their attempts to legitimize white male equality through higher education.

SECTIONAL CONFLICT OVER INTERNAL IMPROVEMENTS

The planter elite of eastern Virginia dominated the legislature from the founding of the Commonwealth of Virginia to 1850, despite the increasing settlement and economic development of western Virginia. Citizens living west of the Blue Ridge attempted to gain stronger political representation in order to achieve their interests, including greater tax support for internal improvements, especially roads. This conflict resulted in new constitutions in 1830 and 1851. At both conventions, western elites sought to increase their political power primarily by establishing universal white male suffrage and changing legislative apportionment. The eastern elite opposed these reforms on the grounds of their republican philosophy that limited suffrage to landholders.[12] Westerners, in response, attempted to redefine citizenship and political authority by introducing a new republican philosophy that grounded authority in a new sense of a common white manhood. They largely failed at the 1829–1830 convention, resulting in an intensification of sectional tensions to the point of westerners threatening secession.

Internal Improvements and Legislative Power

American interest in roads and canals grew along with market expansion following the War of 1812. Much of the country, especially away from the coasts and navigable waterways, had still not made a full transition from a traditional subsistence economy to a market economy by the time of the war. Subsistence farming families were independent. Unlike in much of Europe, they owned their land outright and could use and dispose of it without restriction. Outside of plantations, the subsistence lifestyle required having children serve as labor. An age- and gender-based division of labor ensured the completion of all necessary tasks, including the production and preparation of food, making and mending clothes, and building and maintaining structures on the farm. These needs were largely met by the family, with some needs met by limited trade purchased from small surpluses produced after meeting subsistence needs. But these families needed to buy little. In fact, as historian Charles Sellers describes it, "So long as land was assured for the rising generation, accumulation was pointless and productive effort could be relaxed as soon as conventional standards of consumption were achieved." What little people purchased often came from within the larger community, which contained a few specialists, such as artisans who might create cooking pots or a sawmill operator. The family and community division of labor and the subsistence level of life itself created interdependence and a basic level of equality between families.[13]

Two forces contributed to an increasing desire to shift from subsistence farming to market participation in the late eighteenth and early nineteenth centuries. First, subsistence farmers in the Shenandoah Valley of Virginia and the Susquehanna Valley of Pennsylvania joined more market-oriented farmers of the Atlantic coast in taking advantage of European demand for food imports by growing surplus wheat. Small farmers in the South also produced small amounts of cotton to fuel the new factories of the Industrial Revolution. Second, the American style of prosperous subsistence farming relied upon access to cheap land for the next generation. As population densities increased, land prices increased and landholdings decreased in size. The added costs of land and decreasing productivity on smaller lands pushed men and women to produce greater non-agricultural surpluses for sale and to engage in wage labor. Distance from markets and poor or absent roads made market participation difficult. Internal improvements, including roads and canals, would decrease shipping costs and increase profits. Meanwhile, many Americans found their world changing from a cooperative and interdependent world into a competitive world with increasing class stratification.[14]

Nonetheless, both market expansion and internal improvements faced opposition both nationally and within Virginia. These roads and canals would support western settlement and the inclusion of those settlements in the market economy by enabling them to transport goods to and from the market. Proposals for public support for these improvements, however, generated much conflict. Except for construction of lighthouses and harbor improvements, as well as the 1818 National Road from Cumberland to Wheeling, the federal government ultimately rejected calls for its support. James Madison, for example, vetoed federal support for canal construction in New York in 1817, declaring the appropriations bill unconstitutional. Others expressed concern that federal improvements would benefit manufacturing and commerce at the expense of agriculture, including slave-based plantation production. This growth of commerce would accelerate the growth of the market economy, already seen by many as destabilizing American society by widening the gap between the classes and creating political factions. Consequently, public support for internal improvements would have to come from the states themselves.[15]

Just like the people of western New York who supported the Erie Canal, the people of western Virginia generally supported internal improvements to further their inclusion in the market economy. The Blue Ridge Mountains were a formidable barrier between the people of western Virginia and eastern ports and markets. The people could not rely on river transport and would need to develop roads through mountain passes to connect themselves to the east. There was, however, much conflict over this issue between the people of western Virginia and the planter elite of the east who governed the state. This conflict was, in fact, one cause for Virginia's 1829–1830 constitutional convention, in which westerners tied their desire for improvements to demands for universal white male suffrage.[16]

Privately developed turnpikes did begin to appear in the west in the 1820s. The Lexington-Covington Turnpike, for example, connected Lexington to Covington to the west by a forty-five-mile toll road completed in 1832. This, however, still left Lexington without any turnpike heading directly eastward to more conveniently connect the town to Richmond or the Atlantic coast until after the 1850s. Westerners called for state support for roads and canals and, after the 1830s, railroads. Canals began to appear in western Virginia in the 1830s, but none reached Rockbridge County until the 1850s. Westerners also wanted charters for banks in the west to provide loans and increase the availability of the cash necessary to participate in a market economy. [17]

It isn't, however, true to say that the eastern planters opposed internal improvements. A House Committee on Roads and Internal Navigation stated in 1816 that "open, free and easy intercourse" was in fact a great blessing for the state that would enrich all both materially and in terms of liberty.[18] But westerners expressed great frustration with the speed and limited funds with which the state supported these efforts. After the War of 1812, Virginia's legislature produced a system of mixed enterprise for the development of a transportation system. Its members assumed that locals, those willing to invest money, would know best which projects were worth funding. They created a Board of Public Works in 1816, which included a "principal" state engineer to provide surveys and assistance on projects and would recommend the funding of projects with purchases of up to two-fifths of the stock in the private company that pursued the projects.[19] Moreover, the state would often pay some labor costs on projects by directly purchasing or leasing enslaved black people. This was not minor. In some cases, more than 100 people were enslaved to build canals, railroads, and turnpikes, as many as 170 people on the James River and Kanawha Company canal.[20] So, theoretically, the legislature, dominated by eastern planters, did support internal improvements.

The pace of improvements, however, was slow and for several reasons. The improvements were most needed in the west, but the necessary capital was in the east. The wealth of the planters did not depend on the improvements; they had access to some of the most navigable waterways in America, including the James and York Rivers. Despite this, it was they who would bear much of any tax burden, thus making them reluctant to support any particular improvement project. Proposed projects were often held up by accusations of corruption in the funding process and by competing interests promoting projects at one another's expense. While public support for canals declined, the Board of Public Works did begin promoting road construction by the 1830s.[21] But throughout the 1820s and 1830s, the road projects were generally carried out by men without significant engineering experience. Moreover, the state engineer had little authority to ensure that projects were carried out to the standards he set. Consequently, the roads that were built were often of poor quality, being, for example, too narrow or having grades that were too steep for horse-drawn wagons.[22] So, while the state did provide some support for transportation infrastructure, the pace, placement, and quality of those projects were insufficient or entirely unhelpful for the west.

A New White Manhood

Each county in Virginia sent two delegates to the General Assembly, with the size of counties depending on population, both free and enslaved. With the overwhelming majority of enslaved black people living in the east, eastern counties and their interests had substantially greater representation than western counties in both the General Assembly and at the constitutional convention. Westerners referred to this as the "black basis" for apportionment, as opposed to the "white basis," or the counting of only the white population, which would have increased the proportion of western delegates. Consequently, westerners made the "white basis" a principal demand at the convention.[23] Eastern elites defended the "black basis" on the grounds that it provided a means of gaining representation for property. While this did not increase any individual's vote, it did provide disproportionate representation and, therefore, political power to the counties with the greatest wealth. Able Upshur, a convention delegate from the Tidewater Northampton County, argued that some representation of property was necessary to ensure that not just the numerical majority governed but also those with the "majority in interest" governed. Moreover, "those who have the greatest stake in the government," meaning the property that government is meant to protect and upon which people are taxed, "shall have the greatest share of power in the administration of it."[24]

Virginia's 1776 constitution, to which westerners objected, retained colonial Virginia's standards for suffrage: "that all men, having sufficient evidence of permanent common interest with, and attachment to, the community, have the right of suffrage."[25] The delegates understood "interest" and "attachment" in terms of landownership, following the old requirement of ownership of fifty acres.[26] 1785 legislation extended suffrage to "[e]very white male citizen (other than free negroes and mulattoes) of this commonwealth, aged twenty-one years" who owned either only twenty-five, rather than fifty acres, of land with a house and plantation or a legally designated city or town lot containing a house.[27] This extension of suffrage, however, still left over one-third of white adult Virginia men disenfranchised, with a disproportionate number in the west.[28]

The planter elite of the east legitimated landownership requirements for suffrage through a republican philosophy that advocated representation by the virtuous few in order to protect the liberty of all. One had to demonstrate virtue, the capacity for restraint and self-sacrifice necessary to set aside one's own interests in favor of the common good, in order to govern responsibly. Otherwise, employing government or one's vote to advance one's own interests or personal liberty would create a threat to the liberty of others. Governance by the virtuous on the behalf of all would ensure the long-term security of liberty for all. A Virginia gentleman demonstrated the independence necessary for virtue by acting as if he was free from subsistence labor and, therefore, not needing to subordinate his honor to his personal interests. He did this by assisting the poor, contributing to public services without compensation, and enslaving people.[29]

Since the American Revolution, many men accepted limiting suffrage and office holding to those with the wealth and family background to ensure the independence necessary for virtue in order to prevent the virtueless masses from corrupting democracy for their own interests. Americans, especially white men, generally understood women and all black people as having an innate *incapacity* for public virtue. Consequently, they could not embody the essential quality of independence necessary for political participation.[30] Everyone at the 1829–1830 convention seemed to agree on this. Some eastern delegates feared that arguments for the equality of white men, regardless of property ownership, led inevitably to claims for the equality and enfranchisement of women, children, and all black people. Women and children, Culpeper County (in the Piedmont) delegate John Barbour argued, were excluded from enfranchisement by laws of nature, "for the want of free agency in both, and the want of intelligence in the latter class." The enfranchisement of black men would lead to the slaughter of white people in a revolution like that of Haiti's.[31] But advocates of the white basis and white male suffrage likewise argued that women and black people were disenfranchised by nature. John Cooke of Frederick, just in the mountains, argued it is "self-evident" that "the Creator of the Universe, to render women more fit for the sphere in which He intended her to act, had made her weak and timid in comparison with man, and had thus placed her under his control, as well as under his protection." Consequently, "nature herself had therefore pronounced, on women and children, a sentence of incapacity to exercise political power."[32]

The exclusion of women, children, and black people did not, however, mean that white manhood, while necessary, was sufficient for political participation. Opponents of white male suffrage argued that white men had to demonstrate their capacity for independence in some way, with property ownership providing an important means. Delegates to Virginia's 1776 constitutional convention established that participation in governance required having a stake in society, particularly through landownership. This stake would ensure respect for private property, one of the foundations of liberty. Moreover, property would demonstrate one's independence and, therefore, capacity for governance. Without that ability, landless men would use political power to seize property or at least tax property for their own interests. Eastern delegate Benjamin Leigh of Chesterfield pointed out that universal white manhood suffrage would "put the power of controlling the wealth of the State, into hands different from those which hold that wealth."[33] Suffrage advocate Cooke responded to such arguments, saying that opponents of suffrage claimed in effect that "love of wealth is so strong that the poor are the natural enemies of the rich, and feel a strong and habitual inclination to strip them of their wealth, or, at least, to throw on them alone all the burthens of society."[34] And he was not wrong in his characterization, because Upshur, responding directly to him, argued that were they to "take away all protection from property" by enfranchising the landless, "our next business is to cut each other's throats."[35]

Since before the American Revolution, disenfranchised citizens challenged the above republican insistence on narrow suffrage. Many white men argued against restrictions based on property ownership or taxation and for universal suffrage for white men. In the process, they further racialized citizenship and transformed the meaning of white manhood. While most states adopted universal white male suffrage by the 1820s, Virginia maintained its suffrage restrictions. Western Virginians contributed to this suffrage movement by calling for the 1829–1830 constitutional convention, hoping to achieve both broader suffrage and to eliminate the "black basis" in favor of the "white basis" of legislative apportionment as a means of shifting political power westward. Nationally, disenfranchised white men struggled to broaden suffrage by transforming the meaning of white manhood, identifying it alone with the independence seen as necessary for political participation. Historian David Roediger argues that these men accepted the innate dependence of white women and black people to argue for the innate independence of white men. White men could, by their very nature, exert the restraint and self-sacrifice necessary to set aside their personal interests in order to act for the common good. Advocates of the new white manhood successfully argued for a more intensely racialized sense of public virtue.

The resulting broadening of suffrage for white men often occurred along with greater restrictions on the rights and political participation of free black men, a very few of whom previously could vote upon meeting the same landownership requirements as white men. This was the case, at least legally, if not in fact, in Maryland, Massachusetts, New York, North Carolina, Pennsylvania, and Vermont. As both the free black population and white supremacy grew in northern states in the early nineteenth century, new suffrage reforms that broadened the franchise for white men also either explicitly eliminated voting rights for non-whites or, as in New York, created steeper requirements for black men. Some independent, property-owning white women, such as widows, could vote in New Jersey, but they too lost their rights in 1807 when a new constitution explicitly identified manhood as a requirement for voting.[36]

Enfranchised men of western Virginia supported universal white male suffrage, hoping that it would strengthen the legislative power of the west, making them better able to assert their sectional interests. Disenfranchised men of the middling classes, such as merchants and artisans, even in eastern Virginia, supported broader suffrage of course, as it would include them in political participation. Moreover, they had at least as much interest in gaining internal improvements for the west in order to better integrate them into the market economy. Indeed, western delegates and delegates from eastern cities made the issues of the white basis and broadened suffrage the first item of major business at the convention.[37]

The first substantive debate began with J. Marshall of the city of Richmond reading a memorial from disenfranchised white men of his city. They pointed out that they had been excluded from choosing their representative to the convention, that they were "passed by, like aliens or slaves, as if destitute of interest, or unworthy of a voice, in measures involving their future political destiny" while property-holders held "the exclusive power of new-modeling the fundamental laws of the State; in other words, have seized upon the sovereign authority." They quoted Virginia's own 1776 Declaration of Rights, which states that "all men are by nature equally free and independent."[38] Cooke likewise appealed to the "sovereignty of the people and the equality of men" in arguing for broader suffrage.[39] Philip Doddridge of Brooke County in what is now West Virginia boldly challenged the eastern elite, saying "your doctrine makes me a slave . . . I may still live in the west, may pursue my own business and obey my own inclinations, but so long as you hold political domination over me, I am a slave." Non-freeholding white men "are a majority of individual units in the State, and your equals in intelligence and virtue, moral and political. Yet you say we must obey you."[40] It was, to such men, self-evident that they were the equals of any white men and, moreover, that women and black men were not. It was upon the basis of white male equality that suffrage and representation should be based.

Despite the dominance of the convention by eastern conservatives, they accepted a compromise in the new constitution. The delegates rejected the white basis in a close vote of forty-nine to forty-four. Instead, they compromised by establishing a fixed distribution of fifty-six delegates to the west and seventy-eight to the east. Likewise, the west would have thirteen senators and the east nineteen. While this increased western representation, it maintained strong eastern dominance.[41] When the ratification vote went back to the voters, it fell cleanly along sectional lines, with eastern counties nearly uniformly voting in favor of ratification and western counties against. Counties in the middle were mixed. While Montgomery and Giles Counties voted against ratification, Rockbridge and Botetourt Counties voted for it, accepting the compromises the new constitution offered.[42] The maintenance of eastern legislative domination prevented western elites from achieving their sectional interests, including tax-supported internal improvements. Consequently, with little change achieved, sectional tensions intensified.[43]

It is this sectional tension that provides the primary context for understanding the emergence of the Virginia Military Institute. In the following section, I describe and analyze the 1834–1836 debate in Rockbridge County about founding new educational institutions in Lexington. Although none of the preserved public debate refers to the failures of the constitutional convention, the debate makes most sense in light of that failure. Men of Rockbridge County saw education as a means of promoting universal white manhood suffrage and thereby challenging the eastern planters' domination of the state.

HIGHER EDUCATION AND THE LEGITIMIZATION OF A NEW WHITE MANHOOD

Beginning as early as December of 1834, citizens of Rockbridge County made competing proposals for providing white boys or men with greater access to education. Lexington already served as an important educational center in Appalachian Virginia by being the home of the Ann Smith Academy for girls and Washington College, an academy and college for boys. John Preston, the chief advocate for the founding of VMI, argued that to the presence of these schools and especially to the "influence of Washington College is to be attributed much of the character of our town for intelligence and virtue." Additional schools would enable Lexington to "become the Athens or Boston of Western Virginia."[44] The various education proposals, despite the sometimes-heated arguments over them, shared a common goal of providing an education for poorer white young men, men politically disenfranchised by suffrage requirements reconfirmed in the commonwealth's 1830 constitution.

Antebellum educational institutions for white, hearing children differed, especially in availability, in the various regions of the United States, but, in general, they developed from colonial institutions. In the colonial period, there were a few basic types of schools: elementary or reading-and-writing schools, grammar schools, and colleges. "Latin" and "English" grammar schools merged into academies in the mid-eighteenth century. Reading-and-writing schools evolved into "common schools" following American independence.

State laws attempted to prevent the education of enslaved and often free black people. This was the case especially in slave states but also in some cases in free states. Both black and white people recognized a link between literacy and freedom. Free and enslaved black people in the South saw education as both an expression of freedom and as a means of liberation. Most directly, literacy provided a slave with the ability to write passes that might facilitate free movement to a free state. But literacy also allowed enslaved people to read the Bible, newspapers, and even abolitionist pamphlets that provided them with new language for articulating their own conceptions of themselves and their condition, including their longing for freedom and criticism of the very institution of slavery. As historian Heather Andrea Williams phrases it, "In the Bible, books, and newspapers, literate slaves found a language of liberation." The men who enslaved them often recognized all of this as well. There were many exceptions, but in general, slaveholders viewed literacy and education in general as a fundamental threat to slavery.[45]

Free and enslaved blacks articulated this threat to slavery

through revolts, which slaveholders and state legislators correctly, at least to some extent, associated with literacy. Legislatures responded to both the 1739 Stono Rebellion in South Carolina and the 1831 Turner Rebellion in Virginia with laws limiting or banning the education of enslaved people and even, in some cases, of free black people. Laws throughout the slave states and Washington, DC, variously banned teaching enslaved people to read or, in the case of an 1800 South Carolina law, "mental instruction" in general. Some states, such as Alabama and Georgia, criminalized the teaching of free black people as well. As education continued underground nonetheless, many states created further laws banning the congregation of enslaved and sometime free black people, since those occasions might have—and did—provide space for educating one another. Nonetheless, both formal and informal education continued.

Informal education was most common among enslaved Americans. Moreover, for most people, that education was not in the form of literacy. An important part of education was the development of a powerful ability to memorize information. This ability allowed enslaved people to eavesdrop on white conversations or even to memorize words and letters an individual could not read or understand. People then fed this memorized information into the "grape-vine telegraph" that transmitted information within and between enslaved communities. Nonetheless, literacy was a prized achievement among enslaved people, and many people sought it in bits and pieces whenever and wherever they could get instruction. Fellow slaves or free black people would pass on whatever knowledge they had. Sympathetic mistresses sometimes taught the people they enslaved, usually motivated to teach them to read the Bible. Ministers and missionaries too sometimes taught enslaved people to read the Bible. Enslaved people traded for or bought instruction from literate white people. Sometimes they even tricked the young sons of slaveholders into sharing what they had learned in school in each day.[46]

Remarkably, even when banned by law, free and enslaved black people formed and participated in formal schools. Enslaved people in at least Mississippi established schools in caves or in camouflaged pits dug in the woods. Teachers taught from stolen books, pencils, and chalkboards or even improvised their own chalkboards and made their own pen ink. Schools, as well as informal teaching, usually operated at night. But Sundays were the day when slaveholders forced little work upon people and often left their plantations and homes for church and to socialize, allowing people relative security for education even in broad daylight. Formal schools also operated underground in towns and cities, which provided much cover for free and enslaved black people to move about and cover up their daytime education with other tasks.[47]

Black people risked violent punishment and family separation to attain education. Moreover, they must have worked through the hunger, tiredness, and trauma that makes learning difficult. They did so equating education with liberation. State legislators responded to this threat to white supremacy by banning the teaching of enslaved and often of free black people. All of this was the case in Virginia by the time white men of Rockbridge County began debating establishing a military school in Lexington. Laws and educational institutions in the state reinforced slavery and the broader system of white supremacy. Formal education and especially literacy were for white children and young men.

In colonial America, the three primary forms of formal educational institutions for white people were elementary or reading-and-writing schools, grammar schools that emphasized religion and Latin, and colleges to train clergy. In the eighteenth-century, religious denominations dominated formal education. The Anglican Church promoted both primary and higher education in the colonies. The latter was represented by the College of William and Mary in Williamsburg, Virginia, although the school had begun in 1693 as a grammar school. The church promoted grammar or Latin schools, which tended to teach reading, writing, arithmetic, and religion as well as Latin and Greek to older children. The church employed the Society for the Propagation of the Gospel as a major instrument in establishing especially elementary schools in the colonies. The society exported schoolbooks to the colonies. By the American Revolution, they had succeeded in establishing schools from Georgia to Massachusetts. Quakers, Congregation-alists, Presbyterians, and others also established schools, often free to poor students.[48]

New England colonies created reading-and-writing schools, in theory, for all children, with each town required to create a school or pay a fine. Many towns chose to pay the fine. As it sounds, the schools taught reading and writing and not much else. These were not schools to prepare students for more advanced grammar schools; instead, they were schools for poorer children who would never go to a grammar school. Consequently, the distinction between elementary and grammar schools reinforced existing class distinctions.[49]

Colonial grammar schools were to provide an education for boys for future religious and public service. They also became a means for the middle class to claim social status or provide upward mobility for its sons. Students received a seven-year-long education in especially Latin but also some Greek and Hebrew. The classics in these languages provided training for leadership in government and churches as well as preparation for college. So, while primary schools provided the literacy to read and accept statements from authorities, grammar schools trained those authorities.[50]

During the eighteenth-century, the religious emphasis of the grammar schools declined as Greek and Latin education came to emphasize, instead, a more gentlemanly education. The development of so-called English schools contributed to this process as Latin schools adopted some of their more "practical" subjects, including English, mathematics, history, geography, sciences, and modern languages. By 1750, this new hybrid took shape as the "academy," some for boys and some for girls. These schools tended to be private schools and often prepared male students for college and female students for marriage and running a household.[51]

Private academies continued to provide most secondary education in both the North and the South after the American Revolution. Academies were boarding schools segregated by sex, with more available to boys than to girls. Boarding made it possible for children of dispersed farms and plantations to be educated in a central place and in a school with sufficient enrollment to make it cost-effective.[52]

College was a vague term that could, especially in the colonial era, refer to either grammar schools or higher education. Some institutions provided both. Also, some academies developed into actual colleges for higher education, including Virginia's Liberty Hall Academy, which became Washington and Lee College in Lexington, and Prince Edward Academy, which became Hampden-Sydney College, both Presbyterian schools.[53]

There were just nine colleges in the colonies before independence, but 250 of them between independence and the Civil War. During that great expansion, colleges often struggled financially, and the quality of instruction declined as teaching loads increased and the preparation of incoming students declined. This sparked a long period of debate and reform regarding curricula, the purpose of education, and systems of discipline.[54] These debates continued into the antebellum period, with VMI participating in them.

There was slow movement toward universal public education for white children after the American Revolution. In 1789, Massachusetts reaffirmed its irregularly practiced colonial-era laws requiring towns to provide education supported by property taxes. The new law created school districts that were to provide primary and secondary education for all and to govern standards for the schools. This system spread to other northern states up through the 1820s.[55] Virginia, despite a 1797 law authorizing public schools, left the development of schools under the authority of county magistrates, who wielded great power. They tended to show little interest in public education and almost no schools appeared. The legislature responded with the 1810 Literary Fund to provide some financial support for poor children's education. It did little but did provide some funding for some counties' elementary "pauper schools."[56]

Beginning in the 1830s, a national education reform movement advocated for the expansion of tax-supported common schools as part of a broader social reform movement that included abolitionism and temperance. Supporters of common schools sought to ensure all white children access to education in order to prepare them for citizenship and work by providing them with basic literacy and arithmetic skills as well as training in morality and discipline. At least in the North, interest in this emerged partly in response to anxiety over increasing pluralism through immigration and the social transformation caused by urbanization and the growth of manufacturing and the market economy.[57]

An unknown but surely small number of Virginia's children enrolled in a school in any given year in the 1830s. Much higher proportions of northern children enrolled in schools, but still, perhaps only 20 percent of Pennsylvania and New Jersey's children did so as late as 1840. Those children who did receive education in Virginia did so through one of four ways. First, planters hired private tutors to teach their children English, Greek, Latin, and mathematics. Second, members of the middling classes and planters paid tuition to send their children to academies, such as Lexington's Ann Smith Academy for girls and Washington College. Third, rural communities sometimes "subscribed" to a teacher, often with dubious qualifications, for a fixed period of time to provide a basic education, perhaps even just basic reading and writing. Fourth, parents could sometimes avail themselves of Virginia's Literary Fund to assist them in paying for some education for their children or perhaps attend "charity schools" in cities.[58]

The Franklin Society Proposal for a Military School

John Thomas Lewis Preston, writing to the *Lexington Gazette* as "Cives" in three letters in August and September of 1835, provided the dominant public articulation of the Franklin Society proposal, in which he emphasized both providing an education to those who could not otherwise afford one and employing military discipline to transform the students into ideal and useful citizens. [59] I have not seen any reports on or transcriptions from the Franklin Society debates that can provide an indication of just how faithfully Preston presented the views from the debates or to what extent his "Cives" letters reflected the issues the society raised during the discussion. Regardless, Preston, through these three letters and personal lobbying of legislators in Richmond, provided crucial public support for the proposal.[60] Nonetheless, he denied having originated the idea, claiming that people had proposed it ever since the commonwealth first established the arsenal, though no one has offered convincing evidence for any other originator.[61]

Jennings C. Wise, former commandant of cadets and early historian of VMI, speculated that Claudius Crozet, the school's first president of the Board of Visitors, may have proposed it to local residents while passing through Lexington as part of his work as principal engineer of Virginia. Wise argued that this graduate of the École Polytechnique, a military-engineering school in Paris, and former professor of engineering at West Point would have found the idea obvious.[62] Given Crozet's later role as the president of the Board of Visitors of VMI, I would expect evidence of this claim to have come forward. Possibly, it was Hugh Barclay, who along with James Davidson initially proposed the Franklin Society military school debate and who first advocated for replacing the arsenal with a school. He reportedly became enamored with West Point after accompanying a local boy to the school in the early 1830s. He raved about it to men of Lexington. If Barclay didn't first propose the idea of a military school, perhaps it was nonetheless out of his many conversations about West Point that the idea emerged.[63] Regardless, I suspect that Preston, not Barclay, served as the primary voice in favor of the proposal during the Franklin Society debates because the proposal unanimously failed during the first debate, which occurred in Preston's absence and Barclay's presence, but then succeeded by unanimous vote after Preston's return.[64]

In Preston's letter of August 28, 1835, he reformulated the Franklin Society question as to "*whether it be practicable, so to organize the Lexington Arsenal, that it shall preserve its present character and uses as a military establishment, and be at the same time a Literary Institution for the education of youths.*" Denying any particular political or personal motivation, he claimed to make the proposal "solely by a sincere desire to bring about what we sincerely believe would be beneficial at once to the State, to this community, and to the cause of education." He specifically proposed "to supply the place of the present Guard, by another, composed of young men from sixteen to twenty-four years of age, engaged for four years to perform the necessary duties, who would receive no pay, but in lieu, have afforded to them the opportunities of a liberal education."[65] At least one student would come from each senatorial district, thus distributing the benefits throughout Virginia.[66] He proposed having a tutor to teach "the classics, and the higher branches of an English education," a professor of "the sciences generally," and a captain to maintain the guard and to teach "the military art." Students during their first year would focus on developing military discipline; during their second, have primary responsibility for the guard; during their third, focus on classes at the school; and during their fourth, take classes at Washington College. All students, however, would take some classes throughout, with Latin and other "higher branches of English" during the first year; Latin and mathematics during the second; mathematics and natural philosophy during the third; and natural philosophy, chemistry, and military arts during the fourth. Such a plan would enable students to make up for a lack of earlier education and provide them with one "sufficiently liberal to enable a young man to prosecute it further, unassisted, or creditably to enter upon the study of any of the learned professions."[67]

Preston lamented the number of great minds lost as a result of poverty and lack of access to education, arguing, "Genius knows no fixed locality, and is as often born under a cottage roof, as the dome of a palace; and there are hundreds of young men whose minds thirst for an education which they have not the means of obtaining."[68] Public support generally went to those who did not really need it, while colleges, which might have waived tuition for those in need, still required boarding expenses that most could not afford. Religious institutions might have offered charity, but this generally required a particular religious affiliation on the part of the potential student. Also, many students may have resented charity as a mark of deficiency. Preston, however, proposed the means of offering both an education and boarding but without any charity.

Beyond the benefits of the school to those who could not otherwise afford education, Preston suggested that the military character of the school might offer such benefits as to attract even those who could afford education elsewhere. He argued, "[T]he military discipline of the place would essentially conduce to the formation of good habits, and the exercise to health." Even though the school might offer a more limited or less advanced liberal curriculum than that available at Washington College, parents might find the system of discipline attractive because of its emphasis on moral training and health.[69]

Preston argued that by providing this education, the commonwealth would benefit in several ways. First, the arsenal would remain competently guarded at the same cost as under the previous professional guard. Second, the school would strengthen the state militias through the dispersal of trained military men throughout Virginia. Third, "[t]he State is benefited by everything that promotes the cause of education." Lexington and Rockbridge County would also benefit, because "the soldiery of the Arsenal is the most unpleasant part of our population."[70] Indeed, locals complained that the bored guards, who were not from Lexington, were often drunk in public and got into fights with locals and Washington College students. In 1826, two guards fought, leaving one of them dead.[71] The proposal, therefore, would provide multiple benefits to both the commonwealth and the community at no extra cost.

In contrast to the perceived immorality and disruptiveness of the professional soldiers, a student guard would learn "industry, regularity, and health" through military drilling and discipline.[72] Preston argued,

> How different would be the feeling toward a corps of young men, guided by virtuous principles, ennobled by the ardor of patriotism, and cheered by the proud consciousness that they were, by their own exertions, preparing themselves for the highest posts under their *own free government*, of which they should be capable— mingling with the citizens as their duty might permit upon the *equality of gentlemen*, ready to aid in every enterprise of patriotism or philanthropy, and at last leaving, sorrowing and sorrowed, a community whose confidence and regard they had secured, and whose sympathies and best wishes would continue to follow them in after life.[73]

These young men would not become common soldiers. Instead, they would seek to elevate their positions through their educations. Moreover, they would cultivate the independence understood as so necessary for public virtue, establishing them as the equals of "gentlemen" and beloved by the community.

Preston drew fundamental distinctions between the troublesome soldiers and the future students. The soldiers required military discipline to restrain them and, despite that restraint, the community still saw them as a disturbance. The students, however, would learn to exert self-restraint while not only *not* creating trouble but also proudly serving Virginia. The hill above Lexington would no longer be dominated by the arsenal as a "receptacle to drones, obliged to be restrained by their coercion of military rule, a discordant element in our social system." Instead, it would offer a

> healthy and pleasant abode of a crowd of honorable youths, pressing up the hill of science with noble emulation, a gratifying spectacle, an honor to our country and State, objects of honest pride to their instructors, and fair specimens of citizen-soldiers, attached to their native State, and proud of her fame, and ready, in every time of deepest peril to vindicate her honor, or defend her rights.[74]

The context of east-west sectional tensions in Virginia helps us make sense of Preston's sentiment. The particular method of education or educational environment would transform those seen as vice-ridden and undisciplined into a new form of gentleman committed to the defense of Virginia. Denied enfranchisement and political leadership through a lack of land ownership, these boys would demonstrate their capacity for such leadership by learning to embody the ideals of independence and through demonstrations of their commitment to the commonwealth as a whole, rather than to simply their personal interests or to the interests of those from whom they might receive wages. Through this, the military school would undermine eastern elite claims about the inability of poorer and disenfranchised white men to participate in the governance of others.

A Manual Labor School to Elevate the Manual Laborer

Other residents, including some supporters of the Franklin Society proposal, supported a proposal to bring together the trades and higher education to both provide a means for poor white men to obtain an education and to elevate the respect for and status of manual labor and, therefore, manual laborers. A. B. Davidson, who also voted in favor of establishing a military school during the Franklin Society debate,[75] and J. F. Caruthers proposed in August of 1835 a manual labor school. They advertised the constitution of the Manual Labour Society of Western Virginia and their hopes for the society establishing a relationship with Washington College in order to provide "gratuitous instruction to young men of good moral character and respectable talents." The students would pay for their "cheap and comfortable boarding" by the "wise and prudent application of their hours of recreation to some profitable and healthful employment in manual labour." The society would provide for some of the expenses of the manual labor students through fundraising and by providing land to Washington College, while the students themselves would generate funds by selling the products of their own labor.[76]

Men anxious about social instability and a growing gap between classes as a result of the growth of the market economy and industry participated in the manual labor school movement. They sought to use higher education to create a new class of men that partook of the virtues of both tradesmen and professionals in order to bridge the gap between those classes. Theodore Dwight, spokesman for the Society for Promoting Manual Labor in Literary Institutions, argued that education, or the lack thereof, differentiated the classes. Therefore, enabling a larger proportion of the population to access education would help to minimize class disparities. Although students learned trades, they also received the same liberal education, in classical languages, mathematics, and philosophy, as students of the higher classes. Such schools opened in Pennsylvania, New England, and the West in the 1830s. However, they consistently lost money and failed to provide adequate supplies and tools for the students' manual labor work. Schools generally abandoned this system during the economic decline of

1837. Beyond financial failures, however, these schools failed to create the new class of men for which the manual labor school promoters hoped; provided with a liberal education, the graduates abandoned manual labor and entered into the professions or became merchants.[77]

Following the announcement of the Manual Labour Society in Lexington, someone writing under the name "Agricolus" wrote to the *Lexington Gazette* in October to argue for it as a superior mode of education and, ignoring or challenging the Franklin Society proposal, as the *only* plan for making education accessible to the sons of farmers and artisans. Bemoaning the general denigration of their class, he urged them not to "content [them]selves with being 'beasts of burden'—'hewers of wood and drawers of water,' and doom our sons and our sons' sons, to this condition." They must demand respect and every privilege, with education as the means of doing so.[78] Although manual labor schools provided a liberal education like the colleges, they were superior to colleges because the system of labor provided a system of discipline that "obviated the temptations to vice and promoted habits of order."[79] He surely wrote the preceding claim in response to Preston's similar claims about the benefits of military discipline in his own proposal. Again, parallel to Preston's claims for a military school, Agricolus claimed that "a young man" from South Hanover College, a manual labor school in Indiana, "informed me that the rich, as well as the poor, took pleasure in applying their hours of recreation to useful and healthful employments."[80] Maybe, maybe not. Regardless, Agricolus saw manual labor schools as superior to colleges because they used physical and productive labor to instill manly independence and self-reliance.

Assuming that the members of the Franklin Society voted for more than simply a replacement for an annoying arsenal guard, the manual labor school proposal may appear to have acted as a competitor to the military academy. Many people, however, supported both, including Davidson, the Manual Labour Society's chairman, and Preston, whose name appears in the advertised list of society members.[81] Unsurprisingly then, both proposals emphasize, along with a traditional liberal education for those who could not otherwise afford one, a moral training through physical discipline to turn graduates into "useful" and virtuous citizens. Both proposals also promoted the equality of white men, thus again undermining the eastern planters' domination of Virginia politics.

Proposals to Save Washington College

Members of the faculty, trustees, and alumni of Washington College expressed mixed reactions to the Franklin Society proposal, from voting for it during the society debate and signing a legislative petition to seeing the proposal as a threat to Washington College's survival. Given the condition of Washington College at the time, one might have seen the proposal as either the savior or death knell of the school, as a potential source of income through cooperation or as state-sponsored competition for students. Regardless, advocates of the military school and defenders of Washington College both had to legitimate their institutions through appeals to the elevation of poor young white men through education.

Just as it had periodically since its founding as an academy in 1749, Washington College came near to collapse around the time of the Franklin Society debates, retaining only three or four college students and eight to ten academy students. This decline occurred, in part, because of curricular changes in 1830. Louis Marshall, the new president, abolished formal classes and instituted self-directed studies, with faculty members present only to assist and guide students. Marshall left in 1834 after an inquiry by trustees into the decline of enrollment and complaints by Lexington citizens about the declining reputation of the school. The trustees then re-instituted the old curriculum under the presidency of Henry Ruffner, who had served as a temporary president several times in the past when numerous other presidents resigned or failed.[82]

Some participants in the education debates recommended establishing relationships between Washington College and other institutions, responding to a desire to expand educational opportunities for young white men but also as a means of increasing enrollment and funding for the college. The Manual Labour Society, for example, proposed this. John F. Caruthers, who served as secretary of this society and coauthored its initial announcement, and Captain Robert White, a member of the society, both served as trustees of Washington College. Likewise, Washington College alum John Preston proposed cooperation between the military academy and the college.[83] Trustees John Caruthers and William Taylor, Professor and Acting President Henry Ruffner, and Professor William Armstrong signed the petition to the legislature requesting the establishment of the military school.[84]

Other men proposed adding to Washington College's curriculum, including courses in the military arts and law, in order to attract new students and new sources of funding, especially the Cincinnati Fund for military education. The Society of the Cincinnati, founded in 1783 for officers of the Revolutionary War, established a fund to support educational institutions. The Virginia chapter chose to support Washington College in 1802 and decided in 1807 to require the school to have a professor teach fortification and gunnery in order to qualify for the money. The society handed over the funds to the commonwealth in 1824, granting the treasurer the authority to disburse the money only when Washington College qualified. This potential income encouraged some people to reject the Franklin Society's proposal in favor of Washington College hiring its own military professor. Others, however, hoped to employ a relationship between the military school and the college to qualify for the funds. Ultimately, the initial 1836 act establishing VMI explicitly acknowledged that the school would enable Washington College to qualify for the fund and, moreover, initially formed VMI as the military school of Washington College. The latter, however, exceeded the authority of the legislature because

Washington College was a private school. The legislature amended the act in 1839 to establish VMI, then so named, as an independent institution but one empowered to enter into cooperative relationships with Washington College. It still, however, took some time before Washington College received the funds. The state treasurer, Jerman Baker, embezzled the money, resulting in ongoing legal action by Washington College to obtain the funds, in which they succeeded only in 1848, in part, as a result of its use of VMI professors to provide the required military training.[85]

Other people viewed the Franklin Society proposal as a threat to Washington College. In an open letter to the Trustees of Washington College in the *Lexington Gazette*, anonymous author "Washington" argued that Washington College should revive itself by petitioning the legislature for funds, as unnamed "rival institutions," perhaps including the public University of Virginia, had done. "Washington," however, went beyond expressing concern for just the financial security of the school. He placed his proposal in the context that partially defined the post–Franklin Society debate, that of the expansion of educational opportunities for white men. The author stated, "I do firmly believe that Washington College is now, in every respect, one of the best institutions in the State, for young men of limited means."[86] "Washington" thereby indicates two things. First, young white men could *already* avail themselves of higher education, should they so choose, thus requiring no new and possibly rival institutions, though the costs of boarding probably precluded poor men from actually taking advantage of even entirely free tuition. Second, it indicates satisfaction with the curriculum and organization of Washington College, suggesting that white men of classes lower than those typically attending colleges could and should receive the same liberal education. Regardless, though not a supporter of the new proposals directed specifically toward the elevation of poor white men, even "Washington" had to legitimate his support for the older college through this new discourse.

Common Schools and Asylums for the Lowest of Society

Cornelius C. Baldwin, the owner of the *Lexington Gazette*, personally supported two very different proposals, one for the expansion of common schools for all white children and one for a "deaf and dumb asylum," with both proposals part of larger national education reform movements. These movements emphasized the moral improvement of all whites, especially the poor, through discipline and moral training, in order to improve society as a whole by mitigating supposed causes of crime and disorder. Nationally, or at least in the North, interest in this emerged in response to anxiety over increasing pluralism through immigration and the social transformation caused by urbanization and the growth of manufacturing and the market economy.[87] These movements aimed their work at either all peoples or those deemed in need of training to overcome particular disabilities rather than establishing educational institutions for particularly meritorious members of the lower classes.

Baldwin, while initially offering tentative support for Preston's plan as preferable to the professional arsenal guard, first supported a proposal to use the reorganization of the arsenal as a means of funding common schools.[88] In December of 1835, one year after the Franklin Society meetings, "A Citizen of Lexington," in response to the impending petitioning of the legislature by supporters of the military academy, argued for eliminating the arsenal guard, selling the arsenal property, re-establishing the arsenal in town instead of up on the hill, and having "three or four respectable men" live in the two ground floors beneath the arms, and then using the savings to establish common schools. He argued that this money could provide for the education of "400 CHILDREN WHO ARE NOW GROWING UP IN OUR STATE, ALMOST AS IGNORANT AS THE BRUTES THAT PERISH!" as compared to the twenty or so men he (under)estimated might be educated at the military academy.[89] In the next issue, Baldwin offered his support for "A Citizen's" plan "for the plain reason that the money will do more good in establishing primary schools." However, both Baldwin and "A Citizen" preferred, at least initially, Preston's plan to the current arsenal situation and hoped for its success, if adopted by the legislature.[90]

By the next month, Baldwin and "A Citizen" came to prefer, instead, the use of the savings to establish a "deaf and dumb" asylum on the grounds of the arsenal. These schools emerged along with a broader proliferation of institutions and asylums for those deemed deviant or dependent, including criminals, the insane, orphans, and the poor. Previously, Americans reserved institutionalization for extraordinary circumstances in which individuals and families found it impossible to care for an individual. Criminals were commonly subjected to flogging, stocks, or execution rather than long-term confinement. The new institutions, which increasingly became the preferred mode of dealing with the deviant and dependent, appeared, like common schools, in response to rapid social change and increasing fears of social instability. These institutions emphasized rehabilitation through regimentation and moral training for the purpose of transforming inmates or residents into industrious and orderly members of society, thus ensuring order and stability for the community and nation as a whole.[91]

The first school for Deaf (the capital *D* indicates an identity) Americans was the Connecticut Asylum for the Education and Instruction of Deaf and Dumb Persons, founded in Hartford 1817 and was, by 1820, renamed the American School for the Deaf. Other schools followed. They were bilingual residential schools, teaching primarily in the "manual" method in what is now called American Sign Language (ASL) but also teaching English using ASL. Their purpose, as historian R. A. R. Edwards describes it, "was to allow [the students] to take their place in society as Deaf Americans." ASL was the means of participating in a Deaf culture and even in Deaf families, while English was the means of "integration in a wider society."[92]

In January of 1836, Baldwin published and signed onto a memorial, or citizen petition, to the House of Delegates written by "A Citizen," in which they commented upon the general failure of other military schools, presumably referring to many of the private military schools in especially the North, which routinely closed after a short period of operation. Changing at least their public position, they then unambiguously denounced Preston's proposal, stating, "As a tax paying citizen, I enter my solemn protest against such a foolish expenditure of public treasure as that proposed by [John Preston]."[93] In this memorial, they proposed employing an inexpensive scheme for securing the arms of the arsenal and using the savings to establish a "deaf and dumb asylum" on the old arsenal grounds. Doing so would "elevate to intelligence, and respectability, and usefulness, and happiness, this most unfortunate class of society." Moreover, they appealed to the legislature's pride by identifying Virginia as lagging behind other states in their participation in the reform impulse. Virginia certainly did not lead in broader "asylum" endeavors, with leadership and greatest efforts coming from northern states. While encouraging Virginia to participate in these movements, the signatories also agreed with the goals of the asylum movement, employing institutionalization and education to transform the students into useful members of society.[94] Just three years later, Virginia did establish the Virginia Institution for the Deaf, Dumb, and Blind (now the Virginia School for the Deaf and the Blind) in nearby Staunton. It and VMI admitted their first students in the same year.[95]

Both the common school and asylum proposals reflect a prioritizing of education to raise people out of potential ignorance and immorality rather than to establish an equality of white men. That does not mean, however, that Baldwin and the signatories of the memorial did not believe in and support such equality. In fact, along with much of western Virginia, Baldwin and the *Lexington Gazette* strongly supported, for example, universal white male suffrage by continually printing articles calling for a new state constitutional convention to establish it.[96] Their support of such equality, however, may have manifested, in part, through a distrust of establishing what might have become another elite educational institution, not an unreasonable concern for the Jacksonian Democrats of the *Lexington Gazette*. Instead, they sought to elevate the "common man" and to contribute to social stability and improvement through institutions established for all or for the "most unfortunate class of society" rather than for the most meritorious.

Education to Cultivate Independence

Historian Bradford Wineman observed in Preston's proposals a view of education as capable of promoting a morality and industriousness that would cultivate "independence." This is part of why Preston and other Scots-Irish men of Rockbridge County supported the proposal.[97] But, in the context of the failure of the western elite to secure universal white male suffrage at the 1830 constitutional convention, this independence through education was a subversive idea. It is this post-convention context that helps us make sense of the debate over education in Lexington.

All advocates of education reform in Rockbridge County legitimated their proposals by arguing for the capacity of their plans to elevate the social status of students through an education they could not otherwise afford. In contrast to the eastern planter elite, participants in these debates generally identified poverty as an artificial barrier to the demonstration of virtue. Through education, however, poor white men could overcome this barrier and demonstrate the independence necessary for virtue, regardless of land ownership. The proposals differed, however, in their intended audiences and means of accomplishing their goals.

Advocates of the military school, manual labor school, and Washington College all supported a liberal education that emphasized classical languages, mathematics, and philosophy, the traditional curriculum of colleges attended by the elite. Advocates of the military and manual labor schools called not for distinct curricula but for distinct modes of discipline. "Washington," in contrast, made no suggestion of changing discipline at Washington College. Instead, poor boys would take the same courses and live and work in the same manner as their wealthier classmates. Preston, however, emphasized the military character of his school. The military training would enable the students to serve as arsenal guards and, thus, finance their education, but it would also provide moral training. Through military discipline, students would learn self-discipline. With this discipline, they could then claim public virtue and, therefore, claim a right to participate in governance. Likewise, advocates of a manual labor school saw the use of labor as more than a means of financing an education. Labor served as discipline to transform the students into useful and independent men. In the case of the advocates of both military and manual labor proposals, they saw this discipline as possibly even making their proposals superior to traditional colleges. Even sons of the elite, they believed, would seek out or benefit from this discipline.

Advocates for the military school, a manual labor school, or Washington College as the best means for providing poor white men with education all emphasized providing education only to those boys who had already proven themselves as meritorious in some way, particularly in their morality. Advocates of the military and manual labor schools appeared, however, to express some conflict over this. On the one hand, applicants had to have already demonstrated their morality, but the school would, on the other hand, provide moral training. In contrast, the advocates of the common schools and asylum presumed no particular merit. The common schools would provide educational opportunities for all whites in order to teach and instill morality to elevate that class as a whole. Likewise, the asylum advocates sought out students deemed dependent by defect in order to cultivate discipline that would enable the students to contribute to society.

In the context of the western attempt to gain universal white manhood suffrage, these debates make sense. The education reform advocates sought to use education as a means of either cultivating or even demonstrating an inherent independence of white men. White men did not, they argued, need to own land to be independent. They, in contrast to women and black people, were born independent. All white men were, therefore, inherently capable of voting and governing. At the very least, education would demonstrate that, even if virtue was unevenly distributed among white men, it was not distributed according to class. To limit governance and voting to the wealthy was arbitrary. Virtue existed among the poor as well, but poverty was an artificial barrier to its expression. Regardless, the debates over education revealed a new conception of white manhood that undermined the planters' domination of political power. Expanded education would provide the means of achieving white manhood suffrage, shift political power westward, and secure internal improvements for western Virginia.

LEGISLATIVE CLOSURE AND THE FOUNDING OF THE VIRGINIA MILITARY INSTITUTE

Even though advocates of the military school plan intended to use the school to further their own sectional interests, the legislature, dominated by eastern planters, accepted that proposal. Of the various proposals made in response to the Franklin Society debate, only two made their way to the legislature: the asylum and military academy proposals, doing so by means of citizen petitions. The manual labor school proposal required no legislative action, only local financial support. No substantial support, however, appears to have come forth and nothing like the proposed plan materialized. No available evidence indicates directly why the legislature acted as it did, but the possibilities include interests in strengthening the state militia and appeasing westerners still frustrated by the lack of reform at the constitutional convention.

The military academy proposal arrived at the House of Delegates on January 13, 1836, bearing ninety-three signatures. The petition stated very simply that a military school on the arsenal grounds was practical and "would be highly advantageous to the cause of learning, to the community in which it is hosted, and to some important interests of the State at large."[98] Moreover, eighteen citizens of Fairfield, about fifteen miles north of Lexington, submitted a supporting memorial, employing much of the same wording as the Lexington memorial.[99] These petitions, employing a deferential tone, emphasized unspecified benefits to Virginia, the Lexington area, and to the "cause of learning," the details of which they left to Rockbridge County delegates to provide to the legislature.

Alfred Leyburn, one of the two Rockbridge County delegates and future trustee of both Washington College and VMI, presented the petitions.[100] Charles Dorman, the other Rockbridge delegate, sponsored the legislation and successfully moved to have the petition sent to the Committee of Schools and Colleges on January 16 to "be instructed to enquire into the expediency of establishing, in connexion [sic] with Washington college in the county of Rockbridge, a military school, and substituting said school, in lieu of the public arsenal at that place, as the depository of the public arms, and that said committee have leave to report by bill or otherwise."[101]

After appearing first in the *Lexington Gazette*, the approximately twelve hundred–word asylum proposal arrived on January 19 with only four signatures, including that of Cornelius Baldwin, the owner of the *Lexington Gazette*, and without the support of the Rockbridge delegates.[102] On the twenty-first, the House of Delegates moved both proposals to the Committee on the Militia Laws.[103] Unfortunately, we have no record of who sat on either committee or what they said of either proposal. The safety of the arsenal arms, however must have come up, because Dorman had written to Alden Partridge, a former West Point superintendent and an advocate of military education, to inquire about this some-time in December.[104] Dorman received an enthusiastic reply in the affirmative, which he then had published in the *Lexington Gazette* on January 22, the same day the *Gazette* reported that Dorman had introduced the military academy petition to the House.[105]

With the issue having gone before the legislature, attempts to establish support for either plan continued both in Richmond and in the pages of the *Gazette*. Preston himself traveled to Richmond to lobby the delegates to support the military school petition, giving each delegate a copy of his Cives articles.[106] Throughout February, the *Gazette* published three statements from other papers, including from the state capital Richmond, supporting the asylum plan on the basis of cost, effectiveness, and the honor it would bring to Virginia. They also republished their asylum memorial.[107]

Dorman had the *Gazette* publish a second letter from Partridge in which he extolled the virtues of the commonwealth establishing a military school. He urged Virginia, which he called "the parent State," to "take the lead in [public military education] as she has done on many other important subjects." Such a school would be "in perfect accordance with the principles of our republican institutions" because it would blend "the citizen with the soldier and thereby set an example well worthy of being followed by all her sister States."[108] Like the asylum proposal, quoted previously, this letter called upon the pride of Virginia, pointing to the opportunity for Virginians to lead the nation in the creation of a new type of education, one befitting a republic.

While no available evidence indicates what arguments or whose influence held sway, the Committee on the Militia Laws reported on March 9 that the military academy petition "is reasonable," meaning the proposed reorganization could serve to maintain the security of the arsenal, and rejected the asylum petition.[109] On March 29, the General Assembly created the act "re-organizing the Lexington arsenal, and establishing a military school in connexion [*sic*] with Washington College." While providing the school's Board of Visitors substantial autonomy, the act called only for a professor to teach "military science," with additional courses provided free of charge by Washington College, whose students could, in exchange, receive military training at the military school, making Washington College finally eligible to receive the long-delayed Cincinnati Fund.[110]

So why would legislators, the majority being from the eastern planter elite, support this legislation? I have not seen direct evidence for any answer. Perhaps they saw the school as a means of not only providing an arsenal guard but also inexpensively improving the state militia by spreading trained artillery men and men with officer training throughout Virginia. The legislators would likely have seen this as important for two reasons.

First, the debate over the arsenal arose during debates over the future of militias and the regular army following the War of 1812. After the war, the national debate over militias shifted. No longer did Congress express concern about a professional army taking over the government. Instead, they emphasized the poor performance, whether true or not, of militias in the War of 1812 and the need for a regular, professional force. The "common militia" of universal service declined after the war, largely replaced by a regular army and volunteer local and state militias, which were especially popular in New England. In the Mexican-American War, it was this combination of volunteer militia and professional army that served.[111]

Despite changes in the national debate, some people continued to fear that professional soldiers, unlike militiamen, who had roots in their local communities and states, would be loyal primarily to their officers and the federal military itself, posing the threat of *coup d'état* or military rule.[112] Virginia's 1830 constitution reflected such fears of divided allegiances within a professional military by excluding from suffrage any seaman, soldier, or officer of the US Army or Navy.[113] The Nullification Crises and the passage of the 1833 Force Bill may have renewed Virginia legislators' concerns about a professional army. Even though Virginia's political leaders opposed South Carolina's tariff nullification, they generally opposed President Andrew Jackson's threats to send federal troops to that state to collect the tariffs.[114] By supporting the military school, the planter elite could have helped to stave off any potential threats from the US Army, either by having a militia as a bulwark against that army or by strengthening the militia in order to avoid strengthening a national military for future wars. A larger military meant more men whose stake in society, whether in a local community or in the commonwealth, was questionable because of the possibility of divided allegiances. So, support for the military school may have served to strengthen their more aristocratic republicanism rather than to weaken it by promoting the interests of the men of western Virginia.

Second, the proposal came less than five years after Nat Turner's slave revolt in Southampton, Virginia, during which the rebels killed over fifty white people, including children. Militiamen crushed the revolt and killed over one hundred black people, including many with no involvement in the revolt. This event created such fear of further revolts that the Virginia legislature considered gradually emancipating enslaved blacks and then depatriating them from Virginia, perhaps even forcibly removing them to somewhere in Africa. The militia would again serve as the primary force for reasserting control in the event of such future revolts.[115] Although we have no record of any local advocate of the school ever justifying the school in the context of slavery, Partridge advocated the development of state military schools in the South to prepare specifically for slave revolts.[116] It is possible that the legislators were simply willing to support a proposal that would help to secure white control over black Virginians.

Wineman argues against militia reform as a significant factor. He points out the significant fact that the founding legislation did not require VMI graduates to spend any time in militia service. Nor did the legislation specify any potential role for the graduates in the militia in times of emergency. We should not ignore that. Wineman argues, instead, that education was of greater importance to Virginians than the militia. Education promoted a "free and democratic government." Moreover, he appeals to Scots-Irish enthusiasm for education.[117] Wineman is, I think, right about the motivations of the people of Rockbridge County and perhaps even western Virginia as a whole. However, this enthusiasm for education does not apply to the eastern planters—descendants of English settlers—who dominated the legislature. It was they who could ultimately pass or reject the VMI proposal. Had they a particular zeal for education, they could have, for example, promoted a public school system like that growing in northern states at the time. If we were to choose between two issues that would convince the English planters of the east to support the proposal, I argue that support for the militia was likely a stronger motivation than support for public education.

Alternatively, the eastern legislators could have simply offered the military school as a pittance to quiet western discontent after the 1830 convention, as they did with some western transportation projects.[118] Perhaps they felt that a few internal improvements projects could be worth it to avoid any stronger pressure for the eastern elites to share further power with the west. Such pressure could possibly have led not just to a sharing of power with western elites but also to a broadening of suffrage across Virginia. This, the eastern elite feared, would lead to heavy taxation on landowners and possibly even the abolition of slavery. The eastern elite had re-secured its authority in the new constitution, but they may have seen the military school as part of the price of having done so.

Despite the passage of this legislation in 1836 and regardless of the motivations for it, no cadets arrived until November of 1839, after further legislation in March of that year. Officers of Washington College protested that the legislature overstepped its authority by legislating the operations of a private college when it required the school to provide courses to the cadets of the military school.

In response, the legislature amended the act to simply empower the board of visitors of the military school to negotiate collaboration with Washington College.[119]

Regardless of the motives of the legislature and the eastern elite that dominated it, the western context out of which VMI emerged established the school as a tool of class and ethnic conflict. VMI would become a node in a network of men, both Scots-Irish men of the west and middle-class men of the east, employing a new idea of the equality of white men as a means of legitimizing greater political power for themselves. Education was one means of producing and legitimizing that equality. One of the primary purposes of acquiring power was to establish internal improvements that would expand the market economy of relatively isolated western Virginia. Engineering was necessary for producing transportation infrastructure. Although most engineers did not learn their trade in schools, the new institution, born partly out of a desire for internal improvements, would become the means of creating the very engineers to create that infrastructure. The new school brought together threads of white manhood equality, internal improvements, and class formation, all of which the officers of the future school would weave together to create the cloth out of which engineers were to be made.

CHAPTER THREE

CREATING THE "WEST POINT OF THE SOUTH"

In the winter of 1839, before the Virginia Military Institute (VMI) opened, citizens of Rockbridge County called upon their governor to act quickly to open the school, which they characterized as a school "in which would be taught the principles of Civil Engineering."[1] Eight months later, the Board of Visitors gave form to the school. To teach the principles of civil engineering, the board crafted a curriculum that, along with military training, emphasized mathematics, science, and engineering courses as well as modern rather than classical languages. It was a bare-bones, but thorough, engineering course.

Although engineering came to dominate the curriculum of VMI, it could have turned out otherwise. The initial question posed by the Franklin Society, "Would it be politic for the state to establish a military school at the arsenal near Lexington, in connexion [sic] with Washington College on the plan of the W. Point Academy,"[2] specifically identified West Point as the model for the school. In describing his vision of the school, however, John Preston, writing as "Cives" in the *Lexington Gazette*, never mentioned either West Point or one of the primary characteristics of the school's curriculum: military and civil engineering.[3] Preston's detailed description of his proposed curriculum, moreover, clearly indicates a combination of military training and liberal education. Preston and others at the time would not have necessarily identified formal education as an obvious means of entering engineering; most men learned engineering on the job. West Point, therefore, likely offered to the initial proponents of the Franklin Society plan only a model of military discipline and training and a means of maintaining the arsenal guard.

Nonetheless, VMI did become one of the earliest and most significant sources of formally trained engineers in America and took much of its curriculum, as well as its professors, from West Point. As such, it fulfilled the earliest proposal in ways unanticipated by its initial proponents. We cannot, however, take this outcome for granted and must explain how engineering came to dominate VMI's curriculum. It began with an early intervention by Alden Partridge, an advocate of public military and engineering education, and the appointment of Claudius Crozet (see Figure 3.1), a French-trained engineer and former West Point professor, to the first Board of Visitors of VMI. Partridge never had any connection to VMI, and Crozet soon moved to the background of its leadership, despite his presidency on the board. The board's appointment, however, of Francis Henney Smith (see Figure 3.2), a West Point graduate and admirer of Crozet, as the first superintendent and professor of engineering ensured the maintenance of a strong West Point model of engineering education. The educational backgrounds of these men positioned them to view military training and engineering education as complementary and even as obvious partners within a single school.

The primary context for the founding of VMI was the failure of the Scots-Irish of western Virginia to gain universal white

Figure 3.1. Claudius Crozet (1790–1864). Portrait of Claudius Crozet, Preston Library, Virginia Military Institute, Lexington, VA.

manhood suffrage and the "white basis" of representative apportionment. One of the principal interests driving their struggle
for greater power was their desire for internal improvements to
integrate them into an expanding market economy. Initially, VMI
was to serve as a means of arguing for white manhood suffrage
by revealing poverty to be an arbitrary barrier to the expression

Figure 3.2. Francis Henney Smith (1812–1890). Portrait of Francis H. Smith, Preston Library, Virginia Military Institute, Lexington, VA.

of virtue. Were the western Virginians successfully to do so, they might acquire the power necessary to pass funding for internal improvements. However, because of the intervention of Crozet, Partridge, and Smith, these men also acquired a school that would train the very men who would build the desired roads, railroads, and canals.

WHAT PRESTON PROPOSED: LIBERAL OR ENGINEERING EDUCATION?

As discussed in chapter 2, John Preston, the first public advocate of establishing a military school on the grounds of the Lexington arsenal, laid out his argument for the school in three anonymous letters to the *Lexington Gazette*. Writing under the plural Latin "Cives," he proposed in the first letter that the students "have afforded them, the opportunities of a liberal education," which would include "the classics, and the higher branches of an English education," Latin, a modern language, mathematics, natural philosophy, and military arts.[4] There is nothing in this first letter to indicate a plan to train engineers. In fact, Preston explicitly described the proposed education as "liberal." This matters. Had Preston had his way, VMI, while perhaps providing a means of arguing for white manhood suffrage, would not have provided civil engineers for the internal improvements that were at the heart of the east-west struggle for power in Virginia. This would be true even if, as some historians have implied, Preston did indeed originally envision a school for mechanical engineers instead of civil engineers.

Historian Rod Andrew Jr. argues that Preston's second letter provides evidence of his intent. In that letter, Preston, attempting to assuage concerns about the expense of the school, argued that just a single boy "rescued from the thrall of ignorance" by education could "richly repay the State for all the money ever expended." That is, if the boy had a "mind like that of Clinton, or Fulton, or Arkwright" and could therefore contribute by "developing the wealth of a country, or adding by inventions to its capabilities."[5] New York governor DeWitt Clinton promoted the construction of the Erie Canal. American Robert Fulton made steamboats practical, vastly decreasing shipping costs and time. Englishman Richard Arkwright invented water-powered thread spinning machines that arguably marked the beginning of the modern factory and the Industrial Revolution. Andrew identifies all three men with engineering. From a modern perspective, this is not unreasonable; these men were instrumental in America's and Britain's industrial revolutions. Fulton and Arkwright might even seem to be exemplars of early mechanical engineering. Consequently, Andrew argues that Preston did indeed have engineering, meaning mechanical engineering, in mind as early as 1835.[6]

Historian Bradford Wineman builds on Andrew's argument by placing the founding of VMI in the context of Whig politics in western Virginia. He argues, "Preston anticipated overwhelming public support for an institution whose mission was to produce qualified engineers and teachers who could aid the state and contribute to internal improvements."[7] I will provide further support for the importance of this context in the founding of VMI. Regardless, when considered in the context of antebellum engineering, Preston's statement does not in fact suggest an engineering curriculum like that at West Point or, for that matter, anywhere else.

Recall that the Virginia Military Institute opened within a heterogeneous professional culture that left America with no single national pattern of engineering practice. Men became engineers by a variety of pathways during the antebellum period, including on-the-job training and various academic approaches (see chapter 1). The United States had few engineering schools, and, except for West Point, which provided comprehensive civil and military engineering training, those few offered minimal training and produced few engineers. Most engineers learned their trade through on-the-job craft training under the guidance of more experienced engineers.[8] Consequently, Preston and other early advocates of VMI may not have even thought of a school as a place in which to train engineers.

It must be recalled that for most of the antebellum period, engineering meant civil and military engineering. What we might now, looking back, think of as mechanical engineering was carried out by people who called themselves mechanics. It was only in the 1850s that a subset of these mechanics used education and scientific knowledge to create a professional elite that referred to themselves as mechanical engineers.[9]

So, what then should we make of Preston's comment in his second letter in which he praised Clinton, Fulton, and Arkwright? First of all, were we to think of Fulton and Arkwright as engineers at all, they would be mechanical engineers. But, as I discuss above, there was no professional mechanical engineering until the 1850s. These men were mechanics or possibly inventors. Preston certainly made no proposal to create a school for mechanics. Moreover, the engineering that VMI offered in its first decades was exclusively civil and military. Clinton, however, was involved with the Erie Canal project, certainly a work of civil engineering, but he was not himself an engineer. He was a lifelong politician who merely promoted the building of the canal. So, in the context of antebellum engineering, we cannot turn to any of these three men as examples of engineers or as evidence of Preston's desire to train engineers.

To Preston, these three men represented not engineers but men whose individual genius had enriched America and the world. In his second "Cives" letter, he lamented the number of such great minds that must have been lost as a result of poverty and lack of access to education. He said, "Genius knows no fixed locality, and is as often born under a cottage roof, as the dome of a palace."[10] VMI could identify and cultivate such genius among the lower classes. It was not that these geniuses would go on to be engineers or mechanics, or even necessarily contribute to internal improvements, but that a liberal education would cultivate their minds so as to enable them to express their genius, whatever its direction, and enrich Virginia.

Nonetheless, the Franklin Society members did point to West Point as a model for the school that would replace the arsenal guard. And one of the central features of the West Point curriculum was engineering. Might not this feature have been in the minds of men who thirsted for roads and canals that would expand the market economy in their western part of Virginia? On the one hand, it is, of course, quite possible that they were totally ignorant of that feature of West Point, a school they might have thought of as training merely army officers. On the other hand, after their debates, but before Preston's letters to the *Lexington Gazette*, the paper printed an excerpt from a West Point report on that school's annual examination of its cadets that might have alerted them to the importance of engineering. The excerpt stated the obvious that the knowledge the cadets learned was valuable in wartime, but, less obvious, it was also useful in "times of peace, when applied to the prosecution of the various improvements which are so rapidly developing and enlarging the resources of our country."[11] This statement is somewhat vague and is not illuminated by the rest of the excerpt. The men who read this would've, nonetheless, readily recognized the reference to internal improvements. But they wouldn't have necessarily understood from the report how West Point knowledge contributed to it. Nonetheless, the article might cast doubt on my argument that Preston and others wouldn't have thought of a school as a place to specifically train engineers. This is doubly so because it was probably not an accident that this report appeared in the paper. It seems likely that one of the advocates of VMI arranged for its publication. But we must acknowledge that Preston did not make any mention of an engineering curriculum in his letters. He explicitly identified a liberal education for his cadets, rather than drawing on western sympathies for internal improvements by pointing to West Point's curriculum as a model. No mention of providing an engineering education at VMI appeared until later.

ALDEN PARTRIDGE AND THE ORIGINS OF VMI'S ENGINEERING CURRICULUM

The first suggestion of the proposed military school in Lexington providing civil engineering training to its students came from Norwich University founder Alden Partridge, an advocate of public and private military education. The early advocates of the school made no indication of an intent to provide engineering training. In fact, as discussed above, Preston clearly identified a mix of military and liberal education as the curriculum. Partridge, however, suggested teaching engineering in a January 1836 letter to Rockbridge County delegate Charles Dorman, who had written to Partridge to ask his opinion on the viability of students guarding an arsenal. This education would, Partridge argued, provide the graduates of the school with a practical training that they could apply directly to a career in building a transportation infrastructure to support the expanding nation.

Partridge's Advocacy of Military and Engineering Education

Partridge developed an interest in and plan for a major expansion of military education in the United States while a professor and superintendent at West Point, where he first studied and then taught engineering. He hoped to spread this combination of military and engineering training through networks of public and private colleges that employed military discipline, though not necessarily to produce military officers. These efforts even took him to Virginia, where he briefly taught military courses to students at the University of Virginia and the state militia in Richmond. In the end, however, he had little success in establishing his own schools.

Partridge, of Norwich, Vermont, graduated from West Point in 1806 and received a commission as a First Lieutenant and an appointment as assistant professor of mathematics at his alma mater. He received an appointment as professor of engineering in 1813 and then another promotion to superintendent in 1815, but largely because of a lack of any other willing candidate. Students and instructors soon complained of his authoritarian style of administration. After complaints reached even President James Madison, Partridge received orders to take leave. He returned to duty after a Court of Inquiry cleared him of charges in 1816, but subsequent complaints and intrigues, including an attempt at arresting the new superintendent, Sylvanus Thayer, eventually led President James Monroe to order Partridge removed from his position as superintendent and court-martialed. Found guilty on charges of disobeying orders and mutiny, the chief of engineers placed Partridge on indefinite leave. In response, Partridge resigned from the army in 1818.[12]

Even before the start of his West Point troubles, Partridge had begun what he would later adopt as his life's work: establishing a system of public and private military schools to produce citizen soldiers and to support state militias through military education that emphasized science and engineering. Partridge began with an unsuccessful attempt in 1816 to convince New York governor Daniel Tompkins to support a state-sponsored military academy. After he resigned from the military, Partridge established the American Literary, Scientific and Military Academy in his hometown of Norwich, Vermont, in 1820. He hoped the school, through an engineering curriculum, would fulfill what he saw as a need to train civilians to build a national infrastructure, including canals and roads, though he soon lessened the school's emphasis on engineering in order to accommodate the desires of students and their parents for a more traditional liberal training. He reincorporated the school as Norwich University in 1834.[13]

Partridge repeatedly attempted to establish more schools, to which he, when he succeeded, often appointed former students as their heads. He actively pursued his work in southern states, either personally or through newspapers, because he perceived the South as more receptive to his schemes than the North. He did in fact manage to recruit about one-third of his ALS&MA cadets from southern states. Partridge, a defender of slavery, argued that the schools could serve to provide a guard in case of slave rebellions, an argument he hoped would facilitate the spread of his schools.[14]

Although he did not successfully establish any lasting schools of his own in a southern state prior to the movement to establish VMI, he did establish the Virginia Literary, Scientific & Military

Institute in Portsmouth, Virginia, near Norfolk, after receiving an invitation to visit the town in 1839. It officially closed in 1849, but reopened as a normal school. Partridge, himself, briefly taught in the South, where he offered a military course at the University of Virginia during the spring of 1834 and then again for the state militia in Richmond in 1835–1836.[15]

"The Partridge Connection" with VMI

Probably because of Partridge's enthusiastic advocacy of military education in the South based on the model of West Point and a misunderstanding of the role of the Virginia legislature in founding VMI,[16] some historians, including Terry Reynolds, assume that the legislature took direct inspiration from Partridge when it established VMI.[17] In contrast, historian Dean Paul Baker states, "Although they were working toward similar goals, there is no known evidence of collaboration between [VMI Superintendent Francis Henney] Smith and Partridge or of influence by either in the creation of the other's academy."[18] Although technically correct about the relationship between Partridge and Smith, Baker incorrectly identifies Smith, not appointed until 1839, as the crucial figure in establishing VMI's curriculum. Andrew, in *Long Gray Lines: The Southern Military School Tradition, 1839–1915*, comes closer to describing the nature of the "Partridge Connection," characterizing it as an "indirect" transmission of "the main features of West Point to . . . state-supported institutions in the South."[19] However, while Andrew recognizes and cites letters that Partridge wrote to Rockbridge County delegate Charles Dorman, sponsor of the founding legislation, to enthusiastically support the establishment of the school,[20] Andrew underestimates the importance of these letters, which provide the earliest preserved suggestion to provide engineering training at the school.

Despite eventually providing an engineering curriculum that exceeded all but West Point's after 1839, the first efforts to establish

VMI did not include any emphasis on engineering, and no one has presented evidence that John Preston or any other early advocate looked to Norwich or Partridge for their models. Nonetheless, we cannot disregard the reasonable possibility that Preston did indeed know of Partridge and his work, especially given Partridge's presence in Virginia in 1834, prior to the first discussions of the plan at the Franklin Society meetings in December of that year. Dorman, a close associate of Preston, must have known something of Partridge and his work to have asked him for his opinion on the military school proposal. We do not, however, know when Dorman first heard of Partridge, which may not have occurred until after the first proposals. Regardless, Preston, like Partridge, took direct inspiration for the form of a military school from West Point, even if he did not look to its engineering curriculum as a model. Andrew claims that Preston began to consider establishing a school along the lines of West Point after visiting the school while accompanying a Lexington boy who enrolled as a cadet.[21] Andrew, however, mistakenly attributed this story to Preston, taking it from a posthumous story about Hugh Barclay, a future member of the first Board of Visitors of VMI, given as possible evidence of Barclay as the originator of the idea of establishing a military school.[22] I was unable to find evidence that indicated that Preston ever visited West Point, an event he would have surely noted in his histories of VMI.

Although we have no evidence of Partridge's direct influence on Preston, Partridge did have some influence with Dorman well before VMI's Board of Visitors appointed Smith the first superintendent in 1839. As I described in the previous chapter, Partridge, through communication with Dorman in December of 1835, argued that students could provide better protection for the arsenal arms than the present guard and thus provided important expert support for the school while the legislature debated VMI's founding in 1836. [23] Moreover, Partridge may have instigated the first consideration of providing an engineering education at the new school.

After publishing Partridge's first letter, Dorman then had the *Lexington Gazette* publish a second letter, in which he extolled the virtues of the state establishing a military school. Partridge played to Virginia's vanity by asking it to "take the lead in [state-funded military education] as she has done on many other important subjects, and adopt a system of education in perfect accordance with the principles of our republican institutions." In so doing, Virginia would "set an example well worthy of being followed by all her sister states."[24]

More importantly, Partridge also advocated that the school focus on teaching civil engineering. Engineering, however, had not yet entered into any public discussion as far as the preserved record indicates. But, in publishing this letter, Dorman may have opened a new front of support for the school in the west by now tying the project to internal improvements, something nearly universally supported in western Virginia, including by the *Lexington Gazette*. He emphasized the practicality of training students in civil engineering, about which he said it opened "a wider field for lucrative and useful employment to young men who are properly prepared to enter upon its duties than any other occupation, and [was] rapidly extending every year." Despite this, he pointed out, there were few schools available for "properly preparing young men for the correct discharge of the duties of this department." Like many of the future officers of VMI, he was critical of existing colleges, about which he said, "[T]he course of education is any thing but practical." Although they did teach mathematics, "the mode of instruction is entirely abstract without the science ever being reduced to practice. The consequence is that students after having completed their education are just as ignorant of practical Science as when they commenced."[25]

Beyond providing military training, Partridge argued that military schools should also provide a "useful" training for civilian pursuits, which the colleges and universities of the time, in his estimation, did not provide. Moreover, he did not foresee the graduates of these schools going into professional military service in any substantial numbers and would, therefore, need to pursue some form of civilian work. Of all civilian work, Partridge most favored engineering, for which he, because of the irregular and limited training of American engineers, saw enormous opportunity.

Partridge's 1836 letter to Dorman provides the earliest clear evidence of an association of civil engineering with the school that became VMI. I have seen no such mention in the discussions of the military school proposal in 1834 or 1835. Despite the fact that West Point provided what later became the model for VMI's engineering curriculum, the early advocates of a military school may not have even thought of civil engineering as something to teach in schools. Instead, they likely thought of it as something one learned on one's own or as a craft. While the early advocates of the school probably did not draw their inspiration from Partridge's schools, Partridge did directly generate the initial interest in establishing an engineering curriculum at that school. This, however, occurred over a year after the first efforts to establish the school.

CLAUDIUS CROZET: ARCHITECT OF THE VIRGINIA MILITARY INSTITUTE

Crozet, as the first president of the Board of Visitors, provided the primary leadership to establish an engineering curriculum at VMI. He drew upon his experiences as a graduate of the École Polytechnique and the Imperial Artillery School of France and as a professor at West Point to establish, at VMI, military regulations and a curriculum modeled after those schools.

Claudius Crozet: Educator, Engineer, and Soldier[26]

Prior to his affiliation with the Virginia Military Institute, Crozet's career demonstrated substantial experience with and expertise in education, engineering, and military arts, all of which prepared him for and shaped his administration of the new school. He was born in France in 1790 into a bourgeois family. He graduated from the École Polytechnique, a French engineering school that employed military discipline, in 1807 in the midst of Emperor Napoléon's military successes. After graduation, he qualified for the Artillery Corps (Corps de l'Artillery) and gained admission to the Artillery School at Metz (École d'Artillerie). In 1809, he received an assignment to the First Battalion of Bridge Builders. He gained substantial practical engineering experience, particularly with bridges, while serving in Germany and the Kingdom of Holland. Rising to the rank of captain, he participated in the initial invasion of Russia, probably being taken prisoner in 1812, and remained a prisoner of war for two years. However, he reportedly spent his imprisonment in the home of a Russian noble, teaching French to the nobleman's children and writing a Russian grammar book for French students. The Russians released him in April of 1814, after the abdication of Napoléon. Crozet returned to his father's home and his family in Paris, where he recuperated after he received leave from the military. He resigned in 1816 after a short and uneventful reactivation.

Crozet immigrated to the United States with his new wife, Agathe Decamp, in the summer or fall of 1816. During the voyage, Crozet met American General Simon Bernard, who had received an appointment as a military engineer at West Point. Probably through this contact, Crozet obtained the position of assistant professor of engineering at West Point beginning in September of 1816. There, he became the first teacher of descriptive geometry in America, a subject that became fundamental to American engineering. He also created new courses for principles of artillery, tactics, and topography. Besides these developments, Crozet also participated in the improvement of the overall curriculum, including making the mathematics courses more rigorous and complete. Present for the conflict that led to Partridge's dismissal, Crozet associated himself with the anti-Partridge faction. Regardless, Partridge respected Crozet and nominated him as his replacement as professor of engineering in 1816. Crozet, however, did not like Partridge because of his autocratic manner regarding academic issues. Such issues eventually brought Crozet himself into conflict with the superintendent when Crozet advocated for greater independence for professors from military authority, including what he saw as the overbearing authority of the superintendent. In general, Crozet did not like West Point. He received less pay than the philosophy professor, had no teaching assistants unlike the other professors, and felt he had received less courtesy and respect than other professors, despite the great importance of the subjects he taught. Finally, he disliked the remoteness of West Point.

Crozet left West Point in 1823 after failed attempts to join the faculty of the new University of Virginia. Instead, he took a position as the principal engineer of the Virginia Board of Public Works. He resigned, however, in 1830, probably because of his frustration with his lack of authority to see projects carried out in the manner he recommended and with the interference of the planter elite and legislature in what he saw as a rational development of a statewide transportation network. He would have been accustomed to engineers having such authority in France, which had centralized government control over infrastructure development. He took a new position as the state engineer of Louisiana, where he felt comfortable because of the prevalence of French and the state's interest in developing railroads, a development that Crozet supported. He resigned from this position as well in 1834 after even greater frustration than that experienced in Virginia, largely because of the great distractions of pork-barrel projects. He then took a position as professor of mathematics and president of Jefferson College, a new public academy in Convent, Louisiana. He resigned, however, in February of 1836 to take a surveying position with the city of New Orleans. The following year, Crozet accepted Governor David Campbell's invitation to return to Virginia as the state engineer.

Crozet Establishes an Engineering Curriculum

After several years of delays, the Virginia legislature finally took the action necessary to actually open the new school. This coincided with the return of Crozet to Virginia, who then also accepted the first presidency of the school's Board of Visitors. Much of the leadership in organizing the institution then fell to him. He adopted both the system of discipline and academics of West Point for VMI. However, he emphasized a civil engineering curriculum over even the military curriculum and thus established VMI as primarily an engineering school.

After complaints that the Virginia legislature had not acted to establish the military academy as prescribed by the 1836 legislation,[27] Dorman urged Governor David Campbell, in April of 1837, to appoint a Board of Visitors. He argued, "An Enlightened Board, who will make wholesome regulations, and whose standing will give Character to the institution, is exceedingly desirable. Another suggestion I beg leave to make, viz. that the Board be selected from various portions of the state." He recommended General Botts of Fredericksburg, General William Ligon of Powhatan, General Johnston of Smyth, General Baldwin of Augusta, and General Watts of Botetourt.[28] By the end of March, Governor Campbell appointed Ligon and Johnston as recommended as well as General George Rust Jr. of Loudoun and, as required by the founding legislation, Adjutant General Bernard Peyton.[29] In addition, he appointed Crozet, who had returned to Virginia that year from Louisiana at the invitation of Governor Campbell himself.[30] The rest of the board apparently approved of Crozet's appointment and elected him president at their first meeting on August 7, 1837, in Lexington.[31]

I have seen no evidence that indicates why Governor Campbell appointed Crozet to the board. He may have chosen Crozet for his extensive military and educational background, including employment as a former West Point professor and president of Jefferson

College, both of which Campbell would have seen as exceedingly useful for administering a school inspired by West Point. Campbell may have also chosen him for his position as one of the most experienced and competent engineers in the United States, but only if Campbell already anticipated an engineering curriculum for the new school.[32] I do not, however, know if the decision to provide this curriculum had yet been made or if Campbell had even seen Partridge's recommendation to do so. Regardless, Crozet's assumption of leadership almost ensured his vision of an engineering school based upon the models of West Point and the École Polytechnique.

The first direct evidence of any actual decision to establish an engineering curriculum for the military school comes after Crozet's appointment and the first meeting of the Board of Visitors, for which we have little information. In January of 1839, Rockbridge County delegate Alfred Leyburn introduced a petition to the legislature bearing eighty-seven signatures as well as an additional endorsement from John Preston. In this petition, these citizens of Rockbridge County requested that the legislature act on a recommendation of the Board of Visitors to amend the founding legislation and provide the funds necessary to establish the school, which, as yet, continued to exist only on paper. As part of their justification, they claimed, "A school in which would be taught the principles of *Civil Engineering* would prepare our young men to participate in the progress of a profession at present more lucrative than any other and to aid the state in the prosecution of her plans of public improvement,"[33] using much the same language as that used by Partridge in his letter to Dorman. Presumably, the board had already determined at their first meeting in 1837 that they would pursue an engineering curriculum and that this had become known by the citizens of Lexington, though such information did not appear in the *Lexington Gazette*. Even if Partridge's letter had convinced these citizens of this course, Crozet would have needed little persuasion to advocate it himself. Nor did Crozet require the urging or influence of Partridge, whom he knew intimately from West Point.

With the building of the military school stalled while the Board of Visitors waited for the legislature to act on its recommendations, little work occurred and Crozet continued to focus on his position as principal engineer for the commonwealth. No one, in fact, had even yet named the school. Citizens of Rockbridge County finally prompted the legislature, in January of 1839, to amend the initial legislation, which it did on March 29, 1839. Based on the recommendation of Preston, the legislature adopted the name Virginia Military Institute. Additionally, it reconstituted and enlarged the Board of Visitors, provided additional money for new buildings, and clarified the relationship between VMI and Washington College.[34] Governor Campbell appointed the new board the following month and included Crozet as one of its members. Curiously, Dorman, who again urged the governor to quickly appoint a board, did not include Crozet among his recommendations.[35] Whether or not Dorman had any concerns about or dislike of Crozet, the new board, including Preston, did not. Once again, the members selected Crozet as president,[36] a position he held until he resigned in 1845.[37]

Under Crozet's leadership, the board set to work in Lexington on May 30 to finally bring the school to life. They first worked with a committee from Washington College to establish and make official the relationship between the two schools, which sat adjacent to each other without even a wall or fence between them. The board then continued other crucially important work, including determining that the cadets' breakfasts would consist of "Hot Corn Cakes and Fresh Light Bread" and "Butter, Coffee and cold Meat." More importantly, they spent five days drafting regulations, the governance structure, and academic departments.

The board established four academic departments: Infantry Tactics and Military Police, Mathematics, Science and Practice of

Artillery, and Civil and Military Engineering.[38] In addition to these four departments, they established two additional subjects of study that cadets would pursue at Washington College. The first, English language and literature and French and German languages, emphasized modern, rather than classical, languages and literature. The other subject area, natural and experimental philosophy, included astronomy, chemistry, mineralogy, and geology. The extensive mathematics curriculum included algebra, geometry, trigonometry, mensuration, descriptive geometry, analytical geometry, and differential calculus. Most likely at the recommendation of Crozet, one of the nation's greatest experts on engineering mathematics, the board selected several textbooks for use, including several mathematics texts written by either French authors or else modeled directly after or translated from French texts. [39]

The board established a system for calculating merit rolls that indicate how they valued the various academic courses. As done at West Point, as well as at the École Polytechnique to this day, cadets were individually and publicly ranked by a numerical score so that everyone knew their relative accomplishment compared to the other cadets. Not all courses, however, provided equal weight in these calculations at VMI. Conduct, engineering, mathematics, and natural philosophy weighed heaviest with a multiplier of three. The purely military courses provided less weight, with one's infantry tactics score multiplied by two and artillery, along with English, French, German, and drawing, by only one.[40] These indicate the primacy of engineering over military training.

Through their various actions, the board defined the operations of VMI on the model of West Point in both discipline and curriculum. But, although unanticipated by Preston and others when they first proposed the use of West Point as a model, the board also defined VMI as largely an engineering school. Just as had Crozet at the École Polytechnique, the cadets would learn military and civil engineering while living under military discipline. One other decision would solidify these decisions and bring them into operation. They unanimously selected Francis Henney Smith as the first superintendent and professor of mathematics and engineering.[41] After providing the leadership that created an enduring vision of VMI, Crozet, though he faithfully traveled from Richmond to attend annual board meetings, receded from outright leadership to focus on his role as principal engineer for the commonwealth.[42]

FRANCIS HENNEY SMITH AND THE "WEST POINT COURSE" AT VMI

By selecting Smith as the first superintendent and professor of mathematics and engineering at VMI, the Board of Visitors gave him the responsibility of taking the framework they produced under Crozet's leadership and making it work. Smith accepted this responsibility but immediately sought to build further upon this framework and to turn VMI into the "West Point of the South." Smith had graduated from West Point and always employed it as his standard for all higher education, in terms of both discipline and curriculum. Smith, consequently, solidified VMI's curriculum as a civil engineering course.

Smith was born on October 18, 1812, in Norfolk, Virginia, to an English, slave-owning Episcopalian family. Smith himself enslaved at least one man, Tom Carter. Smith's father first worked as a merchant in the transatlantic tobacco and grain trade, but, after bankruptcy because of embargoes against trade with England leading up to the War of 1812, worked as a "Gauger and Inspector" for the city, introducing Smith to engineering. Smith received a liberal education at a private academy where he studied French, Latin, and Greek. He then went to West Point, New York, to receive private mathematics tutoring from a former boarder of the Smiths. He received an appointment as a cadet at the Military Academy the following year just one month short of seventeen years old. He graduated fifth in his class in 1833 and received an officer's appointment in the army. While there, he developed a close relationship with Professor Charles Davies, author of several mathematics and engineering textbooks, some of which Smith and the Board of Visitors adopted for use at VMI.[43]

After several rapid and uneventful transfers as a member of an army artillery unit, Smith returned to West Point to serve as an assistant professor of geography, history, and ethics.[44] Smith, however, married and wanted to "advance himself in civil life,"[45] so he resigned from the army in 1836 and joined his brother's company to develop land in the West. Smith, however, found it unprofitable and returned east. He then worked as an assistant topographical engineer and conducted surveys between Norfolk, Virginia, and Charleston, South Carolina, which he also did not enjoy. He finally settled as professor of mathematics at Hampden-Sydney College in 1837, where he remained until his appointment at VMI.[46]

Smith, despite initial frustrations, found great happiness in his work at Hampden-Sydney. He taught algebra, geometry, and trigonometry to freshmen, analytical and descriptive geometry and surveying to sophomores, and differential and integral calculus to juniors. He found, however, that the college, like most, did not sufficiently prepare their students for such intensive mathematics. Wanting to establish West Point standards for mathematics, he required his junior students to review the freshmen and sophomore materials, which initially created great hostility and resentment toward him.[47] He said of this, "By great labor and perseverance and after encountering opposition from Trustees and students, I finally graduated the class on Math! and with a credit to them, which would not have been dishonorable to West Point."[48] Moreover, the students developed great respect for him. Even seniors, who had already finished their math course before Smith's arrival, asked to review mathematics, with some even paying to do so through private tutoring.[49]

Besides instituting one of the most rigorous mathematics courses in the United States outside of West Point, Smith also introduced the first public examinations of students in Virginia, a practice he brought from West Point and later carried out at VMI,[50] where Crozet had instituted the practice prior to Smith's arrival.[51]

Smith's appointment at VMI began with an inquiry from John Preston, who received Smith's recommendation from George Baxter, president of the Union Theological Seminary, during his visit to Lexington for a Presbyterian synod. According to Smith's grandson, "Preston told Doctor Baxter that he wanted a Christian gentleman competent to teach mathematics, and one who, in addition, possessed the requisite military qualifications to superintend a military school." Baxter immediately recommended Smith, whom he knew because of the connections between Hampden-Sydney and the Union Theological Seminary. [52] On April 29, 1839, Preston wrote to Smith and claimed he "had my attention drawn to yourself" as a potential candidate to, along with serving as commandant [later titled superintendent], teach "a thorough course of Mathematics, especially as applied to Civil and Military Engineering, and the exercising of the cadets in Military tactics." Preston told Smith that the position "is an important one, which will be occupied by one who will preside over the opening of such an institution, and of course in an important degree, will determine its future character."[53] After substantial consideration, Smith agreed to have the board consider him as a candidate, seeing this as an opportunity for him to develop his reputation and career by building a new institution.[54] Supported by letters of recommendation from General Winfield Scott, commanding general of the US Army; Major Charles H. Smith, paymaster of the army and brother-in-law of Board of Visitors member General Thomas H. Botts; and John R. Triplett of Richmond, friend of board member General Bernard Peyton;[55] Smith received the unanimous vote of the board.[56]

Smith had studied the curriculum at West Point that Crozet helped to create and took well to the framework established for him by VMI's Board of Visitors. The scheme, however, seemed too small in scope to him.[57] More than just realizing Crozet's and Preston's vision of an engineering school under military discipline,

Smith worked to expand the size of the school and to turn it into the "West Point of the South." Like Crozet, he required no influence from Partridge to promote a West Point–style engineering curriculum.

CONCLUSIONS

Although engineering became the dominant feature of the VMI curriculum, it could have turned out otherwise, perhaps with a combination of military drilling and a liberal education obtained through Washington College. However, the public intervention of Alden Partridge and the appointment of Claudius Crozet led to the early adoption of a core mathematics-based engineering curriculum, modeled after West Point and the École Polytechnique.

For Crozet, Partridge, and Smith, engineering had a natural connection to military education, with the need for engineering in fortifications, artillery, and so forth. All three men also saw this training as applicable to civilian careers. Crozet and Smith had themselves applied their training to civilian projects. While most American engineers had no such formal training, the backgrounds of all three men, as well as Crozet's personal frustrations with working with those craft-trained or even entirely untrained engineers, disposed them toward advocating formal education as the best means for training engineers. Moreover, they all advocated a highly mathematical approach to such training, in contrast with, for example, the curriculum at Rensselaer.

Crozet, Partridge, and Smith placed great importance on the need for developing transportation networks and cultivating resources for the growing nation. So, engineering provided not only a career with natural affiliations to the military but also what they saw as greatly needed at the time to support the expansion of the market economy and the state. Concerned about the lack of appropriate training, the new school would, to them, greatly aid both Virginia and the nation by training competent men to carry out these important tasks. This interest in engineering, even if not raised during the initial efforts to found VMI, resonated with the people of western Virginia, who had advocated, with little success, for greater tax and government support for internal improvements during the 1829–1830 constitutional convention. Partridge's advocacy of civil engineering education, therefore, fell on fertile ground, and the citizens of Rockbridge took up the cause as they continued to advocate for the school. Additionally, such training perfectly suited the young men for whom they intended the school, men who did not already have wealth and land upon which to live later and who required an occupation through which to support themselves. The western elite could readily accept an engineering curriculum as one suited both to elevating poor white people by providing men with a profitable profession and to securing western interests in internal improvements. Moreover, the curriculum, quantitative evaluation of students, and discipline would come to serve as the means of legitimizing the school in its competition with liberal colleges (see chapter 4) and of demonstrating the virtue and independence of white men that was at the core of the founding of the school (see chapter 6).

CHAPTER FOUR

ENGINEERING KNOWLEDGE AND THE STRUGGLE FOR AUTHORITY IN HIGHER EDUCATION

Under President Claudius Crozet's and Superintendent Francis Smith's leadership, the new school adopted an engineering curriculum based on those of West Point and France's École Polytechnique, both of which Crozet had been associated with. The officers of the Virginia Military Institute (VMI), building an unusual institution of higher education for a demographically atypical student body, found themselves having to struggle for authority within the field of higher education. They were competing with the liberal colleges of Virginia. Evidence that at least some of the officers saw their new institution as engaged in such conflict and struggle comes from the statements of the officers themselves. Superintendent Smith, for example, wrote, "[O]ur entire neglect of Latin has been a ground of objection to the Institute in the minds of some, which however erroneous, cannot in the infancy of the school and at present day be utterly disregarded."[1] In this statement, he acknowledges Latin as a marker of authority in higher education, which his own school, whether he liked it or not—he didn't—had to acknowledge and contend with. Moreover, he expended much effort criticizing the pedagogical and disciplinary methods of liberal colleges, including through his 1851 *College Reform*, in which he promoted the methods that he and the board employed at VMI as the most effective model for all higher education.

Even fifty years after the opening of the school, Professor John Preston still felt the need, in his 1889 "Historical Sketch" of the school, to defend against reasonable accusations that VMI challenged the colleges. In this sketch, when describing the origins and purpose of the school he helped to found, he emphasized the claim that they sought to do something new "while not antagonizing the established system of classical education."[2] This statement makes sense only if there actually was some antagonism. In fact, from the beginning, there was concern that state funding for a second school—the University of Virginia being the first—could threaten the viability of private schools such as Washington College, which was struggling to stay open at the time VMI was established. The Board of Visitors in 1845 and Superintendent Smith in 1856 had to continue to argue before the public and the legislature that their school was not a threat. The board wrote explicitly that they had no desire to create "a rival institution,"[3] while Smith pleaded to "[l]et both [VMI and the colleges] exist together."[4] Both men also went on to immediately note that VMI was a distinct type of institution. Such statements indicate that the officers of the new school were seeking a place for that school within the field of higher education but that VMI's distinctiveness was seen as simultaneously lacking the markers of authority recognized within the field and as challenging the authority of the dominant colleges.

The officers of VMI attempted to establish their legitimacy in several, sometimes conflicting, ways. They expressed a variety of views regarding liberal education, but some of the officers, especially Superintendent Smith, went beyond legitimizing VMI as providing just one viable mode of higher education; they also criticized liberal education and argued, in fact, for the superiority of VMI. They did this by creating a binary opposition between the "practical" or "useful" education of VMI and what was, by implied contrast, the impractical or useless education of the liberal colleges. VMI could not and would not compete with them through a traditional curriculum and pedagogy, so Smith and others criticized that curriculum and pedagogy and adopted new standards, those that VMI met. In so doing, they attempted to redefine what counted as authority within the field of higher education, doing so in a way that redefined their own weaknesses as strengths and the colleges' strengths as weaknesses. The officers of VMI thus attempted to position themselves and their school as authoritative.

The curriculum and pedagogy employed at VMI reflected the unique mission and student body of the school. The Board of Visitors and superintendent had to adopt lower standards of admission than the colleges in order to accept the poorly educated young men for whom the school was established. Consequently, the school had to provide some remedial training to enable the cadets to succeed in the core curriculum of mathematics and engineering. Moreover, the cadets required some basic training in liberal courses to enable them to fulfill their service as teachers for the commonwealth. But, while the board and superintendent set lower standards for admission, they established higher standards of testing, which they made public in order to legitimate the school before a broader audience.

The board established a curriculum around a core focus on engineering, thus providing graduates of the school with a training that would enable them, lacking the inheritance and land to guarantee wealth, to pursue paying careers. But, unlike most engineers in America, they received a training based on mathematical and scientific principles to provide them with a more universal knowledge of engineering applicable to any situation in which the graduates would find themselves. As part of this training, the cadets received what was probably the most extensive mathematical training available in America outside of West Point. Moreover, their scientific training eventually equaled, if not surpassed, that of most colleges. But rather than pointing to this training to argue for the superiority of VMI graduates over other engineers, the officers of VMI, instead, emphasized the practicality and thoroughness of the training as indicative of VMI's superiority over the liberal colleges. Nonetheless, the school's officers saw the practical theoretical training as enabling the cadets to enter quickly into the role of managers and leaders of engineering projects rather than working their way up from labor positions, as did so many craft-trained engineers. In short, this training was to enable VMI graduates to become, like their peers from West Point and the École Polytechnique of Paris, an elite among engineers. Moreover, their school, again like the École Polytechnique in France, was to become an elite institution in America. While they succeeded to some extent in the former, they failed in the latter, though the school did survive and even thrive.

The distinctiveness of VMI, including the demographic character of the students, the disciplinary and pedagogical system, and the curriculum served particular purposes: (1) creating a new standard for authority in higher education to enable VMI to compete with the colleges; (2) providing remedial training for students and to prepare them for required service to the commonwealth; and (3) training professionals, particularly engineers and teachers. The content of the curriculum, as well as how it was conveyed, was inseparable from the above goals. Curriculum and pedagogy were inherently political, being essential to the argument for white manhood equality.

A DISTINCT AND SUPERIOR INSTITUTION

The framers of VMI, including Superintendent Smith and Professor Preston, saw the school as offering something distinct from that which came before. Indeed, Preston and other early advocates for the school intended it to serve a distinct population from that served by traditional colleges. VMI would provide an education to those young men who previously had little or no chance of obtaining one. But besides arguing for providing education to a new population, the officers also argued that VMI provided a new form of education. This argument served to settle fears that the new state-funded institution competed with the private colleges of Virginia, such as the College of William and Mary or Washington College. These arguments, however, often contained a suggestion of the superiority of VMI. This superiority was predicated on the usefulness of the curriculum and the use of new teaching and disciplinary methods.

At the request of Governor James McDowell in 1838, Preston gave the school its name, which he crafted to emphasize the distinctiveness of the institution, explaining:

> Virginia—as a state Institution, neither sectional nor
> denominational.
> Military—indicating its characteristic feature.
> Institute—as something different from either College or
> University.[5]

Preston justified the use of *institute* as a means of immediately distinguishing the school from the colleges, even for those who knew nothing about the school except for its name. The Rensselaer Institute, for example, provided first an agricultural and then an engineering training, rather than the liberal education of a college. Institute suggested a specialized purpose for the school, though the name did not necessarily suggest what. Even though the name did not make clear the emphasis on engineering education, it did make clear the distinct military discipline under which students lived.

Addressing the Corps of Cadets at the beginning of the 1856 academic year, Superintendent Smith reflected on the beginning and impact of VMI, saying, "It at once broke in upon the established system of college education as they had come down from the monastic institutions of Europe."[6] Here he distinguished the approach of VMI from that of the liberal colleges, which he aligned, whether correctly or not, with medieval traditions of cloistered scholars far removed from the practical considerations of life. Continuing on, he explained that VMI, while having to lower its admissions standards in some ways so as to draw students from the lower classes, still met most college standards, "saving in *Greek* and *Latin*. It omitted *Greek*, as more properly belonging to theological institutions." Cadets, however, did learn Latin because (1) they might need it to fulfill their post-graduation teaching obligations and (2) "of its great value as an auxiliary in the study of the English language." Moreover, "It substituted *French* as the language of science, and opened wide the field of scientific culture, theoretic as well as practical."[7] Here, Smith identified VMI with science rather than the classics that dominated the academies and colleges not because the classics were seen as inferior but because of the school's emphasis on practical scientific training. He reduced the value of what Latin training remained to merely a practical training.

Despite their emphasis on the distinctiveness of VMI, both Smith and Preston also, at least initially, emphasized the need for amity between their new form of education and the old, represented by Washington College, which sat adjacent to VMI and shared board members with VMI. Preston, an alum of Washington College, interpreted the intentions of the founding Board of Visitors as to provide an education suited to what "may be designated the practical pursuits of life . . . while not antagonizing the established system of classical education."[8] Smith spoke similarly, requesting, "Let both exist together, that the wants of all may be supplied."[9] Moreover, the Board of Visitors argued to the governor in 1845, "Neither are they [members of the Board] actuated by the vain ambition of building up a rival institution to any now existing. The peculiarity of the system of discipline and instruction, and the mode of selecting cadets can make it justly a rival to none." They continued the sentence with, "except so far as the peculiar system makes it preferable to those now existing."[10] The board unambiguously stated the distinctiveness of VMI in regards to instruction, discipline, and the intended population of students. That distinctiveness, they argued, precluded any possibility of the state-funded school creating conflict or competition with private liberal colleges. They did, however, indicate an exception to this; the distinctiveness of VMI may in fact have made it superior to the colleges. As they further noted, they were "desirous to extend the benefits of its peculiar institution to the greatest number, and yet we cannot receive all who would come."[11] The fact that the school received more suitable applicants than they could accommodate, in contrast with the floundering enrollment of Washington College, served as proof to the officers of VMI that their own school was superior.

We might assume that any moderating statements on the part of the board reflect simply the recognition of their school's precarious financial dependence on a legislature controlled by the very people any criticisms might antagonize. At least some officers of the school, however, genuinely respected liberal education. Board member General William Richardson, for example, wanted to send his son to VMI but worried that he would not learn sufficient Latin and Greek, which were for him still markers of authority in education and gentlemanly leadership.[12] In addition, Preston, who had originally envisioned a limited classical education combined with military training, expressed some frustration, as the professor of languages, at the relative neglect of Latin training of the cadets. Besides not providing a sufficiently long training, he perceived that, because it did not receive the same priority as other courses, some irregularity in the Latin recitation schedule developed, hindering the progress of his students.[13] Despite his frustrations with some aspects of the curriculum, Preston still recognized and valued the distinctiveness of VMI, the institution for which he was most responsible for founding.

Smith's Criticism of Liberal Education

Although Superintendent Smith cultivated a love of teaching at Hampden-Sydney College before moving to VMI, he also developed a critique of liberal education, judging it against the standards under which he studied at West Point. Besides the insufficient mathematical preparation of the students, he also expressed concern about the lack of discipline among the students, as well as the means of enforcing discipline. He saw suspensions, for example, as "a strange way of correcting idleness and bad conduct," since it essentially imposed idleness on students.[14]

Later, in writing to a recently resigned army officer starting a career as a professor of mathematics at Transylvania University in Kentucky, he warned of the problems with liberal education in scathing terms. In contrast with West Point cadets, at colleges, "each student directs his own course of study without regard to the judgement or wish of his professor." The result was an education "full of generability but producing no permanent good in the pupil."[15] Such concerns occupied Smith for decades afterward, during which he advocated national educational reform. With West Point as his personal model of academic excellence, Smith fit well with the vision of Crozet to bring into operation a military school emphasizing an engineering curriculum.

Along with the distinctive discipline and curriculum of VMI, the Board of Visitors and Smith established pedagogical practices distinct from those of most colleges. They drew many of these practices from their experiences with the École Polytechnique and West Point, the school that, for most of them, set the standard for higher education. Smith, in particular, contrasted these practices with those of the colleges as a criticism of elite liberal education in order to argue for the superiority of VMI and, therefore, of its graduates. The use of annual public exams also showed off the cadets and legitimated the school to the public of Virginia.

VMI professors employed several pedagogical strategies, including recitations and the use of blackboards, the latter of which were used little in America outside of West Point and were initially brought to America from France.[16] Moreover, they minimized the use of lectures, the standard form of instruction at the colleges and which Smith saw as ineffective, a waste of students' time. He divided classes into groups of ten or twelve students for recitations, during which the instructors examined each student orally and through blackboard demonstrations, upon which they were graded quantitatively on the day's lesson.[17] Similar to the system developed for the École Polytechnique,[18] "A weekly report of the recitations is made to the superintendent every Saturday, an abstract from which is recorded, and the total of each cadet's and weekly marks forms an element in his standing at the [semiannual public] examination."[19] In order to employ such thorough quantitative measures of student performance, the professors had to emphasize constant student participation during class and intimacy between students and professors, neither of which lectures facilitated.

Smith advocated the employment of small class sizes in general, in any kind of school. Moreover, he advocated organizing them into groups of comparable ability in any particular subject.[20] At Harvard, in contrast, students entered into classes based on their date of entry and by alphabetical order, without regard to individual ability or prior knowledge.[21] Under Smith's organization, the students could advance as rapidly as suitable to their background and talents, rather than having any individual delayed in his progress by the slower pace of learning of his fellow cadets.

Recitations, employed to some extent at most colleges as well, generally involved either reciting memorized passages from assigned reading or the replication of solutions to mathematical problems as demonstrated in a textbook. The professor or assistant professor would continually quiz the students on their performance in order to gauge their understanding or draw out a greater depth of explanation for the benefit of the rest of the class.

Some educators, however, had begun to criticize this method in the years prior to the opening of VMI. For example, Harvard professor George Ticknor, influenced by his experiences in German universities, sought to reform Harvard in the 1820s, making it more practical and career oriented, as well as reforming the pedagogy. Interestingly, he, like Smith, saw West Point as superior to Harvard in the rigor of its examinations. In contrast, however, he saw recitations as largely a waste of time, requiring the professor's entire attention just to determine if a student had done the assigned reading. But others, including an 1828 Yale commission, defended the use of recitations.[22]

Smith saw the time-intensiveness of recitations not as a liability but as a means of ensuring the thorough education of the cadets prior to their examinations, thus preventing unnecessary failures. But to avoid employing all of a professor's time with this, the board hired assistant instructors. Smith claimed success for recitations, arguing that they and the small class sizes "contributed, in a great degree, to the efficiency of the graduates of the Institute, in their professional pursuits, particularly in the work soon to be given them by law as teachers." Moreover, "every departure from [recitations] has uniformly tended to dilute the instruction, and to increase the number of deficient cadets."[23] Smith's evaluation of the effectiveness of recitations, however, requires reference to his goal. Not only did he want to prepare cadets to succeed at their semiannual and annual exams, but he also wanted to provide a means of producing a quantitative evaluation of the cadets and their learning, allowing for the ranking of cadets according to their individual merit.[24]

Lectures, unlike recitations, could not provide sufficient means by which the professors could evaluate the students, at least not by Smith's standards. He claimed that because of the limited number of recitations in the colleges and attendance was not always required, "the actual number of recitations of a student in any one subject is often less than one a week," which was, he argued, insufficient. Moreover, the disciplinary and evaluation systems of the colleges created little incentive for the students to attend classes and be prepared for their recitations, because the colleges imposed only academic sanctions, such as retaking exams or not earning a diploma, for students who did not perform well. Colleges should have, instead, employed sanctions as strong as expulsion for failure to attend classes. Moreover, he wrote, "No classification is made of the student in order of merit, except to specify those who deserve 'honors' of the class."[25] Smith's use of scare quotes around *honors* suggests his skepticism of the capacity of lectures to evaluate the merit of the students.

During recitations, VMI professors employed blackboards, which were in use at West Point but not often used at colleges in the 1830s and early 1840s. Students had used personal, handheld slates since the colonial period. Blackboards, when used, were generally seen as mere supplements to the students' own slates up until the 1850s. Modern boards first arrived in America through a French priest who immigrated to Boston in 1814. Their first use for teaching mathematics in higher education was probably at West Point and arrived not with the priest but with the future VMI board president Crozet in 1817. There, cadets worked the blackboard as part of their recitation exams, but professors also picked up the practice as a means of demonstration. Its use then spread to other schools.[26] Their use is described by Smith: "The requirement that each member of the section shall demonstrate fully the subject assigned him at the black board—giving as he proceeds detailed explanations of the various steps with the reasons for the operation on the board, as boys sometimes work what they call 'sums,' on their slates—the instructor being satisfied, if the answer be correct."[27] Smith identified the following advantages to student use of the board during recitation: the student gained self-confidence by having to explain his knowledge to others, use of the board provided a good review for both the class and the student, and it provided an opportunity for the instructor to quiz the student as he worked at the board.[28] Thus, it not only enabled the instructor to evaluate the student but also helped to develop his character, in this case, cultivating confidence in his knowledge.

In order to maximize the use of class time for evaluation, rather than instruction, VMI cadets relied heavily on their textbooks to learn. While Ticknor of Harvard criticized recitations as waste of a professor's time, Smith saw lectures as a waste of students' time. Instead, he wrote, "Lessons should as far as practicable be *learned from the text-book*, and each student thoroughly examined each day upon the lessons of the day."[29] This freed all class time for examination of cadets and clarification of the material.

The annual final exam, conducted orally in the presence of the Board of Visitors, the public, and invited guests, provided the crucial evaluation of both the cadets and the professors charged with their education. Their results on this exam, combined with their daily recitation scores and demerits for behavior (discussed in chapter 6), determined their relative standing. Smith saw the oral and public character of the exam, just like the recitations, as a system that "imparts confidence to the student, and stimulates to exertion." This was so because, he said, "No one with proper pride would like to stand up before a board of intelligent gentlemen, and fail to answer the questions proposed to him." By observing the success or failure of the cadets, the board members could then "judge not only the progress of the class, but of the competency and fidelity of the professor."[30] Ultimately, the exam provided an evaluation—a public evaluation—of not just the cadets and faculty but of the institution itself.

The Lexington public took great interest in the annual exams. Although routinely invited, few governors attended, with James McDowell's presence in 1843 an early exception, though not a surprising one given his home in Rockbridge County.[31] Many local residents, including newspaper owners, did, however, regularly attend. Also, the entire faculty of Washington College attended at least the first exam in 1840. Smith, describing board president

Crozet's questioning of the students at that first exam, wrote, "[H]is questions were rigid, close, but clear, and were readily apprehended by the class." Moreover, afterward, "a murmur of satisfaction passed through the crowd of spectators." Smith was satisfied that "on that day the Virginia Military Institute earned for itself the title, which it has ever since proudly borne, of the West Point of the South."[32] The exam satisfied Smith that the professors and cadets had met his West Point standards for education and that they had satisfactorily demonstrated the legitimacy of the new school to the public.

The *Lexington Gazette*, which routinely reported on the exams and commencements of VMI, as well as of the Ann Smith Academy and Washington College, offered a similar assessment. It described the 1842 exam as "thorough and rigid, and is universally conceded that the young gentlemen have thus far acquitted themselves with the highest honor." Moreover, it provided evidence that VMI was "a school which with the encouragement it deserves from the Legislature will soon be equal in every respect to the United States Military Academy at West Point." VMI was "destined to confer the greatest blessings upon Virginia, in sending forth accomplished soldiers to impart skill and discipline, and a military spirit to her militia, and in giving her common schools gentlemen who are educated and capable to instruct the youth of our state."[33] Thus, Smith seems to have correctly read the impact of the exams on the public. Even the newspaper that had challenged the founding of VMI conceded the close comparison of the quality of the school with West Point. Thus, Smith and the board appear to have succeeded in employing public examinations to legitimate the school, the cadets, and their pedagogy.

Emulating the West Point Curriculum

The Board of Visitors and professors of VMI modeled the curriculum after that of West Point but modified it somewhat to lessen the emphasis on military arts and, instead, emphasize civil and military engineering. But they also repeatedly expanded the offerings and even added an additional year in order to better meet West Point standards and increase the scientific courses to support the core engineering training. For Superintendent Smith, this was necessary to establish an institution of sufficient prestige to challenge the authority of the liberal colleges.

Smith had claimed misgivings about initially taking the superintendent position and told Professor Preston nearly forty years later, "I had some ambition and that with the education I had received at West Point, I could not feel satisfied to anchor myself at the simple work of teaching a few young men, say 20, or at most 40."[34] However, given the substantial employment of the West Point system and the permission to admit some additional tuition-paying cadets, he felt that the school had promise, even if Professor Preston, President Crozet, and others did not appear to him to have a vision of expanding the school.[35] But it did grow, with the board and legislature approving the addition of a fourth year of study and the right to confer a degree, "Graduate of the Virginia Military Institute," in 1845, something advocated by Smith and the board since at least 1842.[36]

Smith advocated expanding the course offerings at VMI from nearly the beginning. In the earliest years, the cadets studied chemistry at Washington College, while the college students could and did participate in military drills at VMI. Smith, unhappy at having a subject so important as natural philosophy taught at another school, did not "hesitate to recommend to the Board the propriety of securing at the earliest day possible the service of a Professor in this department."[37] He succeeded in establishing a new professorship in natural philosophy in 1845, though the new professor did not arrive until 1846.[38]

The VMI curriculum and the changes to it resulted also from an ongoing effort by Smith and other professors to more firmly emulate West Point. The curriculum initially resembled West Point's but in a less thorough form, including in both natural philosophy and, especially, the military courses. VMI, instead, emphasized civil and military engineering. The board of VMI also added additional language training beyond French, at first in German and then instead in Latin. Professor of engineering Thomas Williamson, however, proposed in 1848 to further expand the engineering curriculum to make it as much like West Point as possible.[39] Indeed, the curriculum did grow to more closely emulate West Point's scientific and engineering offerings. As part of this, after adding a fourth year, VMI no longer had to rely on Washington College for its chemistry course. In 1851, VMI added a course in geology and mineralogy, the knowledge of which would, among other things, aid in the construction of tunnels and the exploitation of Virginia's natural resources.

In contrast to both VMI and West Point, Washington College offered the following liberal curriculum by 1842: classics, including four years of Greek and Latin; mathematics during the first and second year, including algebra, geometry, some trigonometry and analytical geometry, as well as some surveying and navigational mathematics; physical sciences in the third year, including chemistry, electricity and magnetism, mechanics, optics, astronomy, botany, mineralogy, and geology; and ethics in the fourth year, which included philosophy, the US Constitution, state law, and the study of William Paley's *Evidences of Christianity* or *Natural Philosophy*.[40] Students had the option of supplementing their liberal education with additional courses in calculus and civil engineering,[41] but, almost certainly, at VMI as part of a course exchange agreement between the two schools. I have, however, seen no evidence that any students pursued this option.

Washington College, perhaps out of desperation for students and money or to compete with VMI, also began offering one- and two-year programs that, like the curriculum of VMI, emphasized practicality. They offered a two-year agricultural program "designed to qualify young men to become intelligent farmers [and] men of business." This program consisted of one year of math and rhetoric and a second year of physical sciences and ethics. The college also offered a one- or two-year normal program consisting of one year of math, rhetoric, and, "other auxiliary studies, specially aiming to make the student accurately acquainted with the English Language," and one year of physical sciences, ethics, grammar, and composition, with the option of studying French at VMI. Moreover, they offered a program for students who wanted to attend Washington College but also wanted to take military and engineering courses at VMI. Students who pursued this program would take Washington College's math, science, and liberal arts during the first two years as well as math, engineering, French, and military courses at VMI, especially in the last two years.[42] It isn't evident how many students, if any, pursued these alternative courses.

Despite efforts by the board of Washington College to draw upon VMI as a means of expanding its own curriculum and student body, the two schools offered very different curricula. However, besides its liberal focus, Washington College did offer some training in the physical sciences, upon which VMI cadets relied in their school's first few years, and substantial instruction in mathematics, though not as thoroughly as VMI. But these were generally separate courses within the liberal curriculum at the college. VMI, in contrast, employed the mathematics and science courses as essential background for supporting the core engineering curriculum.

Given the lower- and middling-class origins of their students, VMI would likely not have been capable of matching the prestige and authority of the liberal colleges had it employed a curriculum similar to theirs. But even without such a curriculum, the officers of VMI still had to contend with the authority of those schools. They attempted to rival the authority of the colleges with new pedagogical practices and a new curriculum. But merely establishing an alternative was insufficient; the officers had to craft VMI into a prestigious institution that could prove its superiority in terms of shaping the morals of its graduates (see chapter 5) and by creating more competent graduates. The officers attempted to demonstrate the latter through the public examinations and by building up a robust curriculum. While observers of the exams may or may not have accepted VMI as superior, the exams at least generated respect for VMI as a legitimate institution of higher education.

A CURRICULUM TO OVERCOME THE BARRIERS OF POVERTY

The ongoing expansion of VMI's curriculum enabled the school to offer increased remedial training to a body of students that, because of lesser wealth, entered the school with a poorer educational background than did students of the colleges and, as a result, often experienced increasing difficulties as they progressed through VMI's curriculum, sometimes even failing as a result of inadequate preparation. By changing the curriculum to reflect the needs of the students, VMI officers attempted to better fulfill their school's mission of eliminating poverty as an artificial barrier to the expression of the individual merit of white men and better equip the cadets to succeed in their classes. After all, the original purpose of the school was to use education as a means of elevating poorer white men into the middling classes and, through their successes, to justify white manhood equality and, therefore, white manhood suffrage. The school also changed in order to adapt to the added requirements of teaching service placed upon the cadets by the legislature.

The earliest curriculum of VMI accommodated the relative deficiencies of the cadets, compared to those entering the liberal colleges. An 1845 Board of Visitors report identified the relative poverty of the cadets as having led to their inability to obtain a liberal education prior to attending VMI and that, moreover, their prior education was "so limited as greatly to embarrass and prejudice them in their subsequent course" at VMI.[43] Professor Preston reinforced this perception, claiming that the cadets were, "for the most part young men who have never studied any of the subjects taught at the Institute, and whose minds have not yet been trained by previous education." This created challenges for the cadets because, "[a]s soon as they enter, they are put upon a very trying course of Mathematics, are required to learn two languages, each entirely new, and after January spend two hours every other day in Drawing—add to this occasional exercises in Composition [and] Declamation." Such a demanding curriculum, Preston noted, "requires uncommon capacity or uncommon diligence."[44] Any difficulties the corps as a whole experienced did not reflect any lesser overall merit compared with the students of the colleges. Instead, it reflected the extraordinary conditions of trying to make up for a lack of prior education while also providing a thorough higher education, all in the span of only three years, at least until the addition of the fourth year.

In order to accommodate the poorly educated boys who sought admission to VMI, the board "placed the terms of admission so low as to admit talent from any and every quarter; and yet high enough to meet the usual demands of the colleges, saving in *Greek* and *Latin*."[45] In practical terms, that meant that applicants had to be able to "read and write well" and do arithmetic, including "reduction, of simple and compound proportions, and of vulgar and decimal fractions."[46] This contrasts with the 1842 requirements for admission to Washington College, which included "a competent knowledge of English Grammar, Geography and Arithmetic, especially Vulgar [and] Decimal Fractions and the rule of Proportion." The prospective student had also to be "well versed in the Grammar of the language which he proposes to study," as well as having already read in Latin "Jacobs' Latin Reader, both parts throughout, Ceaser 6 books, Sallust's Jugurthin War; Golds Ovid throughout with the Latin Prosody and [illegible]; Virgils Bucolics, Georgics and 6 books of the Aeneid; and eight orations in Cicero. In Greek, Jacobs Greek Reader throughout and Johns Gospel."[47] Had VMI's board followed Washington College's standards, they would have found very few candidates.

The board added the fourth year partially in response to the cadets' difficulties. The additional year allowed for remedial courses in arithmetic and English. These courses would, the board claimed at the time, save "from discharge many who come unprepared."[48] Again, cadets failed because of poor prior preparation, rather than from their individual merit. The addition of another year, therefore, made up for this and, just as VMI was supposed to do by providing any education at all, served to further limit the effects of poverty as an artificial barrier to the expression of merit.

Most of the English and language course served largely as a remedial education for the poorly prepared state cadets who had to teach in Virginia's schools for two years after graduation. The standards of education set by the liberal colleges of the elite emphasized the study of classics, including Latin, as well as English literature and rhetoric. Academies that hired the cadets expected them to teach the basics of these subjects. By 1846, VMI required the cadets to study English grammar, composition, geography, and history in their first year and rhetoric and English literature in their fourth.[49]

The initial language course included French and German—modern, rather than classical languages—, but the Board replaced German with Latin in 1842 after the legislature added the requirement that state cadets teach in a Virginia school for two years after graduation in exchange for the education they received. These teaching positions often required teaching rudiments of Latin. "Further," Superintendent Smith wrote, "our entire neglect of Latin has been a ground of objection to the Institute in the minds of some, which however erroneous, cannot in the infancy of the school and at the present day be utterly disregarded." The addition of Latin to the curriculum, though not a contribution to the engineering curriculum, was not entirely burdensome. As Smith noted, "Major Preston is fully qualified to teach the Latin course, and will take pleasure in embracing it in his regular duties."[50] Despite the apparent enthusiasm of at least Preston for Latin,

Smith appears to have advocated its teaching for the purely practical reason of enabling the cadets to fulfill their duty to the state. Though later advocating "its great value as an auxiliary in the study of the English language,"[51] Smith did not see much value in teaching Latin, even though West Point, his constant model, included some basic instruction in both Greek and Latin, at least for some time around 1815. But even West Point adopted these courses only to improve the school's academic reputation.[52]

Preston, as Professor of Languages, enthusiastically adopted responsibility for teaching Latin. He complained, however, that the limited time allocated to the course was insufficient to prepare cadets even for their minimal obligation of teaching the basics of Latin. He believed that "even for those who have had no previous advantages, by one years' uninterrupted study" they could learn what they needed. He hoped to reduce the interruptions by decreasing the emphasis on French, a proposal surely not welcomed by Smith, who saw French as the "language of science" that "opened wide the field of scientific culture, theoretic as well as practical."[53] Although both Smith and Preston hoped only to enable the cadets to fulfill their future teaching responsibilities, Smith lacked the enthusiasm for the classics that would convince him to prioritize Latin.

The Virginia legislature founded VMI on the premise that students could guard the Lexington Arsenal and that properly trained graduates could contribute to improvements in the militia. While basic drilling could have enabled the cadets to fulfill the former, more formal courses were necessary for the latter. The board, as they did with much of VMI's curriculum, based the military course on that of West Point but streamlined it to emphasize core courses.

Besides basic drilling and the use of guns, including artillery, the cadets also studied how to organize, manage, and conduct a militia. Professor Thomas Williamson, another West Point graduate, taught these skills during the cadets' final year.[54] Combined with training in military engineering, this course trained the cadets in "the methods of fortifying towns and camps, of making and repelling attacks, crossing rivers, conducting armies during marches, and in general whatever may be useful to the soldier in time of war." In addition, thanks to donations of the proper equipment by the US War Department, Williamson also provided "instruction in *pyrotechny*," which "will embrace the manufacture of signal and war rockets, incendiary compositions of every kind, and the various uses of powder and inflammable substances in time of war."[55] These courses did not train common soldiers; they provided essential training for future officers and military engineers who might find themselves in leadership positions within the Virginia militia.

While the core of the VMI curriculum emphasized engineering and supporting subjects, much of the curriculum provided remedial training for the ill-educated classes of young white men attending the school. These courses in English and arithmetic enabled the cadets to overcome their deficiencies and to compete with better-prepared men, whether at other schools or at VMI itself. Although many of the cadets were poorly educated to begin with, they were still expected to provide several services to the commonwealth both during and after their education. The cadets, consequently, required additional training in order to fulfill these duties, including serving, if they chose, as militia officers and by teaching in Virginia's schools.

A SCIENTIFIC ENGINEERING CURRICULUM

The Board of Visitors and Superintendent Smith crafted a curriculum that provided cadets with an engineering training, the premises for which derived from the elite state schools of France and from West Point. In this context, engineering meant primarily civil and military engineering but also architecture, at least in the cases of West Point and VMI. This approach to engineering training emphasized a foundation of mathematics and mechanics to understand the application of forces within materials in order to determine, for example, the types and thicknesses of materials necessary for construction in any given circumstance. Based on the content of the courses, engineering work consisted of surveying, producing topographic maps, and the construction of buildings, bridges, railroads, canals, roads, and ports. Military engineering included the construction of fortifications, such as trenches, embankments, and walls. Cadets learned these topics in distinct drawing, surveying, civil engineering, and military engineering courses.

French: The "language of science"

The VMI curriculum included the study of French, the language of professional engineering as board president Crozet and Superintendent Smith, as well as other professors, understood it. They, either directly or indirectly through West Point, accepted French formal engineering training as the model of professional engineering, in contrast with the on-the-job training acquired by most American engineers. VMI required the study of French as essential to professional training. The cadets, in fact, needed French to read some of their math and science textbooks.

The cadets relied on many textbooks either written in or translated from French, such that they required their French instruction simply to enter into their higher mathematics and mechanics courses. Cadets used, at least, J.-L. Boucharlat's *Éléments de mécanique* (Elements of mechanics) and *Éléments de calcul différentiel et de calcul intégral* (Elements of differential calculus and integral calculus) in the original French.[56] They, fortunately, could use English translations, including one of Smith's own, for their lower mathematics courses while they first learned the new language.[57] From the above, it is clear why Smith wouldn't sacrifice French instruction for more thorough Latin instruction, despite the needs of the state cadets to later teach Latin in Virginia's schools.

Mathematics

The mathematics curriculum provided a foundation for the engineering courses that made up the core of the VMI curriculum. The Board of Visitors and Superintendent Smith prioritized these courses in order to meet the standards of West Point and to provide the training deemed necessary for engineering. To achieve this, VMI employed textbooks and course formats from both West Point and France's École Polytechnique.

Superintendent Smith described the math curriculum of the early years of the school as "embracing arithmetic, algebra, plane and solid geometry, analytical and descriptive geometry, differential and integral calculus, shades, shadows and perspective, theory and practice of surveying, and mechanics."[58] Students studying engineering in the United States today will still recognize most of this curriculum, but they will have already had at least arithmetic, algebra, and geometry in high school. VMI cadets, on the contrary, often required arithmetic as a remedial course. VMI offered a mathematics training that, although still recognizable today, was not typical of the training of most American engineers at the time. In fact, it surpassed the course of perhaps almost all other American schools except for West Point, which provided the primary model for VMI courses.

The selection of mathematics textbooks indicates the importance of West Point and French engineering schools as the standard for VMI. VMI and West Point professors wrote many of the books but based them on French texts. Beginning in 1845, the cadets used an arithmetic book written by Smith and Assistant Professor R. T. W. Duke. The algebra course initially employed a textbook written by West Point professor Charles Davies, perhaps the most popular mathematics textbook author in antebellum America and who, working with publisher Alfred Smith Barnes (as in Barnes & Noble), set the standard for how to write, publish, and market textbooks in general, turning textbooks into a big business.[59] Davies based his *Elements of Algebra* (1835) on *Éléments d'Algèbre* by M. Bourdon, which had served as a standard text in France and became the basis for "every subsequent work on the subject of Algebra, both in Europe and in [that] country."[60] After 1848, however, VMI cadets used Smith's own algebra text, one also based on French examples.[61] For geometry and trigonometry, cadets used a translation of a French text, though "[r]evised and altered for the use of the military academy at West Point."[62]

Cadets studied calculus from at least two books. For differential and integral calculus, they studied from J.-L. Boucharlat's *Éléments de calcul différentiel et de calcul intégral* in the original French at least up until 1850.[63] For analytical geometry, cadets used Smith's own translations of a book by Jean-Baptiste Biot, a graduate of the École Polytechnique, later professor of mathematics and physics at the Collège de France and then the Université de France. Biot was a renowned physicist who researched magnetism, mineral chemistry, sound, and especially optics. For his research, he was admitted to the French Legion of Honor in 1814, the Académie des sciences elected him vice president in 1835, and the Royal Society of London awarded him a prize in 1840.[64] Smith said of Biot's book that, "It is justly regarded as the best elementary treatise on Analytical Geometry that yet appeared."[65] During an 1858 tour of European "scientific schools," Smith met Biot and gave him a copy of the translation. Of it, Biot said, "Oh! I know your work and you have done me great honor, for when I read it your own improvements were so great that I hardly recognized the original." They spoke for at least an hour. After this, Smith wrote of Biot, joking, "there is no one that I have seen that has interested me so much, and I said to him that if we only had him in America, we should make something out of him."[66]

One early VMI course sticks out as unfamiliar to contemporary American engineering students, despite the subject still being the foundation for mechanical drawing and graphical analysis.

Descriptive geometry is the use of geometric principles to portray three-dimensional geometric shapes or calculate distances and positions from a given knowledge of the shapes. With this method, engineers could make drawings and calculations based upon fundamental mathematical principles (see Figure 4.1 for an example of an analytical geometry homework assignment). Gaspard Monge, one of the discoverers of the method and the man who introduced the subject to the École Polytechnique, saw it as a universal method applicable to all engineering problems.[67] Crozet introduced descriptive geometry to America after his arrival at West Point in 1815 and assessing the inability of his students to proceed with any engineering study until they had learned more mathematics. No textbook was available, so to teach the subject, he employed some sketches he had acquired from his old school.[68] West Point professor Charles Davies remedied this lack by writing the textbook that VMI cadets later used, *Elements of Descriptive Geometry, with Their Application to Spherical Trigonometry, Spherical Projections, and Warped Surfaces* (1826).

Davies, like Smith after him, looked to France as an ideal of mathematics education and engineering. In the preface to this book, which Smith very likely read while a cadet at West Point, Davies lamented the failure of American schools to adopt the teaching of descriptive geometry. In France, the book was "an important element of a scientific education; it [was] taught in most of the public schools, and [was] considered indispensable to the Architect and Engineer," but it had not "been considered in this country as a necessary part of either a polite or practical education." Consequently, it had "not found its way into other Seminaries with a rapidity at all proportionate to its usefulness." For Davies, this mathematical art was a useful rather than theoretical one.[69]

More specifically, VMI professor Thomas Williamson said of descriptive geometry that it will "enable [the cadets] to make, not only military reconnaissances of a country for military purposes; but also drawings of fortification, gun carriages, bridges [etc.] when

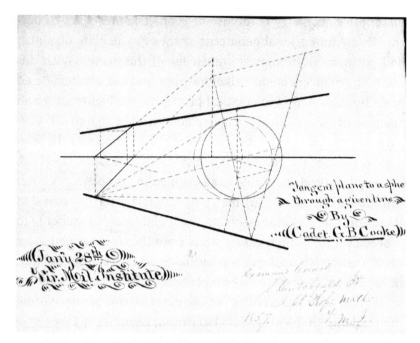

Figure 4.1. Cadet Descriptive Geometry Exercise. B. Cooke, January 28, 1857, "Tangent plane to a sphere through a given line," Cadet Architectural Drawings, MS 203, Virginia Military Institute Archives. Copied from Davies, *Descriptive Geometry*, Plate 9, Fig. 2.

called upon to do so."[70] Monge initially planned for the subject to be used at the École Polytechnique in a series of applied courses in which the students would use the method for a wide variety of topics, including stonecutting, designing ports, machines, and architecture.[71] A universal tool indeed. In a period without calculators and computers, descriptive geometry provided a powerful tool of analysis and design for those engineers who sought to employ scientific principles rather than rule-of-thumb methods. Because of both a minimal mathematical education and the rarity of teaching descriptive geometry in America, few American engineers had the ability to employ this tool. Consequently, graduates of West Point and the southern military schools could claim an elite mathematical education as a credential for both civil and military engineering.

Natural Sciences

Like mathematics, the natural science courses served to support the core engineering curriculum. Superintendent Smith and the Board of Visitors placed great importance on the teaching of these subjects. In general, the sciences were seen as inherently useful within what historian Roger Geiger calls the "useful knowledge tradition." The very principles of science could, they believed, contribute to the improvement of any practical pursuit.[72] It was for such practical pursuits that the faculty of VMI taught the sciences.

The courses in natural sciences initially consisted of mechanics, "[n]atural and experimental philosophy, astronomy, optics and chemistry."[73] The cadets had to employ their knowledge of trigonometry and calculus to pursue these courses. Smith worked to quickly expand the scientific curriculum that he, as the instructor of mechanics, valued so much. After having acquired Professor Thomas Williamson to teach the essential courses in engineering and military tactics in 1841, Smith next prioritized finding a professor to teach the sciences. He argued before the board in 1842 that, "Considering the importance of the physical sciences I cannot hesitate to recommend to the Board the propriety of securing at the earliest day possible the service of a Professor in this department." Moreover, chemistry, for which the cadets relied on Washington College for instruction, "should be particularly taught here, and the facilities we can afford for the operation of a chemical laboratory must engage the attention of the Board."[74] But because of various difficulties in locating and securing a professor, they did not succeed until 1846 when Professor William Gilham arrived.

Smith saw West Point of course as the standard by which to judge VMI's science courses. In order to place VMI graduates "somewhat on an equality with those from West Point," he allocated one hour each day for the cadets in their final year to study mechanics.[75] This mechanics course included statics and dynamics, as well as fluid mechanics, divided into *hydrostatique* and *hydrodynamique* in their French textbook.[76]

Gilham, another West Point graduate, modeled his optics course after that employed at West Point. Moreover, he employed a textbook written by a West Point professor. This course included not only what we now think of as basic optical physics but also extensive practical study of a range of telescopes, microscopes, and other optical instruments, such as the camera obscura, a device used to project images onto paper for accurate tracing.[77] Gilham's chemistry course included recitation and "illustrative experiments,"[78] meaning the students learned largely from a chemistry textbook and observation of experiments, probably meant to demonstrate principles discussed in the text. Like their counterparts at the École Polytechnique, they probably rarely, if ever, performed any of their own laboratory work.[79]

The cadets received a state-of-the-art education in mathematics, at least relative to that available in America, with West Point providing the model and the standard. Although they strove for comparable completeness in the sciences, the Board of Visitors and Smith experienced some frustration in establishing this course, having neither enough instructors nor facilities. Few colleges, however, offered anything more substantial; strong science courses entered college curricula only in the 1840s.[80]

The Engineering Course

Engineering at VMI meant primarily civil and military engineering but also architecture. The engineering courses provided cadets with an empirical knowledge of engineering and also required an extensive foundation in mathematics, mechanics, and mathematics-based drawing. This curriculum emphasized a set of skills and knowledge that craft-oriented engineers could not have obtained through on-the-job training. Based on the content of the courses, engineering work consisted of surveying, producing topographic maps, and constructing buildings, bridges, railroads, canals, roads, and ports. Military engineering included the construction of fortifications, such as trenches, embankments, and walls. Cadets learned these topics in distinct drawing, surveying, civil engineering, and military engineering courses.[81]

The surveying course employed a textbook by, once again, West Point professor Charles Davies. It taught the use of surveying tools as well as specific instruction in laying out the boundaries of land, producing topographic maps, determining and laying out level surfaces, determining elevations, performing surveys and mapping of coasts, and even navigation of ships by various methods.[82]

The curriculum placed great emphasis on drawing, often based on mathematical or geometric principles, just like for French engineers, for whom drawing was an essential tool in "calculation." Historian Antoine Picon describes, for example, how French engineers used mathematically informed drawing in the estimation of the volume of earth to be moved in a construction project. Using drawings for this, the engineers were able to estimate how much labor was required, how to manage that labor, and what the movement of earth would cost. Consequently, the engineers themselves could exert their authority over a labor force that sought to exert its own agency. In addition, it was through drawing that French engineers could learn to "read nature" and, moreover, bring order to it by removing natural barriers to transportation.[83] Besides descriptive geometry, which provided the mathematical principles for engineering drawing, the cadets took two years of other drawing courses. This began with "human figure" drawing during one year and topography and a course titled Shades, Shadows, and Linear Perspective during the next.[84]

This emphasis on drawing contributed to the distinctiveness of VMI's curriculum. Of the art of drawing, Smith said, "There is no part of the education of a man of science more necessary and at the same time more neglected than drawing." Even more so, "To the *soldier* and *engineer*, this art is absolutely indispensable." Given this

Figure 4.2. Cadet Shades and Perspective Exercise. Edward L. Smith, 1856, Untitled, Cadet Architectural Drawings, MS 203, Virginia Military Institute Archives.

importance, Smith lamented, "With the exception of the United States Military Academy, [VMI] is I believe the only institution in the country, in which instruction is given in this useful and ornamental art."[85] Again, according to those who, like Smith, valued mathematics and basic principles as the foundation of engineering, drawing gave VMI cadets an advantage over the craft-trained engineers who dominated American engineering.

Like descriptive geometry, the study of shadows and perspective provided the cadets with a means of drawing and representation with reference to mathematical principles. Davies, of West Point, again emphasized the useful character of the training of engineers in a textbook employed at VMI. He argued that his book would "add something to the common stock of useful knowledge," especially "the architect and draftsman," for whom "a knowledge of them is indispensable." Moreover, drawing with "mathematical accuracy the lines of shade and shadow on a complicated building . . . is certainly a difficult problem, unless it be solved on scientific principles."[86] Figure 4.2 provides an example of a cadet drawing taken from an exercise in Davies's text. The problem the cadet solved required finding "the perspective of the groined arch and the perspective of its shadows," though the cadet added additional detail, including the tiled floor and brick pattern.[87] The drawing indicates the potential usefulness of the study of this particular skill for the production of structural design, including for architecture and fortifications. Figure 4.3 provides, instead, an example of a topographic drawing, copied from some consistently used source, given that cadets produced numerous nearly identical examples up through 1868.[88] Such drawings, though rather elementary, could find use in the production of a variety of maps, including topographic maps and for laying out towns and fortifications.

Professor Thomas Williamson added architecture to the civil engineering course in 1848. He claimed that he could not locate a textbook and did not know of any other courses offered in America. This, however, is almost surely disingenuous. Architecture was taught as part of the engineering course at West Point since 1816, when Crozet introduced the subject there. Starting in 1830, just after Williamson entered West Point as a cadet, Professor Dennis Mahan took over and expanded the course. In 1831, he published his own short architecture textbook.[89] Williamson, trained as an engineer by Mahan, would almost certainly have studied architecture with him and used his textbook.

Regardless, Williamson edited a compilation of architectural drawings and writings and, soon after, published his own textbook. This book, revealing the influence of Mahan, went well beyond what one might expect of the architecture of buildings. Williamson also discussed the construction of bridges, canals, railroads, and roads, work generally considered to be civil engineering. He included even descriptions of the basic mechanisms of locomotive engines. Much of the introduction to his book was an assessment of the accomplishments of French and British engineers and a discussion of the future expansion of transportation infrastructure.[90]

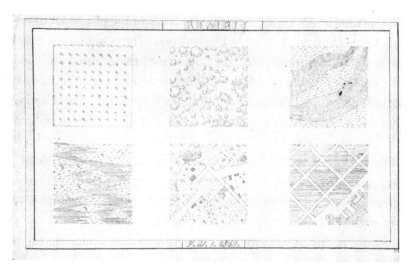

Figure 4.3. Cadet Landscape and Topography Exercise. William E. Kemble, 1851, Untitled, Cadet Architectural Drawings, MS 203, Virginia Military Institute Archives.

Mahan, in his book as well, identified architecture as a discipline of engineering and all structures, including bridges and fortifications, as works of architecture.[91] This identification of architecture with and even subordinate to engineering by Mahan, Williamson, and other students of Mahan was a reversal of the trend in France, where engineering had been a discipline of architecture in the eighteenth century. French engineers had struggled to separate themselves professionally from architects through the cultivation of the mathematical "calculation" described earlier.[92] To Mahan, architecture was distinct from the fine arts. He rejected the use of traditional proportions and conventions in architecture in favor of, as with engineering in general, the application of scientific principles to create designs that were functional. He drew largely on the work of French architects, including Jean Rondelet, Jean-Nicolas-Louis Durand, and Quatremère de Quincy.[93]

Williamson justified the study of architecture by appealing to a desire to produce "native" architects and to provide a "useful" profession for the graduates. Like the construction of roads, American architecture had been left, according to Williamson, to either the incompetent or the foreign, meaning from other countries or even other states. He found these charges to be a "foul reproach upon [Virginia's] intelligence and upon our enterprise." Patriotism demanded efforts to provide for "native" architects for the design of "any public building of any importance, or indeed of any private edifice."[94] VMI cadets, who required some profession and work after graduation, could fill that niche and rival, on the grounds of their basic competence and Virginia births, their competitors. Williamson did not, however, intend for the cadets to serve primarily as architects. They could instead fill the gap until a more professional architecture developed. He wrote that any of his students who pass his course "will avoid, when called upon to furnish a plan, those gross deviations from correct principles everywhere observable throughout the extent of our state."[95] Rather than mastering architecture, they learned the principles that others lacked so that they could simply avoid basic mistakes. This, combined with their general engineering training, enabled them to achieve a basic competence.

Some of those foreign architects surely agreed with Williamson's assessment of American-born "architects." Benjamin Henry Latrobe, an English architect and engineer who arrived in America in 1796, believed himself to be the first, and presumably for a time the only, professional architect in America. In antebellum America, the title of architect was largely confined to those who designed buildings and also mediated between those who commissioned the design and the artisans who actually built the buildings. However, most design was done by craftsmen who generally called themselves "builders, carpenters, or building mechanics." A lesser amount of building design was done by gentlemen amateurs, with Thomas Jefferson being perhaps the most famous of these. The highest prestige professional architects learned their art in the offices of other professional architects. There they were taught to draw, learned by serving as assistants, and engaged in their own study. Increasingly in the early nineteenth century, the builder-architects supplemented their craft training with courses on drawing, mathematics, and science offered by mechanics institutes. Both office and course forms of training, however, was available almost exclusively in northern cities and not in Virginia.[96] A few colleges offered courses in architecture before the 1860s. The University of Virginia, one southern exception, offered some courses since its founding in 1825. A student of Mahan taught some architecture at Yale after 1852. The Massachusetts Institute of Technology, which opened in 1865, is generally cited as providing the first full school training in professional architecture. However, the Polytechnic College of the State of Pennsylvania, which initially offered night courses in 1853, established a full architecture program in 1860.[97] Regardless, until then, VMI and West Point were among those few institutions of higher education that offered architectural training.

The civil engineering course included instruction on the various structures an engineer might design, including bridges, roads, railroads, canals, and river and coastal improvements. For this course, cadets used another textbook by West Point professor Dennis Mahan. The text began with an extensive discussion of various building materials and then went on to explain a variety of structures.[98] Cadets studied from another text by Mahan for their military engineering courses. This work focused on the production of fortifications, including trenches, embankments, and walls.[99]

The cadets drew upon their mathematics training to succeed in their engineering courses. Descriptive geometry received particular emphasis, but the cadets also needed trigonometry, calculus, and mechanics for some of their courses. The surveying textbook, for example, began with an overview of logarithms, trigonometry, and geometry, which Davies used throughout his text.[100] The architecture course and text likewise required trigonometry and descriptive geometry.[101]

The engineering course did, however, include a mix of mathematical and empirical knowledge. One of the civil engineering text-books, for example, included compilations of empirically derived data on the characteristics of materials. Mahan collected this data from research conducted in France and the United States. Mahan also provided empirical formulas for estimating the strength of wood and cast iron. The book did, however, require knowledge of statics and dynamics, trigonometry, and descriptive geometry.[102] Mahan confined the use of integral calculus to an appendix, in which he described how to model the "force producing the rupture of a solid body by a cross strain on its fibres, and the resistance of compression and extension of the fibres produced by the action of the force."[103]

Most of Mahan's discussion of the determination of forces acting on various structures deemphasized the use of basic mathematical and physical principles and, instead, emphasized rule-of-thumb knowledge, such as tables of approximations of materials or dimensions required for any particular construction problem. Few force diagrams derived from the primary principles of mechanics appear in the text. He explicitly justified the use of rule-of-thumb knowledge in the case of retaining walls. Determining the structure and dimensions of such a wall, he said, "is a problem of considerable intricacy." He points out that most of the mathematical solutions for these problems "have generally been confined to particular cases, for which approximate results have long been obtained." These, however, "present sufficient accuracy for all practical purposes within the limits to which the solutions are applicable."[104] Rule-of-thumb knowledge could be acceptable.

Despite Mahan's claim that "[t]he Military Art, in all its branches, is founded upon a comprehensive, and thorough knowledge of the exact and physical sciences; and in no one branch is the importance of this knowledge more felt, than in that of Engineering,"[105] his text, even more so than his civil engineering textbook, emphasized general guidelines and rules-of-thumb for construction and materials, as well as descriptions of various types of structures.

Published in 1836, *A Complete Treatise on Field Fortification* required some trigonometry for calculating the amount of material required for building an embankment, for example, but it did not rely on fundamental mathematical or physical principles. It did, however, require previous knowledge of civil engineering, from which cadets may have drawn more upon such principles.[106]

Regardless of the compromise between empirical and mathematical knowledge, the VMI engineering curriculum offered a formal training that provided basic skills that cadets could transfer from one unique engineering problem to another. This required them to obtain an extensive foundation in drawing, mathematics, and mechanics, which set them apart from both their craft-oriented engineering peers and the students of the colleges.

CONCLUSIONS

The founders and officers of VMI explicitly established what they saw, despite the strong inspiration of West Point and the École Polytechnique, as a new and distinct type of institution for higher education. This distinctiveness included the demographic character of the students, the disciplinary and pedagogical system, and the curriculum. The curriculum served three purposes: (1) create a new standard for authority in higher education to enable VMI to compete with the colleges; (2) provide remedial training for students and to prepare them for required service to the commonwealth; and (3) train professionals, particularly engineers and teachers. The particular content of the curriculum, as well as how it was conveyed, was inseparable from these goals. It is partly from this content and the means of teaching that we can decipher what it meant to the officers of VMI to be engineers. Moreover, the content and pedagogical practices help to reveal the field of struggle in which VMI's officers found themselves.

Having established a new school, the officers of VMI had to establish its legitimacy; they had to give parents a reason to send their sons to the school and give the broader public of Virginia a reason to recognize the school's graduates as authoritative. Consequently, the school's officers found themselves in a contest for authority within the field of higher education, a field dominated by colleges that offered a liberal education to the sons of land- and slaveholders. Given the poor and middling-class backgrounds of the young white men that VMI served and the military and engineering orientation of the curriculum, the officers could not have realistically hoped to compete for authority on the same grounds accepted by the liberal colleges. Consequently, the officers of VMI had to struggle to redefine what counted as authority within the field of higher education and to do so in a way that would transform what would otherwise be weaknesses into strengths.

The class backgrounds of the college students lent authority to the colleges through the cultural capital of the planter class itself. The founders of VMI certainly sought to establish the equality of white men, but they would have, nonetheless, found it difficult to conjure up a superior cultural capital for white people of the poor and middling classes as a counterstrategy to gain authority for their own school. Instead, the officers of VMI sought to define a seemingly universal, rather than class-based, authority for their institution. They carried out the struggle to establish this authority through public testing and constant quantification of student performance. Through such seemingly neutral means, the officers could publicly demonstrate the results of their system. They could prove student learning and competence. To highlight this, some of the school's officers, especially Superintendent Smith, attacked the pedagogy of the colleges. While VMI emphasized recitations in small classes that could ensure student mastery, the colleges offered lectures in which student assessment was limited and for which even attendance was not required. The passive and impersonal approaches of the colleges could not, according to Smith, effectively evaluate students. Not only could VMI create a quantitative measure of performance, both academic and moral (see chapter 6), but the evaluation was also public, allowing other colleges and the broader public to judge for themselves the effectiveness of the curriculum and instructors.

Besides demonstrating that students were learning, perhaps in a manner superior to that of the colleges, the officers of VMI sought to convey a type of knowledge superior to that conveyed by the colleges. In a period of rapid expansion of the market economy and a growing desire for internal improvements to support that growth, VMI would offer a practical training that could be applied to a student's future career and to the benefit of the people of Virginia. Scientific and engineering knowledge could, the officers argued, contribute to the economic progress of Virginia and even, as in the case of architecture, eliminate existing embarrassments and improve the reputation of their state. The colleges, by contrast, offered a liberal education that had been seen as the marker of leadership and authority. VMI's officers recast that form of education as, by implied contrast with the "practical" or "useful" training of VMI, impractical or even useless.

While the curriculum and pedagogy of VMI reveals something of how VMI struggled to gain authority, it also reveals something about what it meant to be an engineer at VMI—being practical and scientific. These terms, however, require explanation. Recall that state engineers of France understood their training and work as "theoretical." They grounded their authority in theory, marking themselves as superior to "practical" mechanics and doctors. Engineering work was, however, practical in the sense that theory was to be applied to provide for the needs of the state and the nation (see chapter 1).[107]

For those men who established VMI's engineering curriculum, they saw that curriculum as entirely practical. They, unlike their French counterparts, never employed "theory" in their discourse. Preston, the most articulate and aggressive of the initial promoters of VMI, later described VMI's curriculum as providing for "the practical pursuits of life."[108] Such an interest in "practical" training or in "useful knowledge" was not uncommon by the 1840s, and the number of schools that offered some version of such knowledge increased throughout the antebellum period. At least the growing middle class of the period saw a scientific education as ideal even for men entering business, let alone the professions.[109] While historian Roger Geiger sees these developments as culminating in new land-grant colleges in the 1860s, historian Jennifer Green has documented that by the eve of the Civil War, eighty-three southern military schools had already provided a "practical" and vocational training, especially in engineering and education, to more than 11,000 boys. All subsequent southern military schools offered a curriculum similar to that described in this chapter. These schools served largely young white southern men of the middling class. These men generally could not afford the classics educations that were prerequisites for admission to the colleges. Military schools did not require this background and, therefore, made higher education available to these men. Moreover, unlike most of their college-bound peers, they did not come from families with land that would provide for their economic futures and generally could not afford the costs of the colleges. These boys had instead to seek out paid careers, making attractive the scientific and engineering training of the far more accessible military schools.[110]

So how do we reconcile this "practical" interpretation of the engineering curriculum at VMI with the employment of a "theoretical" French tradition? The contrast that promoters and faculty of VMI drew was not between theory and practice within the field of engineering but between the practical or useful training of their school and the "monastic" or perhaps even useless education of the colleges. The training provided by VMI was practical in that it provided the skills and knowledge necessary for a career and to serve Virginia through teaching and internal improvements, or whatever other career graduates might pursue.

Although the officers of VMI implicitly and explicitly challenged the colleges and offered VMI as a superior system, they did not have much to say to those engineers with whom the cadets would compete during their careers. Most engineers in America learned engineering as a craft on the job. Arguably, cadets and officers of VMI could have claimed, through the mathematical and scientific curriculum, a more universal set of skills applicable to a variety of engineering contexts rather than an intimate knowledge of a narrower range of materials and projects gained through just experience. But, based on my review of every surviving institutional document and the available papers of VMI's principal officers from the period, the officers were mostly silent about the contrast between these modes of engineering training. Board president Crozet, based on his own experiences with craft-oriented engineers in Virginia, probably had extensive criticisms of the poor quality of work done by many road builders in Virginia, but he did not relay these criticisms in the context of VMI's curriculum. Presumably, such criticisms of self-taught and craft-trained engineers could have served as a further argument for the authority of the school. Professor Williamson, however, did offer some criticism of American architects and argued that through formal training, VMI cadets would prove superior. Nonetheless, the relative silence about competition with other engineers may itself be meaningful.

The silence may have come from either or both of two issues. First, VMI's officers may have seen the opportunities in or need for engineering work as so abundant as to not necessitate real concerns about professional competition. Indeed, America generally lacked a sufficient number of engineers to carry out the construction of the infrastructure of such a large and dispersed country. Criticisms of the means by which most engineers gained their knowledge may have only served to diminish the credibility of the profession as a whole at a time when western Virginians, for example, struggled to acquire the funds necessary for the numerous engineering projects they desired. Second, the officers of VMI may not have seen engineering as the primary field in which they competed for authority. Instead, they sought legitimacy among fellow institutions of higher learning. In order to succeed, they argued for a redefinition of educational authority by emphasizing a practical and scientific education committed to the service of the commonwealth. Indeed, VMI probably did provide the most intensive and formal training in both engineering and mathematics outside of West Point and provided a scientific education that was at least the equal of most colleges before the Civil War. Nonetheless, Crozet and Smith in particular designed a curriculum to produce elite engineers along the lines of West Point and the École Polytechnique. Rather than rise through the ranks of labor, as did so many craft-trained engineers, the cadets skipped the lower ranks and move quickly into roles of leadership on engineering projects.[III]

Crozet and Smith may have recognized the existence of other pathways into engineering besides what they had gone through. Regardless, through the development of a particular curriculum with particular knowledge, they contributed to an engineering tradition in America that identified (1) formal education as the means of producing new engineers and (2) fundamental mathematical and physical principles as the foundation of engineering knowledge and engineering authority. They likely would have wanted to do just that given the chance to create a school anywhere in the United States and in any context. But, given the particular context of VMI, officers of the school's pedagogical and curricular decisions were informed by and gained power through a struggle for political power in Virginia. The officers and the school's local supporters sought to redefine white manhood as a category possessing inherent virtue and independence that legitimated and even demanded the equal political participation of all white men, while simultaneously bolstering claims of the inherent dependence of women and black men. Having chosen education as a front in that struggle, the officers found themselves struggling to redefine authority in a field of higher education that, in Virginia, had served to reinforce a conservative republicanism that defined virtue in terms of property ownership. A mathematically intensive and formal engineering training became the wedge with which partisans in this struggle would crack open the college's claim to exclusive authority in higher education and, therefore, crack open the planters' control of the state.

CHAPTER FIVE

ENGINEERING AS A PROFESSION OF SERVICE TO THE PROGRESS OF VIRGINIA

The officers of the Virginia Military Institute (VMI) justified the legislature's commitment to the school in terms of the service rendered by cadets, but they also emphasized the role of service as a means of training the cadets in public virtue and committing them to Virginia as patriots. This service consisted of guarding the arsenal, teaching in Virginia's schools, providing leadership in the state militia, and working as engineers. In Superintendent Francis Smith's words, "[W]e aim to make the youth entrusted to our care *useful* citizens, who shall be capable of rendering service to their state in war as well as in peace." This was possible because the cadets were "disciplined to habits of economy, industry, promptness and fidelity in the discharge of all their duties." Moreover, "they are taught to respect [Virginia's] laws, and to obey those in authority."[1] The cadets, according to Smith, became "useful" citizens through their service and their training under the disciplinary system of VMI. Cadets did not just fulfill their service as a means of paying for their education; instead, the VMI system transformed them into patriots and citizens sincerely committed to service to Virginia as the guiding principle of their future careers.

Associating engineers with service was nothing new, even in the 1840s. Historian Ken Alder argues that elite state engineers in France—one of the models for engineering at VMI—survived the French Revolution and prospered by positioning themselves as professionals who demonstrated their worthiness through a new form of objective merit and by then serving the French state and, consequently, the French nation. As Alder states, in France, "Engineers were designed to serve."[2] Historian Matthew Wisnioski goes further to argue, "Service is one of the few universal values of engineering." What engineers mean by service, however, is not universal. Wisnioski documents struggles among postwar American engineers to define service to the nation. Despite those differences, engineers claim to possess "special knowledge" and must therefore "use it for the greater good."[3] Whether Wisnioski is right or not about the universality of a culture of service, VMI does provide another data point to make the case. But, in the case of VMI, service was understood in terms of service primarily to Virginia rather than to the United States.

Service to Virginia after graduation could include one of the three major careers or contributions for which VMI's curriculum prepared cadets: militia leadership, teaching, and engineering. The curriculum identified architecture, resource extraction, the building of transportation infrastructure, town planning, mapping, and building military fortifications as the work of engineering. The purpose of this work, along with teaching, was to unleash the productive forces of Virginia. Up to 1856, at least sixty VMI graduates, one-quarter of all graduates, worked directly as civil engineers at some point in their careers, with fifty working in Virginia. They worked as everything from surveyors to railroad company presidents.[4] Beyond these men were surely other undocumented architects and civil and military engineers as well as teachers of mathematics and engineering.

While the cadets did need to pursue paying careers after graduating, they, whether they pursued teaching, engineering, or anything else, were to do so not for their own gain but as a form of service to their home state. Engineering was to be a profession of service. Through their service, they would contribute to the progress of Virginia, including its economic development. The officers of VMI understood this progress in terms of "physical" as opposed to, but not excluding, "moral" progress. The aim of this progress was reestablishing Virginia as an economic leader of America, a leader that was not dependent on men from other states for that development. Moreover, it would be a Virginia with a more diversified economy, one less dependent upon the export of cash crops produced with slave labor. And the men to lead Virginia toward this goal were not the sons of planters but instead the sons of yeomen farmers, mechanics, and merchants, once again legitimizing the equality of white manhood.

FORMAL CADET SERVICE TO VIRGINIA

All cadets had to perform the formal service of guarding the arsenal on the school's grounds. However, formal service after graduation depended upon which of the two types of cadet you were. VMI accepted two classes of students: state and pay cadets. State cadets, in accordance with the original proposals for the school, received an education in exchange for guarding the arsenal. After 1842, the legislature also required state cadets to teach in a school in Virginia for two years. The enabling legislation required the Board of Visitors, responsible for admissions, to ensure that it did not privilege any geographic region of the state in accepting these cadets. The board first had to grant an opportunity for admission of one boy from each senatorial district or, barring a sufficient number of acceptable applicants, at least ensure a reasonable distribution of cadets from the "four great Constitutional Divisions of the State": the Tidewater, Piedmont, Shenandoah Valley, and Allegheny region (see Figure 1.1). Pay cadets received the same education, lived under the same military discipline, and performed the same guard duty as state cadets. However, pay cadets paid tuition and did not have to serve as teachers after graduation. While both classes of cadet came only from Virginia, at least at the beginning, the board did not need to ensure equal numbers of pay cadets from the various districts or regions of the state.[5]

In the first year of operation, the board admitted twenty state and thirteen pay cadets, for a total of thirty-three. Four state cadets came from each of the constitutional divisions, except for the Piedmont, which provided eight cadets. The pay cadets, however, came disproportionately from the counties near VMI, within the Shenandoah Valley or just across the Blue Ridge Mountains, with three from Albemarle and one each from Augusta, Campbell, Fluvanna, Shenandoah, and Rockbridge Counties. The board nearly doubled the number of cadets the following year, admitting six additional state cadets and twenty-two pay cadets, for an approximate total of sixty. Again, the pay cadets came disproportionately from the surrounding region, in fact, more so, with five from Rockbridge County itself, and four from Augusta County and two from Bedford County, both adjacent to Rockbridge.[6] The numbers of state-supported cadets versus pay cadets at VMI was typical of the southern military schools in general. Up until the Civil War, about one-third of all cadets in the state military schools were state cadets.[7]

The cadets began their service to Virginia immediately upon entering the school. They did this by participating in the arsenal guard, a service that justified the very existence of the school to the Virginia legislature. Although pay cadets did indeed pay for the privilege of serving in the arsenal guard, state cadets did not, in Smith's estimation, receive a free education through charity.

Instead, they earned it by providing an arsenal guard superior to that which previously existed. Moreover, they did so at the same cost to the commonwealth as the original upkeep of the arsenal.[8]

In contrast to what Superintendent Smith referred to as the "band of hired soldiers"[9] who first guarded the arsenal and which citizens of Lexington found so troublesome, the commonwealth "substituted the educated and intelligent student, taken, in all cases, from among her own children, and made them the guardian of her means of defense." Moreover, "by educating them and by sending them forth as Instructors throughout the commonwealth she has made even the means of defense less necessary."[10] While the previous professional guard performed their service for pay, cadets instead benefited from their service by using it as an opportunity to learn patriotism and public virtue. The commonwealth, in turn, benefited from the spread of these virtuous young men across the state after graduation.

Beginning in 1842, the legislature added another service requirement for state cadets. They would have to teach in Virginia schools for at least two years after graduating.[11] Unlike the guard service, which applied to all cadets, this new requirement applied only to state cadets. But pay cadets did often serve as teachers as well. This provided a means of improving primary and secondary education in Virginia at a time when few of Virginia's children attended school and, when they did so, often suffered under poor quality teachers with few credentials.[12]

Describing the benefits of the teaching requirement to both the commonwealth and the cadets, William H. Richardson, adjutant general of the Virginia militia and VMI board member, stated, "This valuable institution is, as you will see, rapidly raising up for the state a band of *native born* teachers, of the highest qualifications, in both the pay and state cadets." As for the cadets, "The state gives them the best education (an independence) which they could not otherwise obtain; and they repay her by their services as teachers in her public schools." Through this arrangement, "many meritorious young men, who but for this institution would have lived and died in ignorance and poverty, enter upon life enlightened, useful and independent citizens."[13] Again, the service of the cadets benefited not just Virginia but also the cadet. The commonwealth benefited by obtaining qualified teachers for the slowly expanding common schools. The state cadets, of course, received an education in exchange for their service. This education, according to Richardson, provided them with a means of independence, the hallmark of a virtuous citizen who could participate responsibly in the governance of the state. Besides serving by simply fulfilling their mandatory years of service, the cadets further performed service by participating in a "useful" profession, thus contributing to Virginia rather than just working for personal enrichment.

Smith claimed that, after ten years of operation, VMI did indeed expand education greatly in Virginia by providing teachers. Moreover, the training of the school produced cadets of such high qualification that schools sought to hire more of them than were available.[14] By 1850, VMI provided about 12 percent of all of Virginia's college and academy teachers.[15] Believing in the superiority of the VMI system, Smith saw the spread of its graduates as elevating the quality of schools by spreading elements of the VMI system to other schools. He further claimed that in part due to the increased number of teachers who came out of VMI and, after 1856, the University of Virginia, they increased the number of college students in Virginia from 500 in 1845 to 2,500 in 1860, "thus giving to Virginia the proud pre-eminence of having a larger number of young men attending college in 1860, in proportion to white population, than any other state of this country."[16]

VMI officers, including Richardson in his above quote, also argued that the service of the cadets as teachers benefited the commonwealth by increasing the proportion of native Virginians teaching in schools. This helped to ensure that Virginia's all-white students would learn from teachers who accepted and defended slavery. Smith argued that Virginia, at the time, relied on northern and sometimes British teachers, with a few exceptions of teachers who graduated from the University of Virginia. He explained this in part, by recalling, "At that time it was regarded as an unworthy calling for a young Virginian to teach school."[17] So, by providing high-quality teachers, VMI helped to raise the status of teachers and encourage others to take up the profession. Smith, moreover, extolled the benefit of no longer "being compelled as heretofore to resort entirely to other states for teachers, who are unacquainted with our habits and unaccustomed and too often opposed to our Southern Institutions," meaning slavery.[18] Consequently, by serving the commonwealth as teachers, VMI graduates would defend white supremacy and avoid risking northern teachers turning white southern youth into abolitionists. This would have certainly appealed to the planter-dominated legislature upon whom VMI depended for funding.

Early advocates of the school also promised that VMI would produce leadership for the state militia by sending well-drilled cadets with knowledge of military tactics and leadership to all parts of Virginia. Perhaps convinced of their qualifications in this regard, Governor David Campbell wrote to Smith to express his confidence that the cadets were "qualified to defend its constitutional liberty and its rights."[19] Smith argued for the superiority of the cadets over paid soldiers in their commitment to the defense of Virginia, claiming that the "moral power of an intelligent and disciplined corps of young men, annually sent forth to mix in the affairs of society, will exercise the greatest influence in maintaining respect abroad and peace at home." Moreover, "Young men who are educated in a strong moral sense of the duties of patriotism," as opposed to those who serve as soldiers merely for pay, "will never desert the standard of the commonwealth nor see its flag trailed in the dust; and educated for usefulness and trained to virtue, their influence in all the relations of society must be beneficent."[20] The graduates, according to Smith, did not just train to serve in militias, they also learned, through their military discipline, to become patriots and virtuous citizens in whom the people of Virginia could place their trust. That patriotism, while certainly extending to the defense of the United States against foreign invaders, was also a Virginia patriotism that meant defending the state against domestic threats, including slave revolts.

Service was part of the training of VMI's cadets. They practiced it from their first days at VMI and even after graduation. They guarded one of Virginia's arsenals, they taught in Virginia's schools and professionalized teaching, and they provided a corps of competent officers for Virginia's militia and, later, the Confederate Army. Their service was not abstract or vague rhetoric; it was specific and committed to their home state. That service contributed to the improvement of Virginia's schools and to the military defense of Virginia, the United States, and of slavery. "Native" teachers and competent militia officers would minimize the spread of abolitionism and help assert control over the people white Virginians enslaved. It is important to keep in the forefront that a school predicated upon the egalitarianism of an inherent white male equality was also predicated upon white supremacy and the exclusion of both women and black people from power.

VMI'S CONTRIBUTIONS TO INTERNAL IMPROVEMENTS

VMI cadets were to serve Virginia after their graduation by contributing to internal improvements, including transportation infrastructure. Internal improvements joined the discourse of VMI during the initial struggle to establish the school and soon became a central concern in the institutional discourse of VMI. And, indeed, a minority of VMI cadets did contribute much to Virginia's transportation infrastructure.

In January of 1836, military-school advocate Alden Partridge sent a letter to Rockbridge delegate Charles Dorman to argue that the new school should teach civil engineering, which he called the "most important branch of knowledge," and of "practical Science generally." This was because, as he wrote, "The subject of Internal Improvement engrosses more of the public attention than any other." Moreover, "In consequence of the vast extent of our country a century probably will not be long time enough to complete all that will be required in this department." Given this, engineering "now opens a wider field for lucrative and useful employment to young men who are properly prepared to enter upon its duties than any other occupation, and is rapidly extending every year."[21] Here, Partridge made the connection between formal education and civil engineering, a connection that would have appeared obvious to him because of his West Point training. Moreover, he specifically linked this to the promotion of internal improvements in order to give particular purpose to engineering. Engineers did not simply build railroads and canals for some local or personal interest; they built them to connect and improve the dispersed regions of the nation.

Dorman had the letter published in the *Lexington Gazette* for his constituents, who already largely supported establishing a military school. This would have immediately resonated with the people of western Virginia, given their struggle for internal improvements during the 1829–1830 constitutional convention. Moreover, Partridge's letter made a connection between internal improvements and the use of education to elevate the political status of poor white men, another crucial concern of the military-school advocates. Indeed, Rockbridge County citizens adopted Partridge's language when they sent a petition to the legislature, in which they asked for further progress on the establishment of the school in January of 1839. In this memorial, they identified the training of civil engineers as one of the benefits and purposes of the school. Such training "would prepare our young men to participate in the progress of a profession at present more lucrative than any other and to aid the state in the prosecution of her plans of public improvement."[22] Though, here, they spoke specifically of "public improvement" rather than internal improvement, emphasizing the role of the legislature in supporting these projects through taxes and the development of comprehensive plans. While the legislature offered limited monetary support for a limited number of projects, they had since 1817 employed a "principal engineer" with the Board of Public Works to engage in surveying and planning of roads, bridges, tunnels, and so forth (see chapter 2). Private corporations, however, carried out many of these projects, with the principal engineer having little influence in their actual execution.[23] Claudius Crozet served as the state engineer twice, the second time during his tenure as president of the Board of Visitors.

The officers of VMI did not, at least in their official reports, speak much of internal improvements again from then until the late 1840s. This may, however, reflect concerns about antagonizing the legislature during a period of ongoing sectional conflict over the issue. Support for improvements, especially for transportation but also for education, exploded in the *Lexington Gazette* in 1844 after the legislature rejected the Baltimore and Ohio Railroad Company's proposal to bring a line down into the Shenandoah Valley. This would have provided cheaper transport for the farmers of western Virginia, who at that point had to take their products to Richmond over roads before heading to the coast.[24] Illustrating the intensity of sentiment concerning the issue, "Rockbridge" opened his lengthy anonymous letter to the *Gazette* with the following bold words that invoke the Declaration of Independence:

> The time has arrived when you must assert your rights with the firmness of freemen, or tamely submit to the grossest injustice and tyranny, at the hands of your own State Government. The present is an auspicious moment to demand a redress of grievances, so long endured, that patience under them has ceased to be a virtue. And you have no alternative but to speak out boldly and decidedly, or submit to the disgrace of seeing your just expectations wholly disregarded, and your rights trampled upon, by a government created for the benefit of the whole people of the Commonwealth.[25]

Another writer, whose article appeared immediately below the listing of pro-improvement Whig candidates for the House of Delegates, warned of the possibility of the western portion of the state eventually seceding over the issue if no resolution occurred.[26] This was not, given other outstanding issues from the failures of the constitutional convention, unfounded bluster.[27] Indeed, western Virginia did secede from the state in 1861.

The officers of VMI would likely have had some concern about the school *appearing* as an agent of these sectional interests, even though, in fact, it emerged as exactly that in the context of such heated discourse. They began, however, to speak openly of internal improvements around 1850 after a new constitutional convention, during which reformers, having gained substantial strength from eastern cities, succeeded in establishing universal white male suffrage with little opposition.[28] Regardless, the school, through its emphasis on civil engineering, did in fact serve as an agent for internal improvements throughout its first decades.

After retiring as the final state engineer in 1843 and as the president of the Board of Visitors in 1845, Crozet wrote an *Outline of the Improvements in the State of Virginia* in 1848 to promote further investment in improvements. He criticized the legislature for rebuffing the Board of Public Works's request for reestablishing Crozet's old office of state engineer. "Few states," he wrote, "have natural resources and advantages equal to those of Virginia" given its location relative to the sea and other states, its climate, rivers, mineral wealth, and other geographic factors. Virginia "requires but the execution of some internal improvements to make these advantages available."[29] We can infer that it was the fault of the legislature, dominated by the eastern planter class, that Virginia was not taking advantage of its natural abundance and, instead, lagged behind other states.

Superintendent Smith, looking back on the beginning of the school, identified one of the primary benefits of the school to the state: "Engineers for her works of internal improvement."[30] Many cadets did indeed engage in this work and even provided important leadership in engineering projects, often attaining a high professional status both inside and outside of Virginia. Smith wrote in 1851 that many VMI graduates worked as civil engineers. "There is scarcely a line of improvement in the state upon which they may not be found." He then quoted a letter from the president of Virginia's Southside Railroad Company that employed two VMI graduates as assistant engineers. The president was sufficiently impressed by VMI that he wished to send his own son there to study engineering.[31]

The two VMI cadets identified above were Robert Emmet Rodes of Lynchburgh and Edwin Girard Wall of Winchester, both of the class of 1848. Wall later served as superintendent of the Southside Railroad, while Rodes became a chief engineer of one unidentified railroad and then of the Northeast & Southwest Railroad, both in Alabama. Many VMI cadets followed similar paths to that of Wall and Rodes.[32] Like their West Point peers, the cadets found that employers welcomed their formal engineering training. Graduates of the southern military schools in general found that their careers were accelerated by their formal training. Unlike their craft-trained peers, they skipped the lower labor and sometimes even surveying positions, enabling them to rise quickly to positions of leadership on engineering projects.[33]

Providing a conservative minimum estimate, the *Register of Cadets*, which notes known occupations of former cadets, indicates that forty-seven, or 14 percent of the 338 cadets (graduates or otherwise) from the classes of 1842 to 1851 engaged in some kind of engineering work.[34] Smith, in an assessment of the work of the 226 graduates up to 1856, noted that at least fifty worked as civil engineers in Virginia alone; three worked in western and other southern states; three worked for the US Coast Survey; one surveyed the boundary between the United States and Mexico; one worked in Brazil; and one, after having continued his studies at the École Polytechnique, surveyed a bridge over the Potomac River in

Washington, DC, and served as a military engineer and a chief civil engineer.[35] This amounts to at least 25 percent of just the graduates up to 1856 having worked as civil engineers.

Besides the examples given above, the cadets served as engineers in many capacities. Many served as surveyors, with one helping to lay out Denver, many worked as railroad engineers, and at least one constructed telegraph lines. Many of these cadets attained positions as chief engineer or superintendent, and several even became presidents of railroad companies. Besides civil engineering, one worked as a superintendent at the Tredegar Iron Works in Richmond before becoming president of the Southern Railway Supply Company.[36] Although quantifying the number of cadets who worked as engineers presents some difficulties, the available data attest to the enthusiasm with which the cadets took to the profession of service so emphasized at VMI.

Even more cadets served as teachers than as engineers during some part of their careers. Nearly one-third of all southern military school cadets worked as teachers. Teaching was, in fact, the favored profession among cadets.[37] This, of course, should provide little surprise, at least for VMI, considering that state cadets had to teach for two years to fulfill their obligations to the commonwealth. The cadets, however, did not confine themselves to teaching in the common schools of Virginia. Many also taught at institutions of higher education, including VMI, the Georgia Military Institute, Allegheny College, Randolph-Macon College, and Lynchburg College, often teaching mathematics as their primary subject.[38] Superintendent Smith was proud of the contributions of so many cadets to education and engineering, which he referred to as "important state interests." He noted in 1853 that these teachers and engineers "are *Virginia youths*, who are engaged in this work. What a reform! It is no longer a reproach to a Virginian to teach in our schools, and to labor at the [surveying] rod of the engineer." He implied that it was the professional training of VMI that elevated these professions to respectable status. Moreover, he stated,

"We are no longer dependent upon northern teachers and northern engineers," a dependency that received reproach from several VMI officers. "[B]ut now, with the co-operation of our sister state institution of learning, we are sending abroad the *native teacher* and the native civil engineer, to form the mind and to develop the resources of our own state."[39] Virginians were training their own engineers and teachers who were carrying out internal improvements within their own state to cultivate their own resources to the benefit of their own state.

VIRGINIA'S ENGINEERS AS AGENTS OF PROGRESS

Around 1850, a discourse of "progress" joined together with the discourse of internal improvements. This concept of progress emphasized "physical progress" or the development of transportation infrastructure and natural resources as a means to improve the economic standing of Virginia. Consequently, the officers of VMI made contributing to physical progress part of the service that VMI graduates were to carry out. Moreover, this commitment established, within the discourse of VMI, engineers as primary agents of progress.

Science and technology studies scholars Gary Downey and Juan Lucena argue that engineers purposefully reform their profession in such a way as to position themselves to contribute to the "progress" of their country. In so doing, they legitimize their profession and, they hope, increase their social standing and political power as a profession. Consequently, differences in the "dominant cultural images" of progress held by various nations helps to explain differences in the patterns of engineering among those nations. Engineers in France, for example, do not face the same images of progress as do engineers in the United States and, so, French engineering must serve a different purpose than does American engineering. Engineers within a single nation, however, can also face or accept differing conceptions of progress. This was, Downey argues, the case in the antebellum United States, when engineers faced not only differing conceptions of the progress of the nation but also differing conceptions of the nation itself and of the relationship of engineers to that nation.[40] The officers of VMI found themselves in conflict with an emerging conception of the nation and progress in the late 1840s and early 1850s. In response, they asserted an explicit discourse of progress, one that defined the United States as a collection of states rather than as a single nation-state and for which progress meant the economic advancement of Virginia, to which the primary loyalties of the officers were directed. Consequently, they defined the purpose of engineering as contributing to that progress by providing the transportation infrastructure needed for the expansion of the market economy and the exploitation of Virginia's natural resources. More specifically, Superintendent Smith saw engineers as contributing to the progress of Virginia in the sense of returning Virginia to its position as a leader of the nation, a position it had lost presumably under the leadership of the eastern planters whose authority VMI challenged.

Scientific Education, Engineering, and the Progress of Virginia

When the officers of VMI began to once again openly promote internal improvements in the 1850s, they introduced a new emphasis on the discourse of progress in which they linked the work of engineers to the promotion of the progress of the commonwealth and the nation. They distinguished between intellectual and moral progress, which the knowledge of science among the population would promote, and physical progress, which included the spread of transportation infrastructure and the development of natural resources. VMI's graduates would promote both forms of progress, the former through their service as teachers and the latter through engineering work.

Board of Visitors member Philip St. George Cocke presented

some of the earliest references to progress in the papers of VMI. A West Point graduate, he came to associate progress with internal improvements and scientifically based engineering. Although proud of the growth and accomplishments of VMI, he lamented to Superintendent Smith that its model, particularly with regard to science and engineering, had not spread more. He claimed in 1850, "[VMI] is at present the only school in the whole South in which the physical sciences are exclusively [and] to some extent thoroughly taught." And yet, he continued, using "progress" three times in a single, long sentence:

> It is hardly possible that, in this Country of Progress, [and] in this age of <u>physical</u> progress, such a school will not at all times be crowded, and absolutely forced upward [and] onward by the wants [and] tastes of the whole country, until it shall become <u>the great school</u> of the physical sciences, the great school of the Baconian Philosophy where our young men will go to study Nature [and] all her infinite but immutable laws, and where they will leave [here] learned in sciences [and] skilful in practice, with [illegible] to [illegible] all the laws [and] all the processes of Nature in itself of the physical, intellectual [and] moral progress of this Country.[41]

Here he clearly identified the study and application of scientific knowledge with the progress of the nation as a whole, not just a "physical" progress of expanding railroads and canals but also a moral and intellectual progress. It was upon a knowledge of natural law, which VMI emphasized in its curriculum and used as the foundation of engineering knowledge, that the nation would base its improvement. The teaching of this knowledge in schools, perhaps by VMI graduates, would promote intellectual and moral progress while the application of this knowledge to internal improvements would promote physical progress.

Superintendent Smith likewise referred to his "age" as "one of progress" and, more specifically, "of physical progress." Graduates of VMI, he argued, had opportunities to contribute to the progress of Virginia and "to place her again in the lead of her sister states" by applying science in the development of the state's "immense physical resources." "What state," he wrote, "can compare with this in climate, soil, mineral and agricultural wealth, and in natural channels of intercommunication?" The key to progress was to "[l]et science be applied to direct her energies and to develop her wealth, and we shall soon witness a change in the growing prosperity of our people and state."[42] Again, he emphasizes the importance of applying science to the problems of internal improvements and economic development. He did not see these as tasks for just anyone; the engineer, provided with knowledge of nature, must lead. In other words, the engineer must become *the* agent of progress. Engineers were to serve Virginia, but also lead it towards a renewed position of national prominence.

VMI's discourse of progress extended beyond transportation infrastructure and civil engineering to machinery. Great Britain invited manufacturers and producers from other nations to display their work in London at the 1851 Great Exhibition of the Works of Industry of All Nations, also known as the Crystal Palace Exhibition. Virginia Governor John Floyd asked VMI officers to recommend a commission to observe the exhibition. Cocke was enthusiastic about Virginia's participation. He stated, "If however we have nothing to <u>shew</u> [at the exhibition] we have a great deal to <u>learn</u>." Even if frustrated by Virginia's previous lack of development, he was optimistic, claiming that Virginia was "now just entering upon a grand and glorious career of physical progress [and] development," for which he politely credited "our enlightened public spirited [and] energetic Governor."[43] Here Cocke, in line with the interests of the newly emerging middle class, expressed an interest in manufacturing as part of the physical or economic progress of Virginia. Note, however, that Cocke, as well as Smith, took care to distinguish the progress associated with engineering, internal improvements, and manufacturing from other types of progress.

They spoke specifically of "physical progress," in contrast, but not unrelated, to moral and intellectual progress.

The discourse of a more generalized progress as technological development itself did not develop substantially in America until the 1860s when it, along with railroad construction and westward expansion, exploded.[44] Americans then began to see machines, especially in the form of enormous networks of railroads and telegraphs, as inherently progressive rather than as a means toward, for example, moral progress. But they did not yet employ *technology* as a term until the 1930s, although engineers began using the term in the late nineteenth century as a way of distinguishing their scientifically informed work with machines from the work of uneducated artisans and, therefore, to distinguish themselves from and elevate themselves above the artisans. But engineers intended the term to refer more to their knowledge rather than to machines themselves. However, later engineers began to promote the term in its modern sense, referring to the machines, in an effort to lay claim to progress as their own, arguing that they served as the producers and managers of technology. Because the machines, and therefore technology, constituted progress, the engineers themselves produced and managed the progress of the nation.[45]

Smith and Cocke, however, had no concept of technology, as we understand it. Nonetheless, they still associated engineers, as well as scientific knowledge, with progress, or at least "physical" progress. Rather than thinking primarily of machines, although that played a part in it, they understood physical progress in the older context of internal improvements. But internal improvements, unlike machines in the later discourse of technology as progress, served as a *means* of progress rather than as progress itself. They, like so many in western Virginia and of the emerging middle class, sought internal improvements as a means of developing the economy and resources of the commonwealth and nation. The introduction of this new term *progress*, however, requires explanation. Whereas the discourse of "internal improvements" served the needs of those seeking the development of only the western portion of their state, the new concept of progress emerged in the context of westward expansion and in the context of Manifest Destiny.

The Rejection of Manifest Destiny and a More Constrained Progress

White Americans, especially after the 1860s, understood progress as westward expansion through railroads and telegraph, with the machines constituting progress for the nation as a whole. But, in their westward expansion, they saw this progress opposed by, as well as to, the "wildness" of the West and of American Indians.[46] But they had little fear of this opposition because they saw their progress as inevitable and unstoppable. This technological determinism, however, had roots in an earlier discourse of unstoppable westward movement, the 1840s discourse of Manifest Destiny. Despite the popularity of this discourse, some of the primary officers of VMI rejected it and limited their ideas of progress to only the development of Virginia or to the then existing borders of the United States. This placed them in opposition to the slaveholding planters who dominated the legislature of Virginia and aligned them, instead, with middle-class Whigs, which, in fact, some of them had become.

Historians have interpreted the discourse of Manifest Destiny in various ways.

For example, Frederick and Lois Merk describe it as an ideology underpinning American territorial expansion, comparing it to Islam, Marxism, and Napoleonic revolutionary liberalism. This ideology demanded expansion to erase the arbitrary borders imposed on North America by corrupt European empires, which were to be replaced by the "natural boundaries" of a "self-governed republic" that would serve as a virtuous model for the world. This ideology was, though, an aberration in America, whose true "national spirit" is a mission to "improve the state of the world" through the spread of self-governance. Manifest Destiny, however, was "somehow touched by a taint of selfishness, both national and individual.[47] Thomas Hietala interprets Manifest Destiny as a rhetoric designed by "a small corps of American political figures" to promote a policy of expansion in order to alternately increase the power of slaveholders in Congress, gain ports to gain access to or control of foreign markets, or create a safety valve for the class conflict and urbanization accompanying industrialization.[48] Adam Dahl, perhaps similar to the Merks, interprets it as primarily "a democratic theory of settler colonialism," in which the availability of land made democracy possible by providing a safety valve for the industrializing East, thus preventing the rise of the "poverty and class conflict plaguing European society."[49]

All agree, however, that participants in this rhetoric understood American territorial expansion as divinely ordained and as inevitable. Moreover, it either demonstrated or was driven by American exceptionalism. Americans would create a new type of empire, one that would liberate white people from aristocracy and promote democracy, even if it might require the disappearance or exclusion of non-whites. It was, as Dahl writes, a "world-historical mission."[50]

Manifest Destiny emerged out of the debate over America's annexation of Texas and subsequent war with Mexico in 1846. Historian Reginald Horsman also ties this rhetoric to a changing conception of race in America, particularly the development of a new conception of Anglo-Saxonism. English people had generally referred to everyone living within England as Anglo-Saxon, but during the early nineteenth century, they began to expand this to refer to all English-speaking peoples while also racializing the term. Meanwhile, Americans generally used it to refer to white people, in contrast to black people, American Indians, Chinese people, Japanese people, and Mexicans and Mexican-Americans. The term, however, remained ambiguous and its meaning shifted, depending on context. For example, Anglo-Americans might have seen Irish immigrants as Celts on the East Coast, but as Anglo-Saxons in California, where they could contrast themselves with Chinese immigrants. Regardless, many white Americans and English people had long identified themselves as members of superior nations, explaining this superiority, in part, on the basis of the superiority of their Anglo-Saxon political institutions, such as parliaments and trial by jury. By the 1840s, however, both English people and white Americans began to explain their superiority on the basis of their Anglo-Saxon blood rather than institutions, thus racializing Anglo-Saxonism.[51]

This racial Anglo-Saxonism experienced great popularity in the South, where the *Southern Literary Messenger* of Richmond served as an important publisher of these ideas, including by reprinting German Romantic literature and philosophy that provided the intellectual underpinnings of this discourse. Moreover, throughout the 1840s and 1850s, the publishers of southern periodicals came to increasingly identify themselves as Anglo-Saxons and to identify Anglo-Saxons as the only genuine Americans. This marked a shift from the more generalized idea of whiteness that dominated previously.[52]

The racialization of Anglo-Saxonism took on a particular character that contributed to the doctrine of Manifest Destiny. Drawing on German Romanticism and philology, Anglo-Saxonists came to see themselves as the inheritors of a thousands-year-old racial tradition of westward expansion. Assuming a direct correspondence between language and race, they employed linguistic evidence to construct the Indo-European cultural group and claimed that an elite group within it, with an essentially Germanic language, slowly spread westward across Europe. As it did so, it always invigorated the cultures it came in contact with, thereby spreading civilization and a distinctly Germanic spirit of freedom. For example, the Germanic barbarians brought liberty to a crumbling and decadent Roman Empire and then brought parliaments to the Celtic peoples of Britain. American Anglo-Saxonists took this up and claimed that English colonization of America occurred as the logical extension of this westward expansion. They now had a racial destiny to continue this westward movement and to bring their institutions of freedom and civilization all the way across the continent and perhaps even into Asia, from which the Indo-Europeans supposedly originated, thus completing the cycle begun thousands of years earlier.[53] After the 1840s, spreading Anglo-Saxon civilization westward came increasingly to mean spreading machines and what would become known as technology. Moreover, this spread of railroads and telegraphs, and the settlement that followed behind it, became seen, like the spread of the Anglo-Saxon peoples and their institutions of freedom, as inevitable as progress itself.

The annexation of Texas and the subsequent Mexican-American War are the primary context for the discourse of Manifest Destiny. Southern Democrats supported the war because they hoped to increase the territory of the United States and, thereby, expand slavery westward. In so doing, they would both increase that particular form of economic opportunity and increase the power of slave states in Congress. Whigs, however, wanted to expand the market economy and infrastructure within the existing boundaries of the United States rather than expand the land-hungry, slave-based agricultural economy. So, Whigs, especially in the North, generally opposed the war in order to limit the spread of slavery and, therefore, to limit southern power in Congress.[54] Proponents of the war employed the discourse of Anglo-Saxon superiority and Mexican inferiority as a justification for the war. Opponents of the war, however, often employed this racial discourse as well. Many Whigs feared that westward expansion, particularly by the conquest of Mexico, would actually threaten Anglo-Saxon institutions of freedom, either by turning America into a colonial empire that subjugated others or by introducing large numbers of racially inferior people into the nation. Although they could tolerate black people within the country, because they remained thoroughly under white control, they wanted to maintain America as an Anglo-Saxon nation, which required the exclusion of Mexican people.[55]

Despite the participation of VMI cadets in the Mexican-American War and the praise they received for their service from the officers of their school, many VMI officers expressed opposition to the war. Twenty-five former cadets fought in the war, with some in the regular US Army and others in the 1st Virginia Regiment.[56] Superintendent Smith applauded their performance in a report to the Virginia legislature. He claimed, "It is well known that the efficiency of the Virginia volunteer regiment in the Mexican war was in a high degree promoted by the large number of our graduates who held commissions in it."[57] Whether that was true or not, Smith surely hoped his former students performed well when under the scrutiny of the West Point graduates who led the war and who astounded international observers with their tactical brilliance.

This honoring of the contribution of VMI graduates does not, however, indicate any great support for the war. Smith, in a letter to Cocke, fellow West Point graduate and recent addition to and future president of the Board of Visitors, said he believed "the war to be an unnecessary and unjust one." Moreover, "with every effort to raise some feeling to enable me to defend or justify it, I have been unable to do so." But, expressing his commitment to the values of duty taught at VMI, he also stated, "Had I been drafted, and required by such compulsory process to serve in it, I should have obeyed." Moreover, "[I]t does seem to me that if a foreign power were to invade our soil, as we are invading Mexico, I should agree with Santa Anna, in making 'every mountain pass another Thermopylae.'"[58] For Smith, the war was unjust and was, comparing America to the Persian Empire, the result of American aggression and imperialism.

Board president Crozet, who possessed the personal experience of war that Smith did not, also opposed the war. He wrote to Smith that his "[W]hig principles have been strengthened by the Mexican War." Crozet was about to leave for Europe just when the war broke out. He claimed that his "trunks were actually ready," but he decided to remain in America. He had a strong personal interest in the war; as he said to Smith, "Now my son is in it." His son Alfred, a West Point graduate, fought in the battles of Palo Alto and Resaca de la Parma in May of 1846. But it wasn't just concern for his son's safety that led him to oppose the war. He said to Smith, "Since I have had my surfeit of war, I am for peace. . . . Peace, Peace rises at the top of all my thoughts and the feeling makes me twice a Whig."[59]

Smith's and Crozet's opposition to the war coincided with their Whig politics, which put them at odds with the predominantly Democratic slaveholding planters who dominated the legislature of Virginia. They appear to have rejected claims to a divine American mission, an Anglo-Saxon racial destiny, the need to expand slave power within the Congress, or the need for a safety valve from eastern urbanization and industrialization. Smith's comment that "if a foreign power were to invade our soil, as we are invading Mexico, I should agree with Santa Anna" suggests a belief in some equality between the republics of the United States and Mexico rather than American exceptionalism; the United States had no right or destiny to invade. Nonetheless, the new discourse of progress at VMI after the Mexican-American War suggests the influence of the transformation of the discourse of Manifest Destiny into that of progress. There is, however, no evidence that the discourse of Manifest Destiny itself entered significantly into the institutional discourse of VMI, despite the significant participation of cadets in the war.

CONCLUSIONS

VMI emerged, in part, from sectional struggles over internal improvements in Virginia. Reflecting western interests, as well as emerging middle-class interests, civil engineering became the focus of the VMI curriculum early on and, thus, embedded support for internal improvements in the curriculum. Internal improvements remained contentious in Virginia politics during the first decade of the school, even to the point of westerners threatening secession from Virginia. However, with the adoption of a new constitution enacting universal white male suffrage and strengthening western Virginia in the legislature in 1850, the emphasis on the school's mission to support internal improvements came out more openly among the school's officers.

With this new openness came a discourse of "progress." However, rather than the later technologically deterministic concept of progress as the westward spread of railroads and telegraphs, they emphasized a distinct "physical progress" represented by internal improvements. They give no hint of determinism and, rather than as embodying progress itself, the improvements served as a means of economic, moral, and intellectual progress for Virginia. Moreover, no evidence supports that the expansionist and Anglo-Saxonist discourse of Manifest Destiny entered substantially into the institutional discourse of VMI. Instead, the officers of VMI maintained their emphasis on internal improvements and progress as something for Virginia, emphasizing the need for "native," meaning white Virginian, engineers and teachers to lead these improvements to re-establish Virginia as a leader among the states. As such, they maintained service to the nation, but to Virginia in particular, through civil engineering, the work to which the cadets were to commit themselves. White Virginians could work out of patriotic commitment to the commonwealth and, as opposed to immigrants from the North, would presumably defend slavery and white supremacy.

Science and technology studies scholars Gary Downey and Juan Lucena ask the question, "What is engineering for?" in any given national or, in this case, regional context. The range of approaches to engineering and the diversity of professional identities engineers craft for themselves derives, they argue, from distinctive "images" of progress that engineers must contend with in different countries or, again, regions.[60] The officers of VMI answered the question in terms of service. Engineering was to serve the physical progress of Virginia. Internal improvements would diversify and rationalize the economy of Virginia so that Virginia would return to its prior position as an economic and political leader of the United States. What, at VMI, was engineering for? Creating a new Virginia under the leadership of a new, white middle class committed to, on the one hand, meritocratic competition among equal white men and, on the other, white supremacy.

CHAPTER SIX

THE NECESSARY WHITE MANHOOD OF ENGINEERING

The Virginia Military Institute (VMI) was born out of a struggle for political power in Virginia (see chapter 2). White men of western Virginia, largely of Scots-Irish descent, sought internal improvements to expand the market economy in isolated western Virginia. Having failed to establish universal white manhood suffrage, the means of political power for the growing western population, leaders of Rockbridge County turned to higher education as a means of demonstrating the inherent equality of white men. VMI thus became an institution committed to that principle. Chapter 3 discusses how VMI became a place not just to demonstrate the capacity of white men to vote and wield political power but also, by becoming an engineering school modeled after West Point and the École Polytechnique, in which to train the men who would provide the desired internal improvements. In chapter 4, I argue that the officers of the school used the curriculum and pedagogy to legitimize a new form of "useful" education to compete with liberal colleges and to also legitimize the authority of the lower-

and middling-class white men trained in that curriculum. Chapter 5 explains that the officers of VMI demanded of their graduates more than just that they pursue self-interested careers but instead pursue a career of service, by which they would lead Virginia back toward its preeminent position in the United States through a more diversified and productive economy that challenged the leadership and economic interests of the planters.

This chapter builds further on the above arguments to demonstrate that the officers of VMI used military and pedagogical discipline to transform their cadets into particular types of men. It didn't just so happen that the new servant-leaders, and therefore engineers in general, would be white men. It was necessary that they be so. Descendants of the Scots-Irish had always been unambiguously accepted as white, even by their eastern English-descended neighbors. By the 1840s, as described in chapter 5, whiteness in America had become a less stable category, with the whiteness of, for example, Catholic Irish immigrants being, at most, ambiguous and often even denied entirely. But the whiteness of the Scots-Irish remained unquestioned. It was, however, not the boundaries but the meaning of whiteness and white manhood that the officers of VMI were challenging.

VMI's officers used military discipline to train the cadets to embody a new white manhood, a manhood that differed from that of the eastern elite of Virginia and that served the interests of the men of western Virginia who first proposed the school. The discipline served to subordinate the individual identities and interests the cadets brought with them from across the commonwealth and from across class boundaries. Cadet life allowed for distinctions of only personal merit based on individual character, as measured by one's adherence to military discipline and one's academic accomplishments. VMI, consequently, served as a microcosm of the political order its founders hoped to create. There, innately independent white young men competed with one another on even ground, regardless of class, section, or family. Poverty no longer artificially masked one's virtue, and wealth did not artificially elevate one to positions of leadership. The cadets were to see their society as, or at least turn it into, a space of meritocratic competition but one in which their work meant service to a seemingly neutral conception of the common interests of Virginians rather than personal gain. A principal means of providing this service was through engineering. Being an engineer therefore necessitated being a particular type of person, a particular kind of white man.

RECRUITING THE MERITORIOUS POOR AND ADMITTING FROM THE MIDDLING CLASSES

The founders of VMI and legislators instituted a unique system of admissions, one necessary for the admission of those with a limited previous education but who possessed the physical and moral qualifications for the distinct military discipline of the school. This system resulted largely in the admission of young white men from the middling classes, though also some from the poorer and wealthier classes. It also drew men from across the commonwealth at a time of sectional tensions within Virginia. Consequently, VMI brought together a relatively diverse group of white men who brought with them differing class and sectional values. They were, however, more uniform in their lack of classical education. A scientific engineering curriculum suited men with such limits in their education.

The founders of VMI, from the first debates about its founding to official reports twenty years later, repeatedly justified the school's funding by claiming its ability to provide an education for those boys who could not otherwise afford one. In reality, most of the cadets came from the middling classes, though they too often had difficulty affording a college education. Regardless, the school's founders created a narrative of providing economic mobility to the poor. Though they never said so, nor needed to say so, they intended the school to be only for white men. It would make little sense for an institution that originated out of an attempt to justify the inherent equality and virtue of white men to admit even free black students. Moreover, to do so would lower the prestige of an institution seeking to establish its legitimacy and even its superiority over the liberal colleges of the elite. The poor men the officers claimed to recruit needed to be white otherwise the whole VMI project no longer made sense.

In the second of his three 1835 Cives letters to the *Lexington Gazette*, John Preston explained the necessity of providing an education to poor men. It wasn't just for the benefit of the students; it would provide a benefit to all of Virginia. "It is melancholy to reflect," he wrote, "how much of the energy of the world is crippled up by poverty, and how much of its power is wasted in obscurity." There were, he argued, many poor men everywhere who were frustrated by the limitations that poverty imposed on their intellect and ambition. "Genius knows no fixed locality, and is as often born under a cottage roof as the domes of a palace; and there are hundreds of young men whose minds thirst for an education which they have not the means of obtaining."[1] VMI's officers would seek out and educate these geniuses and, in doing so, would unleash a previously untapped wealth of creative energy to benefit the nation as a whole and Virginia in particular. The school, therefore, would not duplicate the efforts of colleges that already served the wealthy.

Superintendent Francis Smith, six years after the school opened, described the state cadets as coming "from that class of our citizens whose means deny them the opportunity of obtaining a liberal education."[2] He also explicitly identified "Aid furnished to the poor" as one of the advantages of VMI to the commonwealth as a whole, stating, "The assistance which the institute annually confers upon those in indigent circumstances, in affording them the means of an education, is its *noblest* feature."[3] In a period without federal student aid or substantial primary or secondary education opportunities, not having the means of obtaining an education could cover a broad range of people, so we must not assume that the sons of the poorest white farmers filled the school. Historian Jennifer Green has carefully documented the demographics of the cadets of the southern military schools. Despite the rhetoric of VMI officers, most applicants did not come from truly poor families. Some came from substantial wealth and from prominent families. Most, however, came from the emerging middle class.[4] The truly poor could not afford the fees of $90 per year (about $2,450 in 2018) for state cadets and $255 per year (about $7,000 in 2018) for pay cadets. Moreover, the year-round military discipline and summer drilling made it impossible for the cadets to work their way through school to help pay those fees. The parents of "middling" boys, however, often unable to pay full tuition, could afford the fees while also having the capacity to provide the minimal education required to meet VMI's modest admissions standards.[5]

Although the fees remaining for even the state cadets tended to prevent the truly poor from attending the school, the officers of VMI may not have spoken disingenuously when they spoke of the impoverished students who attended the school. "Middle class" appeared in usage in the South by the 1830s but not commonly until the 1850s, when a distinct set of middle-class values and interests solidified into a self-conscious class. Prior to that, people tended to speak of the "middling class" or "middling sorts" to distinguish non-agricultural professionals and employers, "the storekeepers, bankers, clerks, teachers, doctors, editors, ministers, and their families," from wealthy landowning planters on one hand and independent white yeomen farmers on the other.[6] Consequently, founder John Preston, Board of Visitors president Claudius Crozet, Superintendent Francis Smith, and others would not necessarily have conceived of a middle class when they thought of the class of men from which to draw for the new school. Instead, they may have thought largely of poor families and yeomen farmers in contrast to people much like Preston himself, the sons of elite planters and large landholders.

Even though the demographics of the cadets did not perfectly match the vision provided by Preston in 1834 and 1835, at least some board members do appear to have taken very seriously the commitment to education for the meritorious poor. As an example, Smith recounted an incident in which a meritorious but poor young man, whose "thirst for an education induces him to travel on foot over an [sic] hundred miles to press in person before the Board of Visitors his application," lost a position as a state cadet to another competing meritorious and poor man. A sympathetic board member, however, resubmitted the first man's application, but as a pay cadet, and personally paid the expenses from his own pocket.[7] Patronage of students by wealthier family members or acquaintances was not uncommon among cadets of military schools in general.[8] Regardless, even though they may not have come from poor families, many of even the middling boys who went to VMI could not have otherwise afforded higher education.

The officers of VMI publicly proclaimed concern only with the merits of the individual applicants rather than with the family contacts and wealth that might have otherwise led to favoritism in admissions. All applicants, whether they applied for a state or pay cadet position, had to submit themselves to the same application process. At least some people outside of VMI espoused a belief in the integrity of the admissions process. An anonymous writer to the *Richmond Compiler* made the following observation upon the arrival of two applicants and the fair evaluation of their abilities to pay tuition: "One of these young men was the son of independent, if not wealthy, parents—the other was ambitious, but poor, and a strong evidence of his perseverance and enthusiasm was afforded in the fact that he walked all the way to Lexington with his wallet on his back." The writer reported that the board accepted the poor man as a state cadet but not the "independent" man, who then received admission as a pay cadet. The paper praised the decision, stating, "We trust this may be ever the case in such a contest, and that this State Institution may never be liable to the charge of favoring the wealthy."[9]

By employing a new system of recruitment, admissions, and funding, the framers of VMI brought together a diverse group of young white men. Although drawing many pay cadets from central Virginia, the board and Smith admitted men from across the commonwealth, from the Ohio River to the Chesapeake Bay, at a time of great sectional tension. While the costs and year-round schedule of VMI generally precluded the participation of the poorest of white men, the school did draw men from across class boundaries, though most of them came from the vague middling class that was still creating a clear sense of its own identity. Through this diversity, VMI, as a state institution, served all parts of the commonwealth, as well as men from differing and conflicting backgrounds.

The diversity of the cadets and the discourse of the board and other framers of VMI reflected the egalitarian impulse behind the school. This does not mean, however, that the founders intended the school for all white men. They did not imagine the school or future schools like it as a place for all who wanted an education to obtain one. Instead, they hoped to draw the best students by eliminating the barriers of class, admitting students based on their individual merit alone, not by their access to wealth and influence. Moreover, they wanted only men who could fulfill the duties required of them. This meant that they wanted not only the most intelligent and diligent boys but also the healthiest and most moral, regardless of their wealth or connections. Again, the very nature of morality and merit, as conceived of by the school's officers and described later in this chapter, precluded the admission of black students and women. Given the role of militias in policing enslaved peoples and widespread white anxiety about free black people as possible sources of rebellion among enslaved people, no Virginia government would have provided military training to black students. Indeed, VMI enslaved black people to serve the cadets. Regardless, as described in chapter 2, white Virginians largely viewed women and black people as constitutionally incapable of the very independence VMI was meant to cultivate. So, to reiterate, VMI was necessarily a school only for white men.

NO DISTINCTIONS BUT THOSE OF PERSONAL MERIT

Regardless of whether a cadet arrived as a state or pay cadet, the board and Superintendent Smith intended that no one make any initial distinctions between them. Smith claimed, "Both classes of cadets enjoy the same privileges, perform the same duties, dress in the same uniform, and are not distinguishable but by reference to the records of the institution." Moreover, there was no cause for looking down on state cadets as recipients of charity or aid, because they received their education in exchange for the services they performed while students and in teaching after their graduation. However, poverty, though "an indispensable condition for the state cadet appointment, can never be a matter of reflection, when it is so often found accompanied by genius and high moral worth."[10] So, at least ideally, new cadets entered into the school as the equals of all others, with only their individual merit and accomplishments to distinguish between them. To ensure this, the board and Smith established a wide range of practices to test this merit and to suppress distinctions based on wealth and family.

This task of overcoming distinctions required some effort. These young men came from all parts of Virginia, including both sides of the Blue Ridge, at a time of east-west sectional tension. Consequently, they also came from at least Scots-Irish and English backgrounds. Established English settlers and their descendants continued to dominate the Tidewater region of Virginia, while Scots-Irish settlers and lesser numbers of Germans settled the Shenandoah Valley and spread into the Appalachian Mountains. These different ethnic groups brought with them and established competing cultures in their respective parts of Virginia. The English established an intensely hierarchical society in which social inferiors were supposed to defer to their superiors. Social leaders believed that labor was something that had to be extracted from people. Moreover, the lower classes were a source of social chaos, and the control of their labor was a means of controlling that chaos. The Scots-Irish, in contrast, were an independent people. Individuals believed themselves the inferior of no other person and were distrustful of and resented authority.[11] Cadets also included the sons of yeomen farmers as well as the sons of state politicians. They belonged to Baptist, Episcopalian, Methodist, Presbyterian, and possibly other churches. Through military discipline and uniform treatment, the board and professors of VMI attempted to force the cadets to subordinate their class, regional, religious, and ethnic interests to a common interest with the other cadets and to ensure unity among them.

Sociologist Pierre Bourdieu theorizes disciplinary processes as mechanisms for training individuals to employ their bodies in particular ways that identify them as members in social groups, including manhood or womanhood. These uses of the body can include how we hold our arms, our hairstyles, or in what public spaces we place our bodies. Doing so, moreover, excludes from membership those who do not employ their bodies in the appropriate way—those who did not undergo the necessary disciplinary process. Through such disciplinary process, through which everyone in every society undergoes, we literally embody social relations.[12] Although Bourdieu focused on less overt practices of discipline, such as those through which boys and girls learn to become men and women, we can apply this emphasis on the embodiment of particular social categories to more formal disciplinary regimes, such as military discipline.

Superintendent Smith may have found Bourdieu's idea obvious. Indeed, of the regulations and system of military discipline at VMI, Smith said, "It is evident then, that the practice of these important principles for three years, will so fasten themselves upon the cadet as to become *part of his nature*."[13] It is the repetition of physical acts and constant self-monitoring that turns discourse promoting particular values into the lived experiences of the targets of disciplinary regimes. Through discipline, the cadets, challenging their varying backgrounds, would become new men.

Moral and Physical Merit in Admissions

The meritocratic disciplinary process began with admissions to VMI. All applicants had to come in person to VMI to meet with the Board of Visitors and Superintendent Smith, to whom they delivered a written recommendation. The board and Smith had to assure themselves that cadets possessed both the physical and moral qualifications to serve as an arsenal guard, participate in military drilling, and submit to military discipline. Applicants could be no younger than sixteen years old and no older than twenty-five and had to display good physical strength and health. Regarding the latter, they had to be free of "any disorder of an infectious or immoral character."[14] Presumably tuberculosis would have disqualified a cadet in the first case and syphilis in the second.

The board and Smith did not just rely on their own judgment of an applicant's moral qualifications; they required a letter of recommendation attesting to such. The authors of these letters rarely wrote lengthy recommendations and, instead, generally made short statements of the applicant's moral character, as exemplified by the following:

From John Thompson, Jr., regarding George Coleman:

> Young Mr. Coleman is of one of our most respectable families and himself a moral and steady youth, and already has quite a respectable education and I doubt not will conform cheerfully to all the rules of the Institute, and seems so anxious to join the school that I have no doubt, but that he will make a worthy member.[15]

From William Brown, MD, regarding Lawson Botts:

... his conduct has always been highly exemplary. His deportment to his parents [and] friends has ever been kind [and] affectionate. He has been steady [and] regular in his attention to his studies, [and] his progress has given general satisfaction to his tutors. He has a strict regard for truth [and] veracity, a virtue in my estimation of the highest importance, [and] is remarkably exempt from the petty vices which are too often found to exist among youths of his age.[16]

From Nathaniel H. [. . .], regarding William R. Terry:

His moral standing is unexceptionable, his habits industrious, his capacity good . . .[17]

The writers often commented upon the applicants' morality in general as well as their industriousness, previous academic accomplishment, and honesty or other virtues. Again, the school did not admit any and all white men from Virginia; the school was only for those with sufficient merit to fulfill their duties.

Military Discipline: Producing Unity and Suppressing Distinctions

Regardless of one's admission status, or any other status, every cadet had to submit to the same military discipline. This discipline encompassed every aspect of the cadet's life—nearly every day, all year long. Cadets engaged in a constant regime of drills, from marching to parade formations to artillery drills. These exercises taught the basics of the military arts and discipline, taught acceptance of orders, and created a sense of unity among the diverse cadets. The cadets also wore uniforms, of course, and engaged in a regime of personal care and responsibility. All of these features of military discipline increased the sense of unity among the cadets and served to suppress regional and class distinctions between them.

The regulations of VMI imposed a daily regime that made every aspect of the cadets' lives subject to uniform military discipline. They engaged, weather permitting, in either infantry or artillery drilling every day for one to one-and-a-half hours, Monday through Friday between March 1 and December 1. They held dress parade every evening. Cadets marched collectively to and from meals. They also marched to and from the river for bathing on Tuesdays, Thursdays, and Saturdays, which they all did together. These constant and regulated practices limited the free time of the cadets, making even the walk to class a military exercise.[18]

The daily and year-long military discipline made it difficult for the cadets to find opportunities to participate or re-submerge themselves in the culture of their particular regions or social classes. Rather than returning home for the summer, like college students, the cadets remained on post but left the barracks for tents and the classrooms for the field. They usually established the tent camps directly on post or on the surrounding hills. There, the cadets spent the summer drilling, studying, and practicing tactics in the field and went on marches and bivouacs. Second-year cadets could receive leave during this time. But the superintendent held even this privilege subject to the availability of a sufficient guard and the merit of the individual cadet.[19] The drilling produced both visual and tactile clues of uniformity for the cadets. This disciplined them to embody that uniformity, helped to further suppress any distinctions of identity between them, and produced a sense of unity and camaraderie that transcended any differences. The cadets, however, did not simply obey orders during their drilling. Even the lowest ranking cadets had to periodically serve as "Officer of the Day" and lead the marches, providing them the opportunity to gain leadership experience, including leadership over upperclassmen or even over cadets from wealthier families than their own.[20]

Along with military drilling, the board also proscribed behavior that would lead to informal distinctions between cadets on account of wealth and privilege. According to regulations, for example, "No Cadet shall be allowed to keep a waiter [presumably enslaved], horse, or dog." Cadets also could not contract debts, presumably with local merchants; cook or provide their own food; or receive money or items from their parents or anyone else without the permission of the superintendent. As one would expect of a military school, the cadets had to wear prescribed clothing, essentially the West Point uniform, at all times, except in the privacy of their rooms. Uniforms, besides providing a standard visual element for a military institution, also served to prevent distinctions between cadets through richer or poorer dress. Finally, regulations also required common haircuts for the cadets, strengthening the visual unity.[21]

Besides proscribing behavior, the board also prescribed behavior that forced the cadets to learn a disciplined care of themselves. For example, cadets had to make their beds upon waking, clean their own rooms every morning, care for their arms, and regularly deliver their laundry for cleaning by slaves.[22]

All of the above were designed to inculcate self-discipline in the cadets. It also served, however, the crucial function of taking a diverse body of cadets, with distinct interests and backgrounds, and creating a sense of unity among them, a unity that transcended class and regional distinctions. This unity developed, in part, by suppressing the outward signs of those distinctions, whether in appearance or action. Through this suppression, Superintendent Smith and the other professors could discipline young men into embodying the meritocratic and egalitarian white manhood promoted by the founders of the school. Moreover, by requiring cadets to demand the labor of enslaved people, the regime inculcated a participation in and commitment to white supremacy, which, as discussed later, was fundamental to the meritocratic white manhood the school promoted.

The Demerit System and Distinctions of Individual Merit

The officers of VMI did not seek to abolish all distinctions between cadets but only those that arose from wealth, privilege, or region. In fact, they established a method for cultivating and evaluating distinctions of individual merit. Following the models of West Point and the École Polytechnique, the board instituted the demerit system of discipline and the practice of ranking all cadets on a public merit roll. Smith identified this system as the core of the discipline at VMI, stating, "Its tendency is to keep the subject of it constantly upon his guard—to make him watch against trifling indiscretions, for he knows that while the penalty for a single offence may be small, the limit of demerit is reached by the accumulation of these units."[23] This provided a means of regulating the cadets, teaching them to monitor themselves, and of quantitatively evaluating their moral and academic merit.

The board established seven classes of offense, taken from the West Point system, each given demerit values ranging from one to ten. Moreover, upperclassmen earned additional demerits for the same offenses, with the total number increased by one-sixth for second year, one-third for third-year cadets, and after adding a fourth year to the curriculum, one-half for the fourth-year cadets. After a cadet accrued two hundred points in a single year, he was reported to the board for dismissal.[24] Smith gave the following excerpt of one cadet's accumulated demerits as an example of the application of this system: absence from a march to class (3 points), not holding his weapon in the prescribed position (1 point), visiting other cadets during study hours (5 points), smoking a cigar (5 points), and having his coat unbuttoned during guard duty (1 point).[25] A cadet's total number of demerits, modified according to his class, was then subtracted from an initial score of three hundred in order to produce a final score according which to compare cadets. So, a higher score indicated greater merit in conduct. This

MERIT ROLL.—*First Class.*

General merit.	NAMES.	COUNTIES.	Conduct.	Engineering.	Tactics.	Chemistry.	English.	Total.	REMARKS.
*1	H. T. Lee,	Frederick,	300	300	198	100	100	998	Assistant professor of languages.
*2	J. B. Sherrard,	Hampshire,	300	300	200	97.5	97.5	995	Captain.
3	H. B. Hill,	Buckingham,	300	297	198	97.5	99	991.5	Assistant professor of languages.
4	D. A. Langhorne,	Campbell,	297	300	196	98.7	98	989.7	Lieutenant.
5	Caleb Boggess,	Harrison,	300	300	194	98.5	97	989.5	Quartermaster.
5	R. T. W. Duke,	Albemarle,	295	300	196	96.5	100	987.5	Assistant professor of mathematics.
6	R. H. Simpson,	Warren,	300	297	192	98.5	99	987.5	
8	W. H. Wheelwright,	Westmoreland,	300	297	192	95.5	99	983.5	Lieutenant.
9	W. H. Baker,	Frederick,	290	297	192	96	97	972	Lieutenant.
10	H. W. Williamson,	Norfolk,	288	294	196	97	91	966	Lieutenant.
11	J. B. Moorman,	Pendleton,	300	291	187	92	90	960	
12	W. H. Harrison,	Richmond City,	280	294	188	77	96.5	955.5	
13	V. T. Churchman,	Augusta,	293	285	186	95	92	951	
14	W. H. Stith,	Richmond City,	291	282	184	97	95	949	
15	R. M. Wiley,	Botetourt,	294	288	182	86.5	98	948.5	
16	J. R. Cabell,	Pittsylvania,	300	273	185	94	96	948	
17	J. P. Mason,	Rappahannock,	294	270	191	91	93	942	Adjutant.
18	A. H. Powell,	Brunswick,	287.5	288	192	93.5	98	939	Lieutenant.
19	R. L. Walker,	Albemarle,	276	288	190	87.5	97	938.5	Lieutenant.
20	E. M. Anthony,	Botetourt,	273.5	279	183	95	100	930.5	

Figure 6.1. First-Class Merit Roll. "Semi-Annual Report of the Superintendent of the Virginia Military Institute, Together with Accompanying Documents," Doc. No. 28, *Journals of the House of Delegates*, 1845, 11.

score contributed to an overall merit ranking, including academic merit, out of a possible 1,000 points (see Figure 6.1).

Smith argued that this practice produced a constant vigilance in the cadets that trained them to serve as their own police over a range of behaviors from proper dress to smoking to showing up for the assemblies leading to class. But it also provided a quantitative evaluation of the individual merit of each cadet, enabling anyone to compare the merit of any two cadets. Through this, the cadets distinguished themselves from one another through their moral and academic merit, which transcended any other sectional or class distinctions between them.

Creating a Level Field for Competition

The cadets of VMI came from both sides of the Blue Ridge Mountains, from the Ohio River to the Atlantic Ocean, and brought their regional identities and interests with them. Because of the presence of both state and pay cadets, students also came from across class boundaries, from the sons of senators to the sons of poor farmers and middling mechanics. They also came from across denominational boundaries. All of this contributed to an intersection of "local" interests in each cadet that distinguished them from one another. Upon arrival, however, Smith put a *uniform* on them and then made them march, drill, eat, and even bathe in a *uniform* manner. Furthermore, they all studied the same curriculum, obeyed the same orders, did the same guard duty, and accepted the same discipline. Through this, they entered an environment and system that suppressed their local distinctions and encouraged unity and camaraderie among them. They learned, through physical drilling and outward uniformity, to embody unity.

The VMI environment also provided the cadets with the opportunity to compete with their fellow cadets but under a different standard of evaluation than that provided for them outside the school. They competed on only the basis of their individual merit, which was established by a quantitative measure of their morality and academic success, as framed by the board in the regulations of VMI. Rather than relying upon their family connections and wealth, or struggling for lack of them, they had to compete upon equal standing based on their own merit and efforts. This meritocratic competition exemplified the political order of innately equal white men that the founders of VMI had hoped to produce in Virginia as a whole. This more rational social order would not be based on arbitrary wealth and connections. Those were qualitative criteria about *who* you are and to *whom* you're connected. Instead, the new social order would be quantified. Merit would be known through the abstract measurement of particular qualities.

MORALITY AND SELF-DISCIPLINE

Having suppressed distinctions between the cadets, the board and professors were then able to sculpt the cadets into particular kinds of men. They imposed on the cadets a particular morality, one that required and expressed a particular sense of self-discipline. They did this primarily through the disciplinary regime of the school, regulations, and the promotion of evangelical Christianity. This morality and self-discipline were increasingly popular within the growing southern and northern middle classes, who saw self-discipline in particular as necessary for participation in the market economy. It was also necessary for carrying out engineering work as a service to Virginia.

The Necessity of Discipline and the Cultivation of Morality

Superintendent Smith, in a book on education reform, argued that the fact that college students have not yet reached adulthood during their education necessitated a strong disciplinary system to protect their morality. This necessity applied to the students of any institution of higher education. Assuming the average student to be eighteen years old upon entering college, Smith asked, "Is a young man at this age capable of taking care of himself? If so, why does the law of the land trammel his liberty until he is twenty-one?" The answer, according to Smith, is because of the "peculiar temptations" of "[t]his interesting period of his life." After having "been accustomed to all the restraints which parental anxiety and affection deem essential to his welfare, the student enters college, and is at once thrown amid a thousand temptations, which he had not known before, or if known, had been protected from, by parental vigilance and counsel. Must he meet these temptations alone?" No, Smith argues. Instead, should "the authority of the college be thrown around him to shelter him from the dangers which have, alas! but too often shipwrecked the hopes of many a promising youth?"[26] VMI's system of discipline served as a surrogate parent to protect students from immorality. It did this by proscribing immoral activities and, perhaps most importantly, by teaching the self-discipline necessary to resist immoral behavior. Any institution that failed to provide such protection, Smith agued, failed to accept its responsibility to its students.

Similarly, Preston, in his second 1835 Cives letter, argued for the use of military discipline at his proposed school to not just provide military training but also ensure the morality of the students. He argued that the training would do so by restraining the students from immoral behavior but also because "the military discipline of the place would essentially conduce to the formation of good habits and the exercise to health." Consequently, "many a parent anxious about the morals or the constitution of his son, might be glad to send him here rather than to the collegiate institutions of the country and if this scheme should go into operation, it would not be a matter of surprise to see students there upon their own expense, in addition to those supported as a guard by the State."[27] Even before VMI opened and even before the Virginia legislature established the school, Preston proposed military discipline as a means to both ensure the physical health of the students and to teach them moral behavior. Moreover, Preston imagined this as possibly leading to a system of discipline that parents might come to see as superior to that employed by liberal colleges.

Smith identified the demerit system as one of the primary features of VMI discipline that distinguished it from the common system of discipline, such as suspensions, employed at colleges. As Preston hoped, VMI was to not only protect the morality of the cadets but also teach moral behavior. Of the combination of military discipline and the demerit system, Smith said, "It gave discipline in its truest and fullest sense—a discipline which extended to and defined every duty, and provided for every necessity." This system was "a discipline which waited not until a youth became hopelessly vicious, but which aimed to *train* him in habits of order, propriety, study, decency and morality."[28] Military discipline and the demerit system dictated nearly every moment of a cadet's life from his admission to his graduation. VMI, therefore, provided a total discipline that trained cadets in moral behavior in every situation they might experience while students but also protected them from immoral temptations.

VMI, Smith argued, provided a superior system of moral training and discipline to that provided by liberal colleges. In contrast to

VMI, under the usual system of discipline of colleges, "[t]he control is only partial. Young men of notoriously bad habits may be dismissed, but the discipline does not effectively reach offences of a minor grade. The incentives to virtue are not sufficiently urgent, or the restraints to vice sufficiently strong." What is necessary is that "[s]mall offences should be noticed and checked, lest they grow into larger ones; and promptness, punctuality, and system, in the discharge of all duties, should be cultivated as *habits*, the importance of which will be felt in the active business of life."[29] The colleges abdicated their responsibility to students by only punishing immoral behavior and only the most excessive behaviors at that. They failed, in contrast to VMI, to teach morality and discipline in every action.

Regarding the success of the VMI system, Thomas Hoomes Williamson, professor of tactics and drawing, argued for the superiority of the system over that of not only the liberal colleges but even West Point. Williamson had himself attended West Point as a classmate of Smith and, like Smith, looked to West Point as both the model for VMI and as the standard against which to judge higher education in general. Nonetheless, he argued before the Board of Visitors that, in regards to "moral discipline," VMI "is fully equal to West Point, and in many respects far superior to it in its discipline." After four years at West Point as a student and five years at VMI serving as a professor, he could "assert without fear of contradiction, from any competent judge, that the moral discipline of the cadets here is far superior to what it was at West Point when I was acquainted with that institution; that I have witnessed fewer acts of insubordination on the part of the cadets here than I have witnessed there, and none of as violent a character, as I have known to occur at West Point."[30] At both West Point and VMI, military discipline taught the basics of soldiery to their students. But at VMI, it also instructed the cadets in morality and even protected them from immorality. Of course, cadets did willfully break the rules. The merit record records the behaviors for which they were actually reported. But, in reality, the cadets had something of their own code of conduct. They decided among themselves what behavior should be reported.[31] Still, cadets did just outright misbehave. They treated, for example, the not-yet "Stonewall" Jackson badly during his professorship at VMI. Students mocked him, made fun of him, and sabotaged his artillery drills, which he seemingly either failed to notice or patiently endured.[32]

While Smith explicitly criticized the disciplinary systems of liberal colleges, the other officers quoted above did so implicitly, indicating their belief in the superiority of the VMI system. The officers and advocates of VMI emphasized the role of military discipline and the demerit system in cultivating morality and self-discipline, features they described as generally lacking in young men of college age. The officers also implied that, in contrast to VMI, colleges did not check the immorality inherent in students of that age. Consequently, this implied that VMI produced more moral graduates, despite the fact that they came primarily from the middling and even the poorer classes, while college students generally came from the planter class. The possession of virtue served as a prerequisite for participation in governance and voting in antebellum Virginia. So, claims of the moral superiority and virtue of the men who attended VMI challenged the authority of the eastern elite and, therefore, promoted the interests of the western elite by enfranchising the growing population of western Virginia.

Christian Education and Evangelical Morality

As far as we know, all cadets came from a Christian background, regardless of whether or not they themselves professed any religious belief. Superintendent Smith, an Episcopalian, saw this as essential. Consequently, he placed Christianity squarely within the system of discipline and education at VMI. Emphasizing this point, he wrote, in one of his early texts on education reform, that "the object of all education, if limited to this life only, is to make men happy in themselves and useful to others; and it may be assumed as an indisputable point, that we shall most surely secure these ends by laying deep in the youthful mind the principles and precepts of the Christian religion." Moreover, "the *great end* of education is a preparation for another state of existence." Smith could not have been clearer in his insistence on the importance of teaching morality than by tying education to salvation itself. It was not just the curriculum and system of discipline that had to be Christian. "Parents want *Christian* teachers, that they may be sure their children receive a pure morality." Conversely, "The avowed opposer of the Christian religion is unfit for the trust of a public teacher."[33]

Evangelical Christianity had become the dominant religious movement in the South by the time VMI opened in 1839 and, in so doing, had placed Christianity and a strict morality at the center of Southern life, especially for the lower and middling classes.[34] Presbyterian Preston and Episcopalian Smith participated in this movement and sought to teach evangelical values to the cadets. Evangelicals emphasized the need for a spiritual rebirth in order to achieve salvation, attained only through the granting of grace by God. One could, however, seek God's favor through moral behavior after acknowledging and repenting one's sins. Evangelicals rejected the "worldly pleasures" of dancing, drinking, gambling, and hunting, all of which constantly tempted Christians. Resistance required the character traits of humility, self-discipline, and self-restraint. Congregations did not, however, leave this to the individual. Instead, they monitored one another's behavior and sought to enforce morality as a community. They also promoted education to ensure that congregants could read the Bible.[35]

The origins of evangelicalism coincided with some of the tensions that led to the founding of VMI. It first gained popularity in Virginia during the Colonial period among those outside of the Anglican slaveholding class. The emphasis on humility and rejection of the opulence, arrogance, and worldliness of the elite provided an alternative means of legitimation for those unable to afford the expense of elite lifestyles and manners. Besides the opulence, they also rejected as immoral the tobacco smoking, drinking, and sport hunting so popular among the elite. White evangelicals first emerged in conflict with slaveholders but moderated themselves and gained greater acceptance as members of the middling classes, and some elites even converted and joined Baptist and Methodist churches. In Virginia, evangelicalism began to grow into a substantial religious movement during the eighteenth century, particularly among Baptists, Methodists, and Presbyterians. Evangelicals facilitated this growth, in part, by accommodating themselves to slavery and, therefore, to the slaveholding elite. They increasingly accepted slavery as a necessary institution for the paternal care of the souls of black people. Evangelicals employed their various institutions, including educational institutions, to help spread evangelicalism. Presbyterians, for example, founded Hampden-Sydney College and its seminary. By 1820, even the Episcopal Church, which descended from the very Anglican Church against which evangelicals formed in reaction, adopted elements of evangelicalism.[36]

Superintendent Smith, an evangelical Episcopalian, accepted the evangelical responsibility for monitoring and ensuring the morality of the cadets. In practical terms, Christian education for the cadets meant largely that "each class is required to attend recitations in the Bible, or the Evidences of Christianity, on the Sabbath." Also, the cadets were marched every Sunday to one of the four churches in Lexington, with equal numbers of cadets being sent to each in order to avoid the appearance of the school favoring any one denomination. Any cadets committed to a particular denomination needed attend only their own church. Taking responsibility for themselves, "The cadets have also formed themselves into a Bible society, auxiliary to the Virginia Bible society, and promote this cause by annual contributions."[37] Evangelicals, seeing individuals as weak, emphasized the need for members of congregations to observe one another's behavior and enforce morality. Consequently, they believed it necessary for individuals to join an evangelical community to both learn morality and to submit oneself to moral monitoring. Smith's requirement of church attendance, along with his military discipline, ensured this.

In his public writing about education reform, Smith also recommended that "all teachers should, when practicable, open and close their schools by reading a chapter, or part of a chapter, in the Bible."[38] I have seen no evidence as to whether or not this occurred at VMI, either in Smith's own classes or in the classes of other professors. But Smith did punctuate the education of the cadets by handing each graduate a Bible with a personal inscription at the same time he handed them a diploma.[39] In so doing, in his last moment of definite influence over the cadets, he re-emphasized his belief that education served the purpose of preparing students, not just for their earthly careers but also for their afterlife.

Besides preparing students for death, the officers of VMI saw religious observance as directly linked to the maintenance of discipline at the school. Evangelicalism provided the specific model of moral behavior. The board commented on this role for Christianity, noting that it is to their requirement of church attendance "that the Board attribute in a great degree the order, discipline, sobriety and attention which prevails among the numerous body of young men whose character are to shape on a great degree the future destiny of the Commonwealth."[40]

While the board emphasized church attendance, they also emphasized that interdenominational "[i]ntolerance in all matters of opinion is excluded from any influence within the Institute." However, "it must be remembered that while no constraint is exercised, a religious influence is at all times pervading the Corps arising from the knowledge that within the [illegible] of their Institution there is one spot where 'the fire on the altar never goes out.'"[41] While they claimed denominational tolerance, they also asserted an emphasis on evangelical morality by specifically claiming to teach the acceptance of self-discipline. They regulated against much individual conduct, including smoking, playing cards, and drinking alcohol or even entering places that sold alcohol. Beyond specific regulations, "The Cadets are not only required to abstain from all vicious, immoral, or irregular conduct, but they are enjoined on every occasion to conduct themselves with the propriety and decorum of gentlemen."[42]

A great many of the young men who arrived at VMI would likely have already gained great familiarity with some of the values taught to them there. Coming from the middling classes that gave so much support to the evangelical movement, they would likely have already had exposure to the evangelical values of self-discipline and temperance.[43] We can, however, certainly question whether or not they so restrained themselves prior to their arrival. Green argues that some students of the various antebellum military schools did undergo the crucial rebirth experience of evangelicalism during their matriculation. So, once under the strongly Christian discipline and teaching of VMI, it is likely that some VMI cadets did so as well. Green reports that at least one VMI graduate, Robert Gatewood, experienced this rebirth soon after graduating in 1849. He went on to become an Episcopal clergyman and a chaplain for the Confederate army.[44]

The officers and advocates of VMI emphasized the role of military discipline, the demerit system, and Christian education in cultivating morality and self-discipline, features they believed to be generally lacking in young men of college age. The officers also implied that, in contrast to VMI, colleges did not check the immorality inherent in these men. Consequently, this implied that VMI produced more moral graduates, despite the fact that they came primarily from the middling and even the poorer classes, while college students generally came from the planter class. The possession of virtue served as a prerequisite for participation in governance, including voting, in antebellum Virginia. Claims to the moral superiority and virtue of the disenfranchised class of men who attended VMI could have served to challenge the authority of the eastern elite and, therefore, promote the interests of the western elite by enfranchising the growing population of western Virginia.

A New White Manhood

The officers of VMI disciplined their cadets not just to perform or refrain from particular traits but also to become particular types of white men, characterized by independence and self-mastery. Those traits, along with evangelical morality and restraint, productive work, subordination to authority, and personal responsibility were character traits necessary for service to Virginia.

Historians have identified two classes of many competing white manhoods in antebellum America, sometimes labeled "rugged" or "martial" versus "restrained." Both, because they emphasized either mastery over others or mastery over one's self, were expressed by white men as available only to white men. In the former, men might have expressed their manhood as mastery over others, aggression and violence, territorial expansion, rejection of restraint, chivalry, and defense of personal honor. In the latter, men may have expressed their manhood in terms of self-restraint, mastery over one's own emotions and passions, promotion of domesticity and the moral importance of the home, and personal industriousness. White men often racialized these masculinities, seeing black men as inherently incapable of performing either of them. The expression of these two manhoods varied between region and class, and both were sometimes present within the same class in the same region.[45] Green has identified the importance of the struggles between the two manhoods in the context of the emerging southern middle class in general and southern military schools in particular. At the schools, cadets learned to reconcile these two manhoods in particular ways.[46]

An elite, "rugged" southern white manhood emphasized a sense of honor defined by the assertion of independence, mastery over others, genteel manners, fearlessness, and a martial bearing proven through such exploits as horsemanship and hunting. Boys and men expressed their independence through a refusal to submit to authority outside of one's family. For children, deference to one's elders was total but taught them that they too could later expect deference from those younger than themselves or from their social inferiors. In contrast to this subordination within the family, parents taught children to challenge even the authority of their teachers in order, for example, to defend their personal and family honor against attempts to impose punishment. Besides asserting one's honor through independence, boys and men also asserted it through mastery over others, which demonstrated one's capacity to master those one has enslaved or otherwise extracted labor from. This mastery over others frequently took the form of violence against social inferiors, including inferior whites. Despite an emphasis on genteel manners, young men as young as fourteen expressed "rugged" manhood by engaging in drinking and gambling and getting into much trouble. This demonstrated, among other things, one's toughness and fearlessness. An honorable boy or man had to overcome fears of any sort. One exception to this was the constant fear of the shame of failure, whether in hunting or carrying out one's duties or failure of any other sort. Boys and men had to confront any challenge to their honor, often through the use of violence and even lethal duels. Not all of these aspects of honor and elite manhood were confined to the elite. Poorer boys and men performed much of it, except for challenges to authority.[47]

The above manhood derived from the particular English culture that dominated the Tidewater region of Virginia. Although there were important differences between that English Tidewater culture and the Scots-Irish culture of Appalachia, the two cultures did share some important expressions of rugged masculinity. Both shared a violent masculinity and the defense of honor. Whereas English men used violence to defend their honor against insults from their peers and to demonstrate mastery over others,

Scots-Irish men (and women to a lesser extent) used violence to assert a fierce independence and to defend their freedom and dignity against any and all. They also used violence to assert justice through clan networks, circumventing the legal justice that they distrusted. If there was one thing that typical Scots-Irish masculinity was not, it was not restrained.[48]

The cadets of VMI had all faced elite southern masculinity, either as an ideal to achieve or in their inability to perform it. The officers of VMI, however, demanded of the cadets something much more like "restrained" masculinity. Evangelicals taught self-discipline and restraint, and the officers of VMI employed military discipline and the demerit system to train the cadets to embody that restraint. Superintendent Smith observed, "*Habits of economy, method and respect for lawful authority are formed*" through the constant presence of discipline. For example, "At least ten rolls are called each day, at all of which every cadet must be present, and every absence or irregularity at each of these is noted. The cadet is required to examine into his expenses, and being controlled in every dollar which he spends, he learns the importance of care in his expenditures." The long-term usefulness of this discipline is that "the practice of these important principles for three years, will so fasten themselves upon the cadet as to become part of his nature."[49] Likewise, Preston, looking back on the first fifty years of VMI, stated that the military discipline "had special advantages in promoting the health of its pupils, in training them in habits of subordination to lawful authority, to industry and punctuality, and in accustoming them to prompt obedience to every call of duty, small or great, without regard to preference, or self-indulgence."[50] These habits drew upon evangelical self-discipline and restraint, which were necessary for setting aside one's personal preference and subordinate one's self to authority and service to others. While the planter elite, against whom both the early evangelicals and the initial proponents of VMI reacted, engaged in ostentatious displays of their wealth and mastery over others, the cadets, generally coming from much less wealth, learned thrift and restraint. And just as they were to submit to the will of God, cadets learned to submit to the will of earthly authority.

Along with thrift and restraint, cadets learned a particular sense of honor through subordination to authority and through service to others, a sense of honor that the officers of VMI hoped would mark the cadets as valued citizens.[51] Board of Visitors president Crozet, foretelling the success of VMI in 1839, stated, "Here will be a school patronized by the state, and the essential principle of which will be a sense of *honor* and duty. Here the young student will find in each one of his associates the correct deportment of a gentleman and the honorable feelings of a soldier." The system of VMI was to be successful because "[i]mpressions received at this age will rarely fade away, and the youth who shall have learned to perform his duty punctually and to acquit himself honorably on all occasions, may be expected to regulate all his future actions by the same propriety of conduct and to establish for himself the character of a respectable citizen."[52] Respectable and honorable citizens, in Crozet's estimation, fulfilled their duties, whether their duty was to appear for the daily roll on the drill field or to defend the commonwealth against revolt or invasion.

Cadets, armed with self-restraint and a practical engineering and scientific training, also learned that they could fulfill their duty to Virginia through productive work, which would, in turn, prove the cadets as virtuous citizens. Commenting on the success of the VMI system, Preston claimed, "The Institution has, in its history, vindicated the practical value of its training. Energy, Efficiency, Reliability, have been characteristic of its graduates in every pursuit of life, practical and professional—in peace and in war!"[53] Moreover, the system of VMI created "useful, careful, economical, industrious citizens" and "that the necessary restraints imposed lead to virtue and happiness."[54] The planter elite demonstrated their virtue through the independence afforded by property ownership and, consequently, independence from productive labor.

The cadets, in contrast, learned useful work and industriousness as virtues.

Along with clearly stating the intent to employ discipline as a way to instill particular values and character traits, the above statements identify three important classes of traits, those related to subordination to authority, personal responsibility, and productivity, all of which would, according to Preston, make virtuous and happy men. Both Preston and Smith explicitly spoke of subordination to or respect for not just any authority but "lawful authority," which indicated a commitment to law and constitutions, for example, rather than to just any individual in a position of authority or of higher social status. They supported this subordination to authority through the demand for habitual obedience, recognition of duty, and the capacity to subordinate one's own preferences or "self-indulgence" in the fulfillment of that duty.

Although the board prescribed nearly every action of a cadet's day and proscribed so much, they promoted personal responsibility. They did this not by providing the opportunity for the cadets to independently achieve it but through the thorough and constant disciplining of the cadets to it. They had to constantly demonstrate this responsibility through some of the virtues described above, including punctuality, thrift, reliability, and careful action. Beyond any usefulness to the individual cadet, these virtues also provided them all the means to fulfill their obedience to authority.

Green made an extensive study of the cadets of the southern military schools, including how they understood white manhood and adapted to the disciplinary regimes of their schools. Her work provides, as well, much insight into how the officers of the schools, including VMI, cultivated a particular white manhood. The cadets' confrontation with conflicting views of honor and duty reveals most strongly the ways that the cadets, their teachers, and their schools intertwined whiteness and masculinity. Moreover, they did so in ways that reconciled southern "rugged" manhood and "restrained" manhood.

Cadets of southern military schools in general reported experiencing conflicts between cultural expectations of personal honor in which men refused to submit to others and the military discipline of their schools that demanded submitting to authority as part of carrying out one's duty. Moreover, as Green states, "The lifestyle of elite southern honor—the life of the rugged man who dueled, drank, gambled, and possessed property (including guns, servants, horses, dogs, and expensive clothing)—was outlawed, and schools attempted to replace it with regulations." And the cadets accepted these regulations. Sure, they frequently broke the rules, but they also generally accepted their demerits and even their own dismissal as justified punishments for their actions. So, even if they violated the regulations, they accepted the regulatory system.[55]

Green argues that to deal these conflicting demands, cadets redefined independence and honor to reconcile the two visions of masculinity. They came to view "fulfilling their duty" and regulating themselves as demands of their honor. This fulfillment of duty was, through their actual duties of guarding and teaching, a patriotic duty to their home state, which, I suspect, gave greater legitimacy to their submission to authority and regulations. Their new concept of honor through self-restraint and submission to authority contributed to an argument for equality among white men. Moreover, the cadets were white men, not just men. As white men, they were inherently independent, because they, in fulfilling their duty and defending their honor, *chose* to subordinate themselves to discipline. Only independent men could make that choice. They saw black men and all women as inherently dependent people who could not choose to subordinate themselves. Black men and women had to submit by their very natures. Only white men could express the self-discipline, self-restraint, and self-control they learned as cadets and needed to fulfill their duties. While elite southern men of the rugged manhood expressed their masculinity through mastery over others, the cadets expressed their white manhood through mastery over themselves.[56] At the same time, however, they did participate in a collective mastery of white men over black through their institutions' enslavement of people and through their duty to suppress slave revolts.

The officers of VMI taught their cadets to embody a particular expression of white manhood. When this manhood conflicted with that of southern rugged manhood, the cadets reconciled these conflicts by redefining honor and independence in ways that made virtues of the new demands placed upon them. VMI produced a manhood that demanded submission to lawful authority, fulfillment of one's duties, personal responsibility, restraint, self-mastery, and industriousness.

ENGINEERING AND MIDDLE-CLASS WHITE MANHOOD

The white manhood that VMI's officers and cadets created served intertwined political and economic interests. As already discussed repeatedly, the inherent equality and independence of white men that this manhood claimed justified universal white manhood suffrage, which would shift political power in Virginia away from the eastern planter elite. With such power, the men of western Virginia could presumably pursue their interests in internal improvements. More than that, the traits the cadets learned at VMI would enable them to pursue careers in a competitive market economy in general. But the white manhood of the cadets was also essential to future work as engineers in particular.

Again, Green provides essential insights into the meaning of the new white manhood. Men of the emerging middle class throughout the country, including the South, participated in a restrained manhood. The ability to discipline one's self was an important trait for participating in the market economy and engaging in business. Planter men did not labor or see themselves as industrious. Instead, they needed to dominate others to extract labor from them. Men of the emerging middle class, however, depended upon their own efforts in professions and business to make a living.

For them, thrift, industriousness, and self-discipline were virtues. The cadets of VMI were not going to inherit plantations nor were they going to become yeomen farmers or laborers, so they had to prepare for careers in the market economy. VMI provided both a suitable curriculum and a suitable white manhood for that. In a competitive market-oriented economy, thrift, industriousness, and self-discipline could provide an advantage over men who lacked or were weak in such traits.[57]

The above traits applied to engineers as much as members of any other profession or business. Engineers too had to compete in the market. However, the rhetoric of VMI suggests that such traits were necessary for engineers for reasons particular to them. Chapter 5 noted that at VMI engineering was a profession of service to Virginia. The self-discipline and restraint cadets learned at VMI provided them with the ability to serve Virginia. The cadets demonstrated this service in very real ways, including guarding the arsenal, serving as teachers in Virginia's schools, serving in the military, and through their work on internal improvements. But this enactment of service required other character traits, traits built upon the self-discipline of the cadets, including industry, punctuality, subordination to authority, and thrift. Rather than working simply to produce or maintain personal wealth and rather than producing wealth through mastery over others, the cadets were to commit themselves to *productive* or *industrious* work that cultivated the natural resources and infrastructure of the commonwealth.

Their commitment also required the subordination of personal interests to those of Virginia and their fellow citizens. Embedded in the disciplinary practices of the school was the model of an engineer as a particular type of white man, one who demonstrated the self-restraint and self-discipline necessary to carry out the work of an engineer. The purpose of engineering was to serve one's state, rather than just one's own financial interests. Engineers were to participate in the creation of a rational system of internal improvements that would contribute to the common good of Virginia or the "physical progress" of Virginia—the return of Virginia to its status as an economic leader of the country. Setting aside one's own interests in favor of the common good is the definition of public virtue. In short, engineers had to possess public virtue to carry out their work of patriotic service.

To express public virtue, the cadets had to have the necessary character. At the southern military schools, self-mastery, self-discipline, self-restraint provided the means of suppressing one's own interests in favor of the common good. To become an engineer, the cadets had to become a particular type of man. At VMI, it didn't just happen to be so that all of the cadets were white men or that engineers would be white men; it was necessary that they be so. To be an engineer was to be a particular kind of white man.

CHAPTER SEVEN

SECESSION

Realigning Identity and Power

A TEMPORARY RESOLUTION OF CONFLICT

1851 seemed to bring victory to the new middle class and western Virginia; a new constitutional convention brought universal suffrage to adult white men of Virginia. Virginia's citizens convened the convention in 1850 in yet another attempt to resolve the sectional and class tensions that had continued to grow after the 1829–1830 convention. As foreseen during the 1830 convention, the white population of western Virginia had surpassed that of the east in the intervening years, and the eastern Tidewater and Piedmont regions had roughly equal white and black populations. In eastern Virginia lived 410,000 enslaved people, whereas just 52,000 lived in the west. The demographic and political disparities in Virginia had only grown in twenty years.[1] Western dissatisfaction about limited suffrage, power disparities between the east and west, and the slow growth of internal improvements continued to raise the question of the division of Virginia into two states. To give an example local to the Virginia Military Institute (VMI), in 1847, the Franklin Society, in direct response to legislative delays in bringing a canal from Lynchburg to Buchanan, debated dividing Virginia into two states, with the border at the Blue Ridge Mountains. The Blue Ridge was both a formidable transportation barrier, west of which improvements were needed more than in the east, and a historical border between English settlement to the east and Scots-Irish and German settlement to the west. Five slaveholders led the debate. VMI superintendent Francis Smith and John Brockenbrough, both originally from the Tidewater, opposed division. The three westerners, Washington College president Henry Ruffner, Samuel McDowell Moore, and future governor John Letcher all defended division. Their status as slaveholders was insufficient to bind their loyalty to the east. In fact, they also voted in favor of the gradual abolition of slavery and depatriation of black people, a position they further promoted in a published pamphlet.[2] Although there was nothing legal or binding about the debate, the fact that some local leaders were willing to publicly support division was a strong indication of growing discontent, discontent that eastern legislators were taking risks by ignoring.

The most significant result of the 1850 convention was suffrage for all white men, which, along with other changes, redistributed power across the commonwealth and across classes. Westerners wanted and achieved independent branches of government by establishing popular election of the governor, whom the legislature had previously appointed and had little authority. They similarly established popular election of the members of the Board of Public Works, which westerners previously saw as acting more as an obstacle to western internal improvements than as a facilitator. They also eliminated the nearly hereditary county court judges and replaced them with elected judges, which began the process of breaking the hold of the planter elite on the judiciary.

Although the west and middle class made some gains, other things remained unchanged or worsened. Eastern planters, who dominated the new convention just as they did the previous one, created a constitutional limit on taxing slaveholdings, which few western men had, which led to the disproportionate taxing of other forms of property. They then passed a new per capita tax on white men and an income tax. All three tax changes shifted the tax burden of Virginia to the west and increased the profitability of enslaving people.

Easterners continued to fear the abolition of slavery should the commonwealth employ the "white basis" for apportionment of legislators—counting only the white population when determining legislative apportionment. Some eastern delegates to the convention pointed to Rockbridge County delegates John Letcher and Samuel McDowell Moore in particular as advocating abolition through the "white basis," a not unreasonable charge given that both men, along with Henry Ruffner, had advocated gradual abolition in the 1847 Franklin Society debate. However, as historian William Link writes, "In reality, of course, no western delegate arrived at the convention as an abolitionist—or even as overtly hostile to slavery. Most acknowledged that their economies, while modernizing and expanding, remained fully wedded to the eastern slave system." Historian Robert Sutton agrees. Indeed, Letcher and Moore had conveniently denounced their old positions by the time of the convention. Perhaps we might forgive eastern delegates for believing otherwise. Regardless, western delegates insisted that a commitment to liberty required that apportionment derive from eligible voters rather than from property, meaning enslaved, unrepresented black people. They also tried to assure eastern delegates that they had just as much interest in protecting slavery as white people in the east.

The deadlock over this issue resulted in threats of western secession and of a walkout from the convention. As a compromise, the convention gave the west the majority of seats in the House and the east a majority in the Senate, which would allow eastern Senators to veto abolition. Many western delegates considered the compromise and other reforms a victory. With something of a balance of power secured, universal white male suffrage readily passed. The convention approved the new constitution in 1851. Voters then ratified it, with substantial support and even enthusiasm from the west, where it was endorsed by many newspapers, including both Lexington papers. Eighty-six percent of voters, eligible according to the more restrictive 1830 rules, voted for ratification. Only five counties, all of them in the east, voted against it. Following this, the new legislature and Board of Public Works expanded western internal improvements, soon resulting in the arrival of a bank in and a canal near Lexington as well as the Virginia Central Railroad.[3]

Despite the above changes and overwhelming support for the new constitution, important divisions persisted. In particular, westerners resented the tax protections for slaveholders and the new western tax burden. Also, new limitations on the power of the legislature to borrow and spend resulted in unexpected limitations on western improvements, leaving most of what is now West Virginia, except for the northernmost part, without a modern transportation infrastructure. Westerners perceived what improvements that were made as benefiting the east more than themselves. Ironically, those improvements that were made in the north actually increased sectional tensions. Those railroads and roads drew that region tighter into the markets of Maryland, Ohio, and Pennsylvania rather than eastern Virginia. In the late 1850s, Republican Party power and anti-slavery sentiment grew along with these connections, intensifying the tensions between the northern half of the Allegheny region and the eastern elites.[4]

THE NEW POLITICS OF SLAVERY AND SECESSION

The 1851 Constitution resolved some of the worst sources of sectional conflict. While tensions and political disparities persisted, the most intense anti-eastern feelings shifted westward of the Shenandoah Valley and VMI. Soon after, national North-South tensions intersected with the old and now weakening intrastate east-west tensions. As in national politics, it was slavery that dominated the politics of Virginia in the 1850s.

Virginia voters were split between Democrats and Whigs throughout the 1850s. Democrats maintained a small majority while Whig power generally declined through most of the 1850s. But votes for the two were spread across the state. Beyond Whig dominance in cities, it's hard to see a regional pattern. Every region of the state had counties with either party gaining strong majorities. There were counties in which Whigs gained more than 60 percent of the vote and counties where Democrats earned more than 70 percent, sometimes even 90 percent. Again, this was true of every region. Rockbridge County was one of the more evenly split counties.[5]

In the 1850s, white Virginians increasingly developed what Link describes as a "siege mentality." Contributing to this was the perception that northern mobs, northern governments, and the federal government were attacking the property rights of Virginians by insufficiently enforcing the 1850 Fugitive Slave Act or by actively aiding escaped slaves. All of this was, they claimed, an opening attack in a campaign to fully abolish slavery. At the same time, slaves themselves, aware of the politics of abolitionism, increasingly resisted their enslavement by running away and even through violent resistance to their masters, which intensified white anxieties. Such anxiety was felt in Lexington and on the grounds of VMI itself when in 1851 and again in 1856 there came rumors of possible slave revolts in Lexington, and the cadets and officers of VMI discussed how to respond. So, in a period with broadened suffrage and elected governors, slavery became a campaign issue. For example, in the 1851 gubernatorial campaigns, the candidates accused one another, regardless of their party or status as slaveholders, of being abolitionists or hostile to slavery. The Whig vote suffered the most from this. An 1854 insurgent Know-Nothing movement, which dominated the cities, drew false accusations by Democrats of being allies of a northern, abolitionist Methodist conspiracy. By the second half of the 1850s, "extremist" secessionists dominated the leadership, though not necessarily the membership, of the Democratic Party. The "extremists," as Whigs labeled them, saw secession and greater control over both enslaved and free black people as the solution. Although the Whig Party dissolved as a national party, it survived in Virginia as a party defined by opposition to the extremists. While they opposed abolitionism, they believed Democrats' fears were overblown and that secession would bring economic ruin.[6]

The Republican Party had some support in the northernmost counties, from the panhandle on the Ohio River to the easternmost counties on the Maryland border. Especially in the northwest, Republicans expressed anti-slavery views as well as a desire to depatriate or otherwise limit opportunities for free black people so that they could not compete economically with white workers. But Republicans faced attack from their neighbors. Most counties disallowed John C. Frémont from appearing on the 1856 ballot, preventing people from voting for him. Worse, Republican voters faced threats of mob attacks and lynching. Although a Whig-Republican alliance never emerged, Link argues they were nonetheless part of the anti-extremist opposition, which was in fact dominant in Virginia.[7]

The "siege mentality" of white Virginians intensified after John Brown's raid at Harper's Ferry, then in northern Virginia, in 1859. State and local authorities imposed a near martial law environment, including restrictions on travel. Mobs policed their own communities by looking out for strangers who might be northern abolitionists. This new condition made it impossible for Whigs to consider any alliance with abolitionist-tarred Republicans. The extremists intensified their call for secession. In the meantime, they called for limiting interactions between Virginia and the North, including by limiting travel and trade between the two regions. The opposition, while participating in the siege mentality, called for what they saw as a middle way between southern and northern extremists by joining with other moderate border states, in which they included Pennsylvania and New Jersey.[8]

With the coming 1860 presidential election, Virginia Whigs expressed their opposition to secession and extremism through the Constitutional Union Party and its candidate John Bell of Tennessee. Democrats split at the state level, just like they did at the national level. Moderate Democrats, strongest in the cities, the Shenandoah Valley, and the northwest, supported Stephen Douglas of Illinois. He, like the Virginia opposition, saw both abolitionism and secessionism as a threat. The extremists, strongest in the southwest and the east, supported John C. Breckinridge of Kentucky. Douglas Democrats were willing to risk a Lincoln presidency by splitting the Democrat vote. Whigs, however, argued that it was Bell, not Douglas, who was the real moderate alternative to the extremist Lincoln. The election results show a real contest between extremists and the opposition, even in the east. The Tidewater just barely voted for Bell (48 percent) over Breckinridge (47 percent). The Piedmont too was split, with Breckinridge (47 percent) just barely beating out Bell (46 percent). It was only the southwest that voted heavily in favor of the extremist candidate, giving Breckinridge 56 percent to Bell's 42 percent. The rest of the west was heavily in favor of the opposition but split their vote. The Shenandoah Valley, including Rockbridge County, gave 60 percent of its vote to the opposition, with 44 going to Bell and 16 to Douglas, leaving Breckinridge with 39 percent. The northwest gave 41 percent to Bell, 12 to Douglas, and 44 to Breckinridge. They also gave 4 percent of their vote to Lincoln. The cities gave 55 percent to Bell, 18 to Douglas, and only 27 to Breckinridge. The split Democratic vote gave the state to Bell. Overall, the strong opposition showing confirmed the strong moderate, unionist sentiment of Virginia.[9] Secessionism, even without considering disenfranchised black sentiment, was the minority view.

Political divisions intensified after the election of Lincoln. Slave resistance may have intensified even further in the face of the new political situation they hoped would lead to their emancipation. White Virginians increasingly feared—perhaps for good reason—slave insurrection. The northwest saw its interests as increasingly separate from those of the rest of Virginia. Enslaved and free black Virginians along with white people of the northwest represented the position of secession under no circumstances. The extremists wanted immediate secession. The moderate opposition desired union but did see the South as under attack, opposed any weakening of the rights of slaveholders, and rejected "submission" to Lincoln and the Republicans. They hoped to remain in the Union but also warned that they would support secession if the federal government used force to prevent states from seceding. The secessionist position grew after Lincoln's inaugural address, in which he rejected the right of secession and suggested the use of force to prevent it.[10]

In February of 1861, moderate Governor Letcher of Rockbridge County convened a special legislative session to discuss secession. The legislature voted to require a convention, preferred by the extremists, instead of a popular vote, but with the delegates chosen on the "white basis," as demanded by the west. They also rejected the right of the federal government to forcibly return states to the Union and declared Virginia's intention to secede if that happened. While even most moderates supported the latter position, the northwest threatened to leave the state if Virginia seceded. A coalition of moderate Douglas Democrats and Bell Whigs dominated the convention by two to one. Only the Piedmont sent a predominantly secessionist delegation. But, while meeting, Lincoln ordered the US Navy to break South Carolina's blockade of Fort Sumter. Delegates suspended the convention. When they reconvened, they voted 88 to 55 in favor of secession. The Rockbridge County vote was split, while their neighbors to the north and west voted for union and their eastern and southern neighbors voted for secession.[11]

In June, Unionists convened their own convention in Wheeling and created a separate Union government in the northwest. In 1863, that territory became the new state of West Virginia. Delegates to the constitutional convention of the new state instituted changes that western Virginians had sought for decades. They established the "white basis" for legislative apportionment, reaffirmed universal white male suffrage, prohibited bringing new slaves into the state, prohibited free black people from living in the state, and made provisions for state support of private corporations engaged in internal improvements.[12]

SECESSION'S CHALLENGE TO THE MEANING OF VMI

VMI emerged out of Virginia's sectional conflicts but then also came to serve in the statewide conflict between the middling classes and the planter elite. While imperfect in the view of the western and middle-class coalition, the 1851 Constitution did resolve some of the tension by establishing universal white male suffrage and by increasing the political power of the west. This resolution created changes in the discourse of VMI officers. For example, officers spoke openly of the role of the school in promoting those internal improvements previously so contentious but seemingly made politically acceptable by the new constitution. But the new and ongoing political conflicts of the 1850s strained the coalition at VMI. Although no one questioned the defense of slavery that was central to Virginia's politics in the 1850s, questions of secession brought out differences between the eastern English and western Scots-Irish backgrounds of the officers and students. These splits challenged the meaning and purpose of the engineering identity they had created to serve the old coalition. The Civil War necessarily changed the meaning of VMI and its cadets.

Cadets and officers, having for so long suppressed explicit *east-west* distinctions among themselves through the use of military discipline and quantification of merit, began, like many Americans, to discuss and participate in *North-South* sectional tensions in the 1850s.[13] Just after the 1850–1851 constitutional convention, the Board of Visitors finally succeeded in obtaining funding for an additional professor of natural philosophy and artillery. Already by this time, North-South sectional tensions had already increased such that Board of Visitors member and constitutional convention participant Corbin Braxton said of the pending appointment, "It matters not the qualifications of a Northern man at this time, the state of public feeling is such in this State that none could be acceptable." So, in 1851, they hired Thomas, later "Stonewall," Jackson, another West Point graduate from Virginia.[14]

As the mutual fears of the "slave power" and abolitionists intensified, Superintendent Smith made clear in his 1856 report to the Board of Visitors that VMI was "essentially a *Virginia* school" that would defend slavery. Along with teaching students the basis of the American and Virginian governments, it was "especially" important that students "should understand and believe the foundation of that divine institution of *slavery* which is the basis of the happiness, prosperity and independence of our southern people." Consequently, the board agreed to add a course that would teach VMI cadets these topics.[15] The cadets and the institution had been served by slaves all along, some owned by VMI itself and others rented from local slaveholders. While cadets learned to care for themselves as part of their discipline, "[a]ll the menial but essentially necessary work was done by negro slaves." These enslaved people are largely invisible in the records of VMI, but they do record the first names of three men: Stephen, Anderson, and Henry.[16] Moreover, VMI officers had hinted at their support of slavery in the past. Recall, for example, that both Smith in 1846 and board member William Richardson in 1849 had emphasized the importance of VMI training "native" teachers. But they did not at that time of lesser sectional tensions mention slavery by name. Smith, who by 1860 enslaved nine people, referred instead to Virginia's "habits" and "Southern institutions."[17] Smith's 1856 comments, however, include slavery by name and without apology. They appeared as a deliberate and open defense of slavery in the context of the new North-South tensions and the all-importance of slavery in Virginia's 1850s politics.

In 1859, the cadets, Jackson, Preston, and Smith participated in the martial law atmosphere that arose after John Brown's raid by serving as the guard at his trial and execution.[18] After this, Smith ordered greater military training for the cadets, including more shooting practice with modern guns, more marches carrying full loads, and training with bayonets and swords. Presumably this would prepare cadets to suppress slave revolts and defend Virginia against raids by abolitionist northerners. Moreover, Virginia formally recognized VMI as part of the Virginia militia. In response, the Board of Visitors made clear to all incoming cadets that they were not mere students; they were "in the service of the State, under the military command of those appointed to govern it" and no longer "subject to the control of [their] parents."[19] Smith was preparing his young engineers, teachers, businessmen, and doctors to defend slavery from internal and external attack.

Talk of secession from the Union seemed absent or muted at VMI throughout the 1850s. But VMI could not escape the extremist-moderate debate after the John Brown raid. In 1860, VMI's officers, students, and community members spoke openly and diverged in their views, revealing the regional or ethnic character of the issue and the limits of class interests in overcoming those differences. Most of the native citizens of Rockbridge County, Scots-Irish and German, few of whom owned slaves, opposed secession. The Franklin Society, so instrumental in establishing VMI, held a debate, in which the speakers voted nine to three in opposition to secession. The majority of the cadets, in contrast, were of English descent and from the east. They supported secession.[20]

The elite John Preston, the primary force in establishing VMI, aligned himself with the interests of his Scots-Irish countrymen and the west that they dominated. Consequently, he opposed the extremists. Smith reported that Preston expressed a belief in the "sympathy between the Scotch Irish of the Valley & those of Pen-n[sylvania] as necessarily deeper & more natural, than the sympathy with S[outh] Carolina." Moreover, South Carolina was "hasty" in seceding and he "rebuked" that state.[21] Preston had become a slaveholder only in 1852, after enslaving people who had been held by a family member who had died. He came to support slavery in the years before the war, believing that slavery would be a means of bringing black people to civilization and, ultimately, something of equality with white people. After the war, however, he supported emancipation, including by personally teaching black children and with public statements of support for black leaders and their efforts to establish themselves as free people.[22]

Superintendent Smith was of English descent and from Norfolk, in the heart of the Chesapeake Bay area of Virginia. While he had become an exemplar of the new middle class and had done much to promote its interests against the eastern planters, he took up a position perhaps halfway between the secessionists and the conditional secessionists. Like the secessionists, Smith placed the blame for "disunion" on the North. It was not South Carolina that dissolved the Union by its secession, he argued; the Union dissolved when the North abandoned "the spirit of union." South Carolina's secession was justified by northern threats and unconstitutional acts. Like the conditional secessionists who were dominant in Virginia in 1860, he believed that South Carolina and any other southern state should be allowed to secede "without interference on the part of the Federal Gov't." If the government did try to interfere, Virginia should resist. Smith saw Virginia's interests as aligned with the South as a whole. In fact, like the secessionists, he believed Virginia would prosper in the Confederacy because Virginia's cities and ports would become the industrial and shipping centers of the new country when southern shipping and trade avoided northern ports and cities. It appeared that it was in the new Confederacy, not the old United States, that his vision of Virginia as an economic leader, based on an economy more diverse than the cash crops cultivated by enslaved people, would find fulfillment. Smith supported Virginia's efforts to prepare for war. Governor Letcher appointed Smith to the state's mobilization advisory board after Virginia seceded.[23]

Unsurprisingly, many men of Lexington and Rockbridge County saw Smith's views on secession as extreme. Smith himself reported that at a meeting of a local committee, of which he was a member, the other members saw his views as "suited only for the atmosphere of S[outh] Carolina." While Smith had to express his dissent respectfully to his social equals and superiors, he could more freely express his contempt for the lower classes, revealing his sympathies for the aristocratic republicanism of the eastern planters. He criticized the local "working people [and] mechanics" for their opposition to secession and unwillingness to "fight for the slave holders." Perhaps as important, he rebuked them for their organizing to "express their sentiments on the crisis" after they were not represented in the local committees debating the issues. Smith saw them as being manipulated by demagogues and "yankey mechanics." Smith demanded allegiance to the state from every citizen and called the workers' sentiments "treasonable." He wrote, "[H]e, who should resist her call to arms where my property was invade[d] would be a traitor & would deserve to receive a traitor's doom." Nonetheless, Smith was sure that, despite all of this talk, when war began, "the uprising" against the federal government would be "universal [and] spontaneous."[24]

Perhaps Smith was more right than wrong. Rockbridge County, despite its largely Unionist population, chose to remain within Virginia after secession. This made VMI an institution of the newly Confederate, though smaller, Commonwealth of Virginia. VMI, its cadets, and its officers contributed to the Confederate war effort, despite any prior differences over secession. During the war, the school, operating intermittently, continued to train some cadets as well as students from other schools. Classroom studies declined while drilling and other military training intensified. Most cadets, however, were mobilized elsewhere. For example, cadets spent 1861 training new soldiers in Richmond. After a period of mobilization, Smith returned to VMI in 1862 to continue training the officers the Confederate Army needed. VMI cadets and graduates served throughout the war, most famously at the 1864 Battle of New Market, in which the cadets are credited with much responsibility for the Confederate victory. There, cadets served in both infantry and artillery battalions with a casualty rate of over 25 percent. VMI cadets and alumni provided 1,800 soldiers to the war.

The month after the Battle of New Market, Union soldiers burned and pillaged VMI. Superintendent Smith wrote in 1877 that VMI "left more of its alumni on the battle-field among the slain" in that war than did "West Point in all the wars of the United States since 1802," when the academy was founded. VMI reopened in the fall of 1865. Threatened with closure by the new state legislature during the military occupation of the Reconstruction, Smith persuaded them and the military commander of the occupation that the engineering and scientific training offered by the school would support the economic reconstruction of Virginia. The school survived, but cadets then drilled without arms and no longer guarded an arsenal.[25]

VMI emerged from sectional conflicts that pitted eastern and western Virginia against each other. Western Scots-Irish elites, such as John Preston, allied themselves with the lower classes of the west to gain greater political power and internal improvements for the west. Under the leadership of Superintendent Smith, VMI became a node in the network of a growing southern middle class. This middle class, from Lexington to Smith's hometown of Norfolk, sought universal white manhood suffrage and greater internal improvements. The ethnic and regional interests of the Scots-Irish west and the class interests of Virginia's middling classes coincided at VMI in the first twenty years of the school. But just as the westerners and the middle class made important gains, North-South sectional tensions heightened the ethnic and sectional differences present at VMI, an institution serving the whole state and that had, at least rhetorically, claimed to represent some objective and neutral interest of all Virginians. While the founders of the school placed engineering training at the center of VMI, secession and war brought the military character of the institution to the foreground. But, under Reconstruction, it was engineering and science that enabled the school to survive. Nonetheless, the war changed the meaning of VMI. With most of western Virginia no longer part of the state, the school could no longer serve sectional interests; it was captured by the English, eastern planter elite.

The contributions of VMI, like that of other military schools, to the Confederacy during the war elevated the status of the school and created heroes of its officers and cadets, especially martyrs such as Stonewall Jackson and the fallen cadets of the Battle of New Market. But as historian Rod Andrew Jr. argues, the schools no longer served southern military preparedness. After the war, they drew on their Confederate contributions to provide "legend, myth, and cultural notions of what it meant to be an honorable man" in ways that tied military training and war-fighting to civic virtue, patriotism, loyalty, and useful citizenship. While the ideal of the Confederate veteran resonates with the prewar and even founding purpose of VMI, the school was to become partly a monument to a united, though smaller, white Virginia resisting northern aggression and supporting segregation rather than a subtle node in an east-west sectional conflict. But this was not an argument Superintendent Smith could or ever intended to make to the new Unionist Reconstruction government. Instead, he had to minimize the military purpose of the school, which was not out of line with the pre-1859 role of the school. He emphasized instead the practical training it could provide to aid the physical reconstruction of Virginia.[26]

CONCLUSIONS

The founding purpose of VMI was to argue for the innate independence and equality of all white men, to prove that, rather than wealth being an expression of virtue, poverty was an artificial barrier to its expression among men of any class. Education, so valued by the Scots-Irish of western Virginia, was to be a means of gaining greater political power for the west so they could obtain internal improvements to gain greater access to the growing market economy.

With its emphasis on a meritocratic competition and a practical education, the school became a node in an alliance between the Scots-Irish of the west and an emerging middle class that wanted to diversify the economy of the state. Engineering, internal improvements, and new leadership would contribute to the "physical progress" of Virginia and return the state to its former status as an economic leader of the United States. The particular white manhood they mobilized drew upon a growing middle-class culture. But the officers attempted to naturalize or universalize that identity by linking it to disinterested service to Virginia as a whole. That service, however, was not at all disinterested; it served the class interests of the small middle class of Virginia and the regional interests of the west. These local or particular interests drove professional identity formation at VMI. The broader class, gender, and racial identities deployed at antebellum VMI were not ancillary to engineering; they were integral to it.

To achieve their goals, the officers of VMI cultivated a white manhood of self-mastery, morality, industriousness, and submission to lawful authority. These traits were necessary to pursue a career of service to Virginia rather than self-interest. The traits and commitment to disinterested service were also markers of the virtue and independence that had long defined the character necessary for participation in governance. The curriculum and pedagogical practices of the school would provide the means of quantitatively proving the equality or even moral superiority of the cadets over the sons of planters who attended Virginia's colleges. At the very least, it was to demonstrate that the planter class did not have a monopoly on virtue and, therefore, should not have a monopoly on political power.

Given all of the above, admitting women or black men to VMI would make no sense. Nor would it make sense to see women or black men as capable of becoming engineers. The officers and cadets had, instead, to distinguish themselves and, therefore, all white men from women and black men to prove their own fitness for governance and leadership. Independence was to be an inherent feature of white manhood rather than a consequence of property ownership. Conversely, dependence had to be an inherent feature of womanhood and blackness. Moreover, VMI's claim to service and patriotism was partly built upon a commitment to slavery and white supremacy.

There is no separation between identity, engineering work, and engineering knowledge. Identity construction and maintenance requires struggle. Such struggle occurs in the context of broader class, political, and social struggles. It occurs in the context of and interwoven with struggles for other kinds of identities, such as gender and racial identity. Contexts also change, creating challenges to existing identities that demand the continual reconstitution of identity. The case of VMI suggests that to be an engineer in any given cultural and historical context is to be, whether consciously or not, a certain kind of person engaged in particular struggles for authority and power. Moreover, it is only in the context of those struggles that engineers' identities, what they claim as authoritative knowledge, and what they claim as the work of engineers makes sense. At VMI, it didn't just happen to be that engineers were white men;

it was necessary that they be so and that women and black men not be engineers. Moreover, engineers had to be a particular kind of white man if their identities as white men and as engineers were to be effective or even to have meaning in the struggle for political power in Virginia. Identity and struggle are one.

Notes

INTRODUCTION

1. Francis H. Smith, *Introductory Address to the Corps of Cadets of the Virginia Military Institute, on the Resumption of Academic Duties, September 2nd, 1856* (Richmond, VA: Macfarlane & Fergusson, 1856), 18–19.

2. Patrick R. Grzanka, "The (Intersectional) Self and Society," in *Intersectionality: A Foundations and Frontiers Reader*, ed. Patrick R. Grzanka (Boulder, CO: Westview Press, 2014), 67–72.

3. Stephanie A. Shields, "Gender: An Intersectional Perspective," *Sex Roles* 59, nos. 5–6 (September 2008), 302.

4. Michael Kimmel, *Manhood in America: A Cultural History* (New York: Free Press, 1996), 2.

5. For examples, see David G. Pugh, *Sons of Liberty: The Masculine Mind in Nineteenth Century America* (Westport, CT: Greenwood Press, 1983); Susan Jeffords, *The Remasculinization of America: Gender and the Vietnam War* (Bloomington: Indiana University Press, 1989); Anthony E. Rotundo, *American Manhood: Transformations in Masculinity from the Revolution to the Modern Era* (New York: Basic Books, 1993); Mark E. Kann, *The Gendering of American Politics: Founding Mothers, Founding Fathers, and Political Patriarchy* (Westport, CT: Praeger, 1999); Ruth Oldenziel, *Making Technology Masculine: Men, Women and Modern Machines in America, 1870–1945* (Amsterdam: Amsterdam University Press, 1999); Kristin L. Hoganson, *Fighting for American Manhood: How Gender Politics Provoked the Spanish-American and Philippine-American Wars* (New Haven, CT: Yale University Press, 1998); Dana D. Nelson, *National Manhood: Capitalist Citizenship and the Imagined Fraternity of White Men* (Durham,

NC: Duke University Press, 1998); Craig Thompson Friend and Lorri Glover, eds., *Southern Manhood: Perspectives on Masculinity in the Old South* (Athens: University of Georgia Press, 2004); bell hooks, *We Real Cool: Black Men and Masculinity* (New York: Routledge, 2004); and Amy S. Greenberg, *Manifest Manhood and the Antebellum American Empire* (New York: Cambridge University Press, 2005).

6. Harry Brod and Michael Kaufman, eds., *Theorizing Masculinities* (Thousand Oaks, CA: Sage Publications, 1994); Tim Carrigan, Bob Connell, and John Lee, "Toward a New Sociology of Masculinity," in *The Masculinity Studies Reader*, ed. Rachel Adams and David Savran (Malden, MA: Blackwell Publishers, 2002), 111–112.

7. Rotundo, *American Manhood*, 2–6.

8. Thomas F. Gossett, *Race: The History of an Idea in America*, 2nd ed. (New York: Oxford University Press, 1997), 29–31, 84; Ivan Hannaford, *Race: The History of an Idea in the West* (Washington, DC: Woodrow Wilson Center Press, 1996), 182–184; Matthew Frye Jacobson, *Whiteness of a Different Color: European Immigrants and the Alchemy of Race* (Cambridge, MA: Harvard University Press, 1998), 31, 40, 46; David R. Roediger, *The Wages of Whiteness: Race and the Making of the American Working Class*, rev. ed. (New York: Verso, 1999), 27–30, 135–136.

9. Nikhil Pal Singh, *Black Is a Country: Race and the Unfinished Struggle for Democracy* (Cambridge, MA: Harvard University Press, 2004), 19–20, 34.

10. National Center for Education Statistics, "Degrees Conferred by Sex and Race," https://nces.ed.gov/fastfacts/display.asp?id=72; Philip Cohen, "More Women Are Doctors and Lawyers Than Ever—but Progress Is Stalling," *The Atlantic*, December 11, 2012, http://www.theatlantic.com/sexes/archive/2012/12/more-women-are-doctors-and-lawyers-than-ever-but-progress-is-stalling/266115/; National Action Council for Minorities in Engineering, *2013 NACME Data Book: A Comprehensive Analysis of the "New" American Dilemma* (White Plains, NY: NACME, 2013), 1, 4; National Action Council for Minorities in Engineering, *2011 NACME Data Book: A Comprehensive Analysis of the "New" American Dilemma* (White Plains, NY: NACME, 2011), 2, 5, 7, http://www.nacme.org/research-publications; United States Census Bureau, "STEM Occupations by Sex, Race, and Hispanic Origin: 2012–2016 ACS 5-Year," https://www.census.gov/data/tables/time-series/demo/industry-occupation/stem.html.

11. Oldenziel, *Making Technology Masculine*, 13.

12. Amy Sue Bix, *Girls Coming to Tech! A History of American Engineering Education for Women* (Cambridge, MA: MIT Press, 2013), 2, 4, 16.

13. Sue V. Rosser, "Using POWRE to ADVANCE: Institutional Barriers Identified by Women Scientists and Engineers," *NWSA Journal* 16, no. 1 (2004): 57–58, 61; Cynthia Burack and Suzanne E. Franks, "Telling Stories about Engineering: Group Dynamics and Resistance to Diversity," *NWSA Journal* 16, no. 1 (2004): 82–85; Karen L. Tonso, *On the Outskirts of Engineering: Learning Identity, Gender, and Power via Engineering Practice* (Rotterdam: Sense Publishers, 2007), 2; Wendy Faulkner, "Doing Gender in Engineering Workplace Cultures. I. Observations from the Field," *Engineering Studies* 1, no. 1 (2009): 4–6, 9; Wendy Faulkner, "Doing Gender in Engineering Workplace Cultures. II. Gender In/authenticity and the In/visibility Paradox," *Engineering Studies* 1, no. 3 (2009): 174, 177–179; Amy E. Slaton, *Race, Rigor, and Selectivity in U.S. Engineering: The History of an Occupational Color Line* (Cambridge, MA: Harvard University Press, 2010), 77, 208; Erin A. Cech and Tom J. Waidzunas, "Navigating the Heteronormativity of Engineering: The Experiences of Lesbian, Gay, and Bisexual Students," *Engineering Studies* 3, no. 1 (2011): 2.
14. Faulkner, "Doing Gender in Engineering Workplace Cultures. II," 174, 170.
15. Faulkner, "Doing Gender in Engineering Workplace Cultures. I," 15–16; Faulkner, "Doing Gender in Engineering Workplace Cultures. II," 174, 170.
16. Oldenziel, *Making Technology Masculine*, 13; Lisa M. Frehill, "The Gendered Construction of the Engineering Profession in the United States, 1893–1920," *Men and Masculinities* 6, no. 4 (April 2004): 394.
17. Sally L. Hacker, "Mathematization of Engineering: Limits on Women and the Field," in *Machina Ex Dea: Feminist Perspectives on Technology*, ed. Joan Rothschild (New York: Pergamon Press, 1983), 39, 46–49, 53–54.
18. For the pre–World War II exclusion of women and their admission during and following the war, see Bix, *Girls Coming to Tech!*
19. Alissa Falcone, Scott Gabriel Knowles, Jonson Miller, Tiago Saraiva, and Amy E. Slaton, "Continuous Reinvention: A History of Engineering Education at Drexel University," in *Building Drexel: The University and Its City, 1891–2016*, ed. Richardson Dilworth and Scott Gabriel Knowles (Philadelphia: Temple University Press, 2017), 39–66.
20. Slaton, *Race, Rigor, and Selectivity*, 20.
21. Ibid., 82, 98, 108.
22. Ibid., 10.
23. Marie Hicks, *Programmed Inequality: How Britain Discarded Women Technologists and Lost Its Edge in Computing* (Cambridge, MA: MIT Press, 2017), 4, 5–7, 12–13.
24. For comparative approaches to engineering and engineering knowledge,

see Melvin Kranzberg, ed., *Technological Education—Technological Style* (San Francisco: San Francisco Press, 1986); Peter Meiksins and Chris Smith, eds., *Engineering Labour: Technical Workers in Comparative Perspective* (New York: Verso, 1996); Eda Kranakis, *Constructing a Bridge: An Exploration of Engineering Culture, Design, and Research in Nineteenth-Century France and America* (Cambridge, MA: MIT Press, 1997); John K. Brown, "Design Plans, Working Drawings, National Styles: Engineering Practice in Great Britain and the United States, 1775–1945," *Technology and Culture* 41, no. 2 (2000): 195–238; Antoine Picon, "Technological Traditions and National Identities: A Comparison between France and Great Britain During the XIXth Century," in *Science, Technology, and the 19th Century State*, ed. Efthymios Nicolaidis and Konstantinos Chatzis (Athens, Greece: Institute for Neohellenic Research/ National Hellenic Research Foundation, 2000), 13–21; Gary Lee Downey and Juan C. Lucena, "Knowledge and Professional Identity in Engineering: Code-Switching and the Metrics of Progress," *History and Technology* 20, no. 4 (2004): 393–420; Yiannis Antoniou, Michalis Assimakopoulos, and Konstantinos Chatzis, eds., "National Identities of Engineers," special issue, *History and Technology* 23, no. 3 (2007): 193–208; Gregory K. Dreicer, "Building Bridges and Boundaries: The Lattice and the Tube, 1820–1860," *Technology and Culture* 51, no. 1 (2010): 126–163; and Irina Gouévitch and Peter Jones, eds., "Theme Issue: Becoming an Engineer in Eighteenth-Century Europe: The Construction of a Professional Identity," *Engineering Studies* 3, no. 3 (2011): 149–253.

25. Downey and Lucena, "Knowledge and Professional Identity," 395.

26. Ibid., 407–408.

27. See Frehill, "Gendered Construction"; Hacker, "Mathematization of Engineering"; Oldenziel, *Making Technology Masculine*; and Slaton, *Race, Rigor, and Selectivity*.

28. Oldenziel, *Making Technology Masculine*, 22–26.

29. Alice L. Pawley, "What Counts as 'Engineering': Toward a Redefinition," in *Engineering and Social Justice: In the University and Beyond*, ed. Caroline Baillie, Alice L. Pawley, and Donna Riley (West Lafayette, IN: Purdue University Press, 2012), 60, 71.

30. Ibid., 66–69.

31. Donna Riley, *Engineering and Social Justice: Synthesis Lectures on Engineers, Technology, and Society* (San Rafael, CA: Morgan and Claypool, 2008), 35–37.

32. Pawley, "What Counts as 'Engineering,'" 60–61, 71, 76.

33. Riley, *Engineering and Social Justice*, 80, 86; Pawley, "What Counts as 'Engineering,'" 61, 71.

CHAPTER ONE

1. Gary Lee Downey, "Low Cost, Mass Use: American Engineers and the Metrics of Progress," *History and Technology* 23, no. 3 (2007): 293; Robert F. Hunter, "Turnpike Construction in Antebellum Virginia," in *The Engineer in America: A Historical Anthology from* Technology and Culture, ed. Terry S. Reynolds (Chicago: University of Chicago Press, 1991), 43; Peter Meiksins, "Engineers in the United States: A House Divided," in *Engineering Labour: Technical Workers in Comparative Perspective*, ed. Peter Meiksins and Chris Smith (New York: Verso, 1996), 63; Terry S. Reynolds, "The Engineer in 19th-Century America," in *The Engineer in America: A Historical Anthology from* Technology and Culture, ed. Terry S. Reynolds (Chicago: University of Chicago Press, 1991), 7–8, 10–11, 13.

2. Jennifer R. Green, "'Practical Progress Is the Watchword': Military Education and the Expansion of Opportunity in the Old South," *Journal of the Historical Society* 5, no. 3 (2005): 363, 365.

3. Daniel Hovey Calhoun, *The American Civil Engineer: Origins and Conflict* (Cambridge, MA: Technology Press, 1960), 55–60, 68, 78–79.

4. Hunter, "Turnpike Construction," 44, 49–51, 67.

5. Aaron Hall, "Slaves of the State: Infrastructure and Governance through Slavery in the Antebellum South," *Journal of American History* 106, no. 1 (June 2019): 43.

6. John B. Rae, "Engineers Are People," *Technology and Culture* 16, no. 3 (July 1975): 412, 414–415.

7. Monte A. Calvert, *The Mechanical Engineer in America, 1830–1910: Professional Cultures in Conflict* (Baltimore: Johns Hopkins University Press, 1967), 29, 43–45; Reynolds, "Engineer in 19th-Century America," 15.

8. Calvert, *Mechanical Engineer in America*, 3–4, 19–21.

9. Ibid., 5, 14–15.

10. Calhoun, *American Civil Engineer*, 10.

11. Rae, "Engineers Are People," 416.

12. Calhoun, *American Civil Engineer*, 13, 25, 27, 29–30, 35, 49.

13. Frederick B. Artz, *The Development of Technical Education in France, 1500–1850* (Cambridge, MA: MIT Press, 1966), 234–235; Bruno Belhoste, "The École Polytechnique and Mathematics in Nineteenth-Century France," in *Changing Images in Mathematics: From the French Revolution to the New Millennium*, ed. Umberto Bottazzini and Amy Dahan Dalmedico (London: Routledge, 2001): 22–26; Stephen Crawford, "The Making of the French Engineer," in *Engineering Labour: Technical Workers in Comparative Perspective*, ed. Peter Meiksins and Chris Smith (New York: Verso, 1996), 104–106; Antoine Picon, *French*

Architects and Engineers in the Age of Enlightenment, trans. Martin Thom (Cambridge: Cambridge University Press, 1992), 132, 135, 229, 338; Antoine Picon, "The Engineer as Judge: Engineering Analysis and Political Economy in Eighteenth Century France," *Engineering Studies* 1, no. 1 (2009): 30–31.

14. Reynolds, "Engineer in 19th-Century America," 10–11, 16.

15. Report of the Board of Visitors of the Military Academy, 1833, Annual Report of the Board of Visitors (1819 to 2002), United States Military Academy, Special Collections and Archives, West Point, New York, 1.

16. Reynolds, "Engineer in 19th-Century America," 11–20.

17. Calhoun, *American Civil Engineer*, 44.

18. Dean Paul Baker, "The Partridge Connection: Alden Partridge and Southern Military Education" (PhD diss., University of North Carolina at Chapel Hill, 1986), 139–140, 148, 230, 249.

19. Terry S. Reynolds, "The Education of Engineers in America before the Morrill Act of 1862," *History of Education Quarterly* 32, no. 4 (Winter 1992): 466.

20. Calhoun, *American Civil Engineer*, 45.

21. Amos Eaton, *Prodromus of a Practical Treatise on the Mathematical Arts* (Troy, NY: Elias Gates, 1838), iii, 29.

22. Palmer C. Rickets, Introduction to *Extracts from the Report of Director B. Franklin Greene Upon the Reorganization of the Institute* (Troy, NY: Rensselaer Polytechnic Institute, 1931), 3–4.

23. Rensselaer Institute, *Rensselaer Institute* (Troy, NY: Prescott & Wilson, 1847), 6–7.

24. Reynolds, "Education of Engineers," 467–471.

25. Burton J. Bledstein, The Culture of Professionalism: The Middle Class and the Development of Higher Education in America (New York: Norton, 1976), 163, 171–172; Calhoun, American Civil Engineer, 13.

26. Laura Fairchild Brodie, *Breaking Out: VMI and the Coming of Women* (New York: Vintage, 2000), 11, 17, 21, 29.

27. For VMI, see merit rolls in 1846 Semi-Annual Examination of the Cadets of the Virginia Military Institute Archives; "The Institute," *Lexington Gazette*, March 21, 1850, 2. For Washington College, see Ollinger Crenshaw, *General Lee's College: The Rise and Growth of Washington and Lee University* (New York: Random House, 1969), 50; and "Washington College," *Valley Star*, September 13, 1849, 2. Hampden-Sydney numbers from an 1838 petition and for 1849, see John Luster Brinkley, *On This Hill: A Narrative History of Hampden-Sydney College, 1774–1994* (Hampden-Sydney, VA: Hampden-Sydney College, 1994), 157, 188n11. For UNC numbers for 1835 and 1861, see William D. Snider, *Light on the Hill: A History of the University of North Carolina at Chapel Hill* (Chapel

Hill: University of North Carolina Press, 1992), 59. UVA numbers taken from an average enrollment for the years between 1825 and 1842, see Philip Alexander Bruce, *History of the University of Virginia, 1819–1919* (New York: Macmillan Company, 1920), 2:71–72. Princeton numbers for 1835, 1847, and 1860, see Thomas Jefferson Wertenbaker, *Princeton, 1746–1896* (Princeton, NJ: Princeton University Press, 1946), 250. Yale numbers for 1839 and 1850, see George Wilson Pierson, *A Yale Book of Numbers: Historical Statistics of the College and University, 1701–1976* (New Haven, CT: Yale University, 1983), 4, 6.

28. Michael David Cohen, *Reconstructing the Campus: Higher Education and the American Civil War* (Charlottesville: University of Virginia Press, 2012), 6.

29. The 2000 Register of Former Cadets of the Virginia Military Institute (Lexington, VA: VMI Alumni Association, 2001).

30. Jennifer Green, *Military Education and the Emerging Middle Class in the Old South* (New York: Cambridge University Press, 2008), 145.

31. Francis H. Smith, Introductory Address to the Corps of Cadets of the Virginia Military Institute, on the Resumption of Academic Duties, September 2nd, 1856 (Richmond, VA: MacFarlane & Fergusson, 1856), 22; for the cadet graduating from the École Polytechnique, see Alfred Landon Rives in 2000 Register.

32. Calhoun, *American Civil Engineer*, 45.

33. Rensselaer Polytechnic Institute, Forty-Fifth Annual Register of the Rensselaer Polytechnic Institute, 1868–1869 (Troy, NY: William H. Young, 1868), 41–46; Henry B. Nason, ed., Biographical Record of the Officers and Graduates of the Rensselaer Polytechnic Institute, 1824–1886 (Troy, NY: William H. Young, 1887), 176–212.

34. The 1850 census, the earliest to distinguish engineers from other occupations, counts 11,626 men working as engineers, with 425 of them residing in Virginia. Census reports provide no definition of engineer, so it's unclear if this number overcounts or undercounts engineers. Given the time period and the use of other categories, such as "mechanics," it is likely that "engineers" is predominantly civil and perhaps mining engineers but probably does not include military engineers, who were certainly counted as army for their occupation. Regardless, there is much uncertainty here. See J. D. B. DeBow, *The Seventh Census of the United States: 1850* (Washington, DC: Robert Armstrong, 1853), lxx.

35. Calhoun, *American Civil Engineer*, 45, 52–53.

36. Ibid.; Reynolds, "Engineer in 19th-Century America," 7–26; Reynolds, "Education of Engineers," 459–482; Meiksins, "Engineers in the United States," 61–97.

37. Calhoun, *American Civil Engineer*, 41–46.

38. Reynolds, "Engineer in 19th-Century America," 7–26; Reynolds, "Education of Engineers," 464.

39. Rod Andrew Jr., *Long Gray Lines: The Southern Military School Tradition, 1839–1915* (Chapel Hill: University of North Carolina Press, 2001); Green, *Military Education*; Jonson Miller, "Pathways and Purposes of the 'French Tradition' of Engineering in Antebellum America: The Case of the Virginia Military Institute," *Engineering Studies* 5, no. 2 (2013): 117–136.

40. Green, "'Practical Progress,'" 363–365.

CHAPTER TWO

1. 1830–35 Secretary Book, 5 December 1834, Franklin Society and Library Company Papers, Collection 103, Special Collections, James Graham Leyburn Library, Washington and Lee University.

2. Cited in Charles W. Turner, "The Franklin Society, 1800–1891," *The Virginia Magazine of History and Biography* 66 (October 1958): 433.

3. 1830–35 Secretary Book, 12, 20, 27 December 1834, Franklin Society and Library Company Papers, Collection 103, Special Collections, James Graham Leyburn Library, Washington and Lee University.

4. Turner, "Franklin Society," 435.

5. 1830–35 Secretary Book, 5, 20, 27 December 1834, Franklin Society and Library Company Papers, Collection 103, Special Collections, James Graham Leyburn Library, Washington and Lee University; General Assembly of Virginia, Earl G. Swem, and John W. Williams, *A Register of the General Assembly of Virginia, 1776–1918, and of the Constitutional Convention* (Richmond, VA: Commonwealth of Virginia, 1918), 140. *Journal of the House of Delegates of the Commonwealth of Virginia* (1836), 79.

6. An act re-organizing the Lexington Arsenal, and establishing a military school in connexion with Washington College, Acts of the General Assembly of Virginia, 1835–1836 (March 20, 1836); Cives, "The Lexington Arsenal," *Lexington Gazette*, August 28, 1835, 2.

7. Col. J. T. L. Preston, Historical Sketch of the Establishment and Organization of the Virginia Military Institute, Prepared at the Request of the Board of Visitors, 4 July 1889, MS 240 (facsimile), Virginia Military Institute Archives, 12.

8. Bradford Wineman, "J.T.L. Preston and the Origin of the Virginia Military Institute, 1834–1842," *The Virginia Magazine of History and Biography* 114, no. 2 (2006): 235.

9. Ibid., 240.

10. Ibid., 227–228.

11. Charles Sellers, *The Market Revolution: Jacksonian America, 1815–1846* (New York: Oxford University Press, 1991), 5.

12. Robert P. Sutton, *Revolution to Secession: Constitution Making in the Old Dominion* (Charlottesville: University of Virginia Press, 1989), 65; William G. Shade, *Democratizing the Old Dominion: Virginia and the Second Party System, 1824–1861* (Charlottesville: University Press of Virginia, 1996), 60–61.

13. Sellers, *Market Revolution*, 5, 9, 11–15.

14. Ibid., 16–19.

15. Carol Sheriff, *The Artificial River: The Erie Canal and the Paradox of Progress, 1817–1862* (New York: Hill and Wang, 1996), 16–18, 20–21; Harry L. Watson, *Liberty and Power: The Politics of Jacksonian America* (New York: Noonday Press, 1990), 8, 61–62.

16. Shade, *Democratizing the Old Dominion*, 66–69; Sutton, *Revolution to Secession*, 24–26.

17. Robert F. Hunter, "Turnpike Construction in Antebellum Virginia" in *The Engineer in America: A Historical Anthology from* Technology and Culture, ed. Terry S. Reynolds (Chicago: University of Chicago Press, 1991), 44, 59; Oren F. Morton, *A History of Rockbridge County, Virginia* (Staunton, VA: McClure, 1920), 165; Sutton, *Revolution to Secession*, 59, 108.

18. Quoted in John Lauritz Larson, *Internal Improvement: National Public Works and the Promise of Popular Government in the Early United States* (Chapel Hill: University of North Carolina Press, 2001), 93–94.

19. Claudius Crozet, *Outline of the Improvements in the State of Virginia* (Philadelphia: C. Sherman, 1848), 4–5; Larson, *Internal Improvement*, 91–95.

20. Aaron Hall, "Slaves of the State: Infrastructure and Governance through Slavery in the Antebellum South," *Journal of American History* 106, no. 1 (June 2019): 39–43.

21. Larson, *Internal Improvement*, 96–97, 238.

22. Daniel Hovey Calhoun, *The American Civil Engineer: Origins and Conflict* (Cambridge, MA: Technology Press, 1960), 31.

23. Shade, *Democratizing the Old Dominion*, 60–61.

24. *Proceedings and Debates of the Virginia State Convention of 1829–1830* (Richmond, VA: Samuel Shepherd, 1830), 66.

25. Virginia Constitution (1776), sec. 6.

26. Sutton, *Revolution to Secession*, 26.

27. William Waller Hening, *The Statutes at Large: Being a Collection of all the Laws of Virginia, from the First Session of the Legislature, in the Year 1619*, vol. 12 (Richmond, Virginia, 1823), 120.

28. Shade, *Democratizing the Old Dominion*, 4.

29. Rhys Isaac, *The Transformation of Virginia: 1740–1790* (Chapel Hill: University of North Carolina Press, 1982), 131–132; Robert E. Shalhope, "Republicanism and Early American Historiography," *The William and Mary Quarterly* 39, no. 2 (1982): 335; Watson, *Liberty and Power*, 45; Gordon S. Wood, *The Radicalism of the American Revolution* (New York: Vintage Books, 1991), 104.

30. Ruth H. Bloch, "The Gendered Meanings of Virtue in Revolutionary America," *Signs* 13, no. 1 (1987): 41–42; Matthew Frye Jacobson, *Whiteness of a Different Color: European Immigrants and the Alchemy of Race* (Cambridge, MA: Harvard University Press, 1998), 22, 26–27, 31; Watson, *Liberty and Power*, 6, 43, 45, 49; Robyn Wiegman, *American Anatomies: Theorizing Race and Gender* (Durham, NC: Duke University Press, 1995), 48–49.

31. *Proceedings and Debates*, 67–68, 91–92.

32. Ibid., 55.

33. Ibid., 53; Shade, *Democratizing the Old Dominion*, 66–69; Sutton, *Revolution to Secession*, 24–26, 45.

34. *Proceedings and Debates*, 59.

35. Ibid., 70.

36. Alexander Keyssar, *The Right to Vote: The Contested History of Democracy in the United States*, with a new afterword (New York: Basic Books, 2000), 20, 28–29, 54–59; David R. Roediger, *The Wages of Whiteness: Race and the Making of the American Working Class*, rev. ed. (New York: Verso, 1999), 56–59.

37. Shade, *Democratizing the Old Dominion*, 66–69; Sutton, *Revolution to Secession*, 24–26.

38. *Proceedings and Debates*, 26.

39. Ibid., 54.

40. Ibid., 88.

41. Shade, *Democratizing the Old Dominion*, 4, 52, 58–61, 64. Sutton, *Revolution to Secession*, 85, 87–88, 90–92.

42. *Proceedings and Debates*, 903; Sutton, *Revolution to Secession*, 106.

43. Shade, *Democratizing the Old Dominion*, 65, 103, 107.

44. Cives, "The Lexington Arsenal-No. II," *Lexington Gazette*, September 4, 1835, 1.

45. Heather Andrea Williams, *Self-Taught: African American Education in Slavery and Freedom* (Chapel Hill: University of North Carolina Press, 2005), chap. 1, ebook.

46. Ibid.

47. Ibid.

48. Stuart G. Noble, *A History of American Education*, rev. ed. (Westport, CT: Greenwood Press, 1970), 70–73.

49. Joel Spring, *The American School: From the Puritans to the Trump Era*, 10th ed. (New York: Routledge, 2018), 30.

50. Ibid., 20, 23–24.

51. Noble, *History of American Education*, 77–78, 80–81, 84.

52. Ibid., 131–134.

53. Ibid., 73–74.

54. Spring, *American School*, 77, 79–80.

55. Noble, *History of American Education*, 127–128, 130.

56. Ibid., 130.

57. Carl F. Kaestle, Pillars of the Republic: Common Schools and American Society, 1780–1860 (New York: Hill and Wang, 1983), 75, 77, 81; David J. Rothman, The Discovery of the Asylum: Social Order and Disorder in the New Republic (Boston: Little, Brown, 1971), xiii, xviii–xix.

58. Kaestle, Pillars of the Republic, 24, 75, 80–82, 100, 106–107, 194–200.

59. Col. J. T. L. Preston, Historical Sketch of the Establishment and Organization of the Virginia Military Institute, Prepared at the Request of the Board of Visitors, 4 July 1889, MS 240 (facsimile), Virginia Military Institute Archives, 4.

60. Ibid., 11.

61. Cives, "The Lexington Arsenal," *Lexington Gazette*, August 28, 1835, 2.

62. Jennings C. Wise, *The Military History of the Virginia Military Institute from 1839–1865* (Lynchburg, VA: J. P. Bell Company, 1915), 31–32.

63. Wineman, "J.T.L. Preston," 231.

64. 1830–35 Secretary Book, 20, 27 December, 1834, Franklin Society and Library Company Papers, Collection 103, Special Collections, James Graham Leyburn Library, Washington and Lee University; Randolph P. Shaffner, *The Father of Virginia Military Institute: A Biography of Colonel J.T.L. Preston, CSA* (Jefferson, NC: McFarland & Company, 2014), 37.

65. Cives, "The Lexington Arsenal," *Lexington Gazette*, August 28, 1835, 2.

66. Cives, "The Lexington Arsenal-No. III," *Lexington Gazette*, September 11, 1835, 2–3.

67. Cives, "The Lexington Arsenal," *Lexington Gazette*, August 28, 1835, 2.

68. Cives, "The Lexington Arsenal-No. II," *Lexington Gazette*, September 4, 1835, 1.

69. Ibid.

70. Ibid.

71. Wineman, "J.T.L. Preston," 226–261.

72. Cives, "The Lexington Arsenal," *Lexington Gazette*, August 28, 1835, 2.

73. Cives, "The Lexington Arsenal-No. II," *Lexington Gazette*, September 4, 1835, 1. Emphasis added.

74. Cives, "The Lexington Arsenal-No. III," *Lexington Gazette*, September 11, 1835, 2–3.

75. 1830–35 Secretary Book, 27 December 1834, Franklin Society and Library Company Papers, Collection 103, Special Collections, James Graham Leyburn Library, Washington and Lee University.

76. A. B. Davidson and J. R. Caruthers, "Constitution of the Manual Labor School of Western Virginia," *Lexington Gazette*, August 21, 1835, 2.

77. Jeffrey A. Mullins, "'In the Sweat of Thy Brow': Education, Manual Labor, and the Market Revolution," in *Cultural Change and the Market Revolution in America, 1789–1860,* ed. Scott C. Martin (New York: Rowman & Littlefield, 2005), 144, 147, 151–152, 155, 166–169; Frederick Rudolph, *The American College and University: A History* (1962; reprint, with an introductory essay and supplemental bibliography by John R. Thelin, Athens: University of Georgia Press, 1990), 217–218.

78. Agricolus, "To the Farmers and Mechanics of Western Va.," *Lexington Gazette*, October 2, 1835, 2. "Hewers of wood and drawers of water" is a quote from Joshua 9:21 indicating menial labor and subordinated laborers.

79. Ibid.

80. Ibid.

81. A. B. Davidson and J. R. Caruthers, "Constitution of the Manual Labor School of Western Virginia," *Lexington Gazette*, August 21, 1835, 2.

82. Ollinger Crenshaw, *General Lee's College: The Rise and Growth of Washington and Lee University* (New York: Random House, 1969), 48, 50–51, 55, 92.

83. Cives, "The Lexington Arsenal," *Lexington Gazette*, August 28, 1835, 2.

84. 13 January 1836, folder 63, box 222, Virginia General Assembly Legislative Petitions, Rockbridge County, 3 February 1834–1864, Library of Virginia, Richmond, VA.

85. Crenshaw, *General Lee's College*, 31–33, 51; An act re-organizing the Lexington Arsenal, and establishing a military school in connexion with Washington College, Acts of the General Assembly of Virginia, 1835–1836 (March 20, 1836); An act amending and reducing into one the several sets concerning the re-organizing the Lexington Arsenal and establishment therewith a military school at Washington College, Acts of the General Assembly of Virginia, 1838–1839 (April 10, 1839).

86. Washington, "To the Trustees of Washington College," *Lexington Gazette*, July 17, 1835, 2.

87. Kaestle, *Pillars of the Republic*, 75, 77, 81; Rothman, *Discovery of the Asylum*, xiii, xviii–xix.

88. "Lexington Arsenal," *Lexington Gazette*, December 25, 1835, 3.

89. A Citizen of Lexington, "Lexington Arsenal," *Lexington Gazette*, December 18, 3. Emphasis in original.

90. "Lexington Arsenal," *Lexington Gazette*, December 25, 1835, 3.

91. Rothman, *Discovery of the Asylum*, xiii, xviii–xix, 237–239.

92. R. A. R. Edwards, *Words Made Flesh: Nineteenth-Century Deaf Education and the Growth of Deaf Culture* (New York: New York University Press, 2012), 1, 3, 27.

93. A Citizen of Lexington, "To the Honorable the Senate and House of Delegates of Virginia," *Lexington Gazette*, January 8, 1836, 2.

94. Ibid.

95. Edwards, *Words Made Flesh*, 38.

96. Shade, *Democratizing the Old Dominion*, 58.

97. Wineman, "J.T.L. Preston and the Origin of the Virginia Military Institute, 1834–42," 242.

98. 13 January 1836, folder 63, box 222, Virginia General Assembly Legislative Petitions, Rockbridge County, 3 February 1834–1864, Library of Virginia, Richmond, VA.

99. Ibid.

100. *Journal of the House of Delegates of the Commonwealth of Virginia* (1836), 79.

101. Ibid., 82.

102. A Citizen of Lexington, "To the Honorable the Senate and House of Delegates of Virginia," 2. 19 January 1836, folder 82, box 222, Virginia General Assembly Legislative Petitions, Rockbridge County, 3 February 1834–1864, Library of Virginia, Richmond, VA.

103. *Journal of the House of Delegates of the Commonwealth of Virginia* (1836), 92.

104. Dean Paul Baker, "The Partridge Connection: Alden Partridge and Southern Military Education" (PhD diss., University of North Carolina at Chapel Hill, 1986), 290; George S. Pappas, *To the Point: The United States Military Academy, 1802–1902* (Westport, CT: Praeger, 1993), 77.

105. A. Partridge, "Military Academy: To Col. C. P. Dorman, of the House of Delegates, Dec. 31, 1835" and "Virginia Legislature," *Lexington Gazette*, January 22, 1836, 1–2.

106. Col. J. T. L. Preston, Historical Sketch of the Establishment and Organization of the Virginia Military Institute, Prepared at the Request of the Board of Visitors, 4 July 1889, MS 240 (facsimile), Virginia Military Institute Archives, 11.

107. "Lexington Arsenal," *Lexington Gazette*, February 5, 1836, 3; "Lexington Arsenal," *Lexington Gazette*, February 26, 1836, 2.

108. A. Partridge, "Mr. Partridge's Letter to Col. Dorman, Jan. 6, 1836," *Lexington Gazette*, February 12, 1836, 1–2.

109. *Journal of the House of Delegates of the Commonwealth of Virginia* (1836), 199.

110. An act re-organizing the Lexington Arsenal, and establishing a military school in connexion with Washington College, Acts of the General Assembly of Virginia, 1835–1836 (March 20, 1836).

111. Lawrence Delbert Cress, *Citizens in Arms: The Army and the Militia in American Society to the War of 1812* (Chapel Hill: University of North Carolina Press, 1982), 172, 174, 176–177; Allan R. Millett, Peter Maslowski, and William B. Feis, *For the Common Defense: A Military History of the United States from 1607 to 2012*, rev. and exp. ed. (New York: Free Press, 2012), 121, 133.

112. John K. Mahon, *History of the Militia and the National Guard* (New York: Macmillan, 1983), 42, 78–79.

113. Article III, Sec. 14, Constitution of Virginia, 1830.

114. Watson, *Liberty and Power*, 128.

115. Louis P. Masur, "Nat Turner and Sectional Crisis," in *Nat Turner: A Slave Rebellion in History and Memory*, ed. Kenneth S. Greenberg (New York: Oxford University Press, 2003), 154–156; Sutton, *Revolution to Secession*, 54.

116. Baker, "Partridge Connection," 310–311.

117. Wineman, "J.T.L. Preston," 240.

118. Shade, *Democratizing the Old Dominion*, 108.

119. An act amending and reducing into one the several sets concerning the re-organizing the Lexington Arsenal and establishment therewith a military school at Washington College, Acts of the General Assembly of Virginia, 1838–1839 (April 10, 1839).

CHAPTER THREE

1. 19 January 1839, folder 82, box 222, Virginia General Assembly Legislative Petitions, Rockbridge County, 3 February 1834–1864, Library of Virginia, Richmond, VA.

2. 1830–35 Secretary Book, 12 December, 1834, Franklin Society and Library Company Papers, Collection 103, Special Collections, James Graham Leyburn Library, Washington and Lee University.

3. Cives, "The Lexington Arsenal," *Lexington Gazette*, August 28, 1835, 2; Cives, "The Lexington Arsenal-No. II," *Lexington Gazette*, September 4, 1835, 1; Cives, "The Lexington Arsenal-No. III," *Lexington Gazette*, September 11, 1835, 2–3.

4. Cives, "Lexington Arsenal," *Lexington Gazette*, August 28, 1835, 2.

5. Cives, "Lexington Arsenal-No. II," *Lexington Gazette*, September 4, 1835, 1.

6. Rod Andrew Jr., *Long Gray Lines: The Southern Military School Tradition, 1839–1915* (Chapel Hill: University of North Carolina Press, 2001), 14–15.

7. Bradford Wineman, "J.T.L. Preston and the Origins of the Virginia Military Institute, 1834–1842," *The Virginia Magazine of History and Biography* 114, no. 2 (2006): 241.

8. Daniel Hovey Calhoun, *The American Civil Engineer: Origins and Conflict* (Cambridge, MA: Technology Press, 1960), 10.

9. Monte A. Calvert, *The Mechanical Engineer in America, 1830–1910: Professional Cultures in Conflict* (Baltimore: Johns Hopkins University Press, 1967), 29, 43–45; Terry S. Reynolds, "The Engineer in 19th-Century America," in *The Engineer in America: A Historical Anthology from* Technology and Culture, ed. Terry S. Reynolds (Chicago: University of Chicago Press, 1991), 15.

10. Cives, "The Lexington Arsenal-No. II," *Lexington Gazette*, September 4, 1835, 1.

11. "West Point Academy," *Lexington Gazette*, August 7, 1835, 1.

12. George S. Pappas, *To the Point: The United States Military Academy, 1802–1902* (Westport, CT: Praeger, 1993), 49, 53, 73, 77, 80, 82, 83, 85, 91, 94.

13. Dean Paul Baker, "The Partridge Connection: Alden Partridge and Southern Military Education" (PhD diss., University of North Carolina at Chapel Hill, 1986), 40, 44, 55, 113, 120, 127–128, 292, 294, 302, 335, 366–367.

14. Baker, "Partridge Connection," 290, 310–311, 380.

15. Ibid., 385, 389, 394, 411–412.

16. Ibid., 134–135, 164.

17. Terry S. Reynolds, "The Education of Engineers in America before the Morrill Act of 1862," *History of Education Quarterly* 32, no. 4 (Winter 1992): 464.

18. Baker, "Partridge Connection," 394.

19. Andrew, *Long Gray Lines*, 10.

20. Ibid., 12.

21. Ibid., 12.

22. Colonel William Couper, *One Hundred Years at V.M.I.*, 4 vols. (Richmond, VA: Garrett and Massie, 1939), 1:15n11.

23. A. Partridge, "Military Academy: To Col. C. P. Dorman, of the House of Delegates, Dec. 31, 1835" and "Virginia Legislature," *Lexington Gazette*, January 22, 1836, 1–2.

24. A. Partridge, "Mr. Partridge's Letter to Col. Dorman, Jan. 6, 1836," *Lexington Gazette*, February 12, 1836, 1–2.

25. Ibid.

26. For biographical information on Crozet, I rely on Robert F. Hunter and Edwin L. Dooley Jr., *Claudius Crozet: French Engineer in America, 1790–1864* (Charlottesville: University Press of Virginia, 1989).

27. C., "The Arsenal," *Lexington Gazette*, January 13, 1837, 2.

28. C. P. Dorman to Governor David Campbell, April 26, 1837, RG 3 Executive Papers, April to June, 1837, Box 349, Library of Virginia, Richmond, VA.

29. The 1794 Uniform Militia Act required all states to appoint an adjutant general to oversee their militias and to ensure their compliance with the act; John K. Mahon, *History of the Militia and the National Guard* (New York: Macmillan, 1983), 52.

30. "Lexington Arsenal," *Lexington Gazette*, May 26, 1837, 2; An act re-organizing the Lexington Arsenal, and establishing a military school in connexion with Washington College, Acts of the General Assembly of Virginia, 1835–1836 (March 20, 1836); Hunter and Dooley, *Claudius Crozet*, 30, 51, 103.

31. Hunter and Dooley, *Claudius Crozet*, 126.

32. Ibid., 17, 98–100.

33. 19 January 1839, folder 82, box 222, Virginia General Assembly Legislative Petitions, Rockbridge County, 3 February 1834–1864, Library of Virginia, Richmond, VA. Emphasis added.

34. An act amending and reducing into one the several sets concerning the re-organizing the Lexington Arsenal and establishment therewith a military school at Washington College, Acts of the General Assembly of Virginia, 1838–1839 (April 10, 1839).

35. 6, 13 April 1839, box 358, RG 3 Executive Papers, April to July 1839, Library of Virginia, Richmond, VA.

36. "Virginia Military Institute," *Lexington Gazette*, June 1, 1839, 3.

37. Board of Visitor Minutes, vol. 2, 1839–1853, Virginia Military Institute Archives.

38. 30 May to 12 September 1839, Board of Visitors Minutes, vol. 2, 1839–1853, Virginia Military Institute Archives.

39. Ibid.

40. Board of Visitors of the Virginia Military Institute, *Regulations of the Virginia Military Institute at Lexington* (Richmond, VA: Shepherd & Colin, 1839), 10, 13.

41. 8 June 1839, Board of Visitors Minutes, vol. 2, 1839–1853, Virginia Military Institute Archives.

42. Hunter and Dooley, *Claudius Crozet*, 129.

43. F. H. Smith III, "Old Spex of the VMI," Francis H. Smith, Superintendent, 1839–1889, Virginia Military Institute Archives, 11–12; United States Military Academy, *Register of the Officers and Cadets of the U.S Military Academy, June, 1833*, 6.

44. James L. Morrison Jr., *"The Best School in the World": West Point, the Pre-Civil War Years, 1833–1866* (Kent, OH: Kent State University Press, 1986), 23; Department of Mathematical Science, "Francis Henney Smith, USMA 1833,"

United States Military Academy, http://www.math.usma.edu/people/Rickey/ dms/00711-Smith-FH.html; United States Military Academy, *Register of the Officers and Graduates of the United States Military Academy, from 1802 to 1837*, 20.

45. F. H. Smith III, "Old Spex of the VMI," Francis H. Smith, Superintendent, 1839–1889, Virginia Military Institute Archives, 28.

46. Ibid., 28; United States Military Academy, *Register of the Officers and Graduates of the United States Military Academy, from 1802 to 1837*, 20.

47. F. H. Smith III, "Old Spex of the VMI," Francis H. Smith, Superintendent, 1839–1889, Virginia Military Institute Archives, 33.

48. F. H. Smith to Benj. Alvord, 20 August 1840, Superintendent (Francis H. Smith) Correspondence, Outgoing Letter Book, 1840 July 25–1844 Feb 8, Virginia Military Institute Archives.

49. F. H. Smith III, "Old Spex of the VMI," Francis H. Smith, Superintendent, 1839–1889, Virginia Military Institute Archives, 33.

50. Ibid.

51. Board of Visitors of the Virginia Military Institute, *Regulations of the Virginia Military Institute at Lexington* (Richmond, VA: Shepherd & Colin, 1839), 12.

52. F. H. Smith III, "Old Spex of the VMI," Francis H. Smith, Superintendent, 1839–1889, Virginia Military Institute Archives, 9, 15, 53.

53. J. T. L. Preston to F. H. Smith, 29 April 1839, Preston-Smith Letters, Virginia Military Institute Archives.

54. F. H. Smith III, "Old Spex of the VMI," Francis H. Smith, Superintendent, 1839–1889, Virginia Military Institute Archives, 56.

55. Ibid., 55.

56. 8 June 1839, Board of Visitors Minutes, vol. 2, 1839–1853, Virginia Military Institute Archives.

57. F. H. Smith III, "Old Spex of the VMI," Francis H. Smith, Superintendent, 1839–1889, Virginia Military Institute Archives, 63–64.

CHAPTER FOUR

1. F. H. Smith, 1842, Superintendent's Report, Superintendent's Annual Reports to the Board of Visitors, Virginia Military Institute Archives, 10.

2. Col. J. T. L. Preston, "Historical Sketch of the Establishment and Organization of the Virginia Military Institute, Prepared at the Request of the Board of Visitors," 4 July 1889, MS 240 (facsimile), Virginia Military Institute Archives, 19.

3. 4 July 1846, 1845 Board of Visitors Report to the Governor, Board of Visitors Minutes, vol. 2, 1839–1853, Virginia Military Institute Archives, 159.

4. Francis H. Smith, *Introductory Address to the Corps of Cadets of the Virginia Military Institute, on the Resumption of Academic Duties, September 2nd, 1856* (Richmond, VA: MacFarlane and Fergusson, 1856), 20.

5. Col. J. T. L. Preston, Historical Sketch of the Establishment and Organization of the Virginia Military Institute, Prepared at the Request of the Board of Visitors, 4 July 1889, MS 240 (facsimile), Virginia Military Institute Archives, 12. Emphasis in original.

6. Smith, *Introductory Address*, 10–11.

7. Smith, *Introductory Address*, 11. Emphasis in original.

8. Col. J. T. L. Preston, Historical Sketch of the Establishment and Organization of the Virginia Military Institute, Prepared at the Request of the Board of Visitors, 4 July 1889, MS 240 (facsimile), Virginia Military Institute Archives, 19.

9. Smith, *Introductory Address*, 20.

10. 4 July 1846, 1845 Board of Visitors Report to the Governor, Board of Visitors Minutes, vol. 2, 1839–1853, Virginia Military Institute Archives, 159–160.

11. Ibid., 159.

12. William Richardson to Francis Smith, 7 September 1840, letter 1840 024, Superintendent (Francis H. Smith) Correspondence, Incoming Numbered Letters Series (1839–1844), Virginia Military Institute Archives.

13. Prof. J. T. L. Preston, 13 June 1844, 1 July 1847, and undated [1848?], Report of the Professor of Languages, Faculty and Departmental Reports, 1843–1844, Virginia Military Institute Archives.

14. F. H. Smith III, "Old Spex of the VMI," Francis H. Smith, Superintendent, 1839–1889, Virginia Military Institute Archives, 34.

15. F. H. Smith to Benj. Alvord, 20 August 1840, Superintendent (Francis H. Smith) Correspondence, Outgoing Letter Book, 1840 July 25–1844 Feb 8, Virginia Military Institute Archives.

16. Peggy Aldrich Kidwell, Amy Ackerberg-Hastings, and David Lindsay Roberts, *Tools of American Mathematics Teaching, 1800–2000* (Baltimore: Johns Hopkins University Press, 2008), 21–24.

17. F. H. Smith, 1845 Superintendent's Semi-Annual Report, Superintendent's Annual Reports to the Board of Visitors, Virginia Military Institute Archives, 7.

18. Frederick B. Artz, *The Development of Technical Education in France, 1500–1850* (Cambridge, MA: MIT Press, 1966), 237.

19. F. H. Smith, 1845 Superintendent's Semi-Annual Report, Superintendent's

Annual Reports to the Board of Visitors, Virginia Military Institute Archives, 7.

20. Francis H. Smith, *The Regulations of Military Instructions, Applied to the Conduct of Common Schools* (New York: John Wiley, 1849), 15.

21. Frederick Rudolph, *The American College and University: A History* (1962; reprint, with an introductory essay and supplemental bibliography by John R. Thelin, Athens: University of Georgia Press, 1990), 119.

22. Rudolph, *American College and University*, 118–120.

23. Francis H. Smith, *The Virginia Military Institute: Its Building and Rebuilding* (Lynchburg, VA: J. P. Bell Company, 1912), 67.

24. Smith, *Regulations of Military Instructions*, 17.

25. Francis H. Smith, *College Reform* (Philadelphia: Thomas, Cowperthwait & Co., 1851), 16–17.

26. Kidwell, Ackerberg-Hastings, and Roberts, *Tools of American Mathematics Teaching*, 21–25; George S. Pappas, *To the Point: The United States Military Academy, 1802–1902* (Westport, CT: Praeger, 1993), 32, 41.

27. Smith, *College Reform*, 16.

28. Smith, *Regulations of Military Instructions*, 13–15.

29. Smith, *College Reform*, 28–29. Emphasis in original.

30. Ibid., 28–29.

31. Governor John M. Gregory to Francis Smith, 22 May 1841, letter 1841 016; Governor David Campbell to Francis Smith, 17 June 1844, letter 1844 011, Superintendent (Francis H. Smith) Correspondence, Incoming, Numbered Letter Series, 1839–1844, Virginia Military Institute Archives; "Commencement Week," *Lexington Gazette*, July 6, 1843, 2.

32. Smith, *Virginia Military Institute*, 63–64.

33. "Virginia Military Institute," *Lexington Gazette*, July 7, 1842, 2.

34. Francis H. Smith, 1886, Report of the Superintendent, Report of the Board of Directors, Superintendent's Annual Reports to the Board of Visitors, Virginia Military Institute Archives, 7.

35. Ibid.

36. 8 July 1845, Board of Visitors Minutes, vol. 2, 1839–1853, Virginia Military Institute Archives, 95; Francis H. Smith, 1842, Superintendent's Report, Superintendent's Annual Reports to the Board of Visitors, Virginia Military Institute Archives, 8; Francis H. Smith, 1845 Superintendent's Semi-Annual Report, Superintendent's Annual Reports to the Board of Visitors, Virginia Military Institute Archives, 7.

37. Francis H. Smith, 1842, Superintendent's Report, Superintendent's Annual Reports to the Board of Visitors, Virginia Military Institute Archives, 7–8.

38. Francis H. Smith, 1845, Superintendent's Semi-Annual Report, Superintendent's Annual Reports to the Board of Visitors, Virginia Military Institute Archives, 7; William Couper, *One Hundred Years at V.M.I.*, 4 vols. (Richmond, VA: Garrett and Massie, 1939), 1:157–158.

39. Thomas H. Williamson, 21 June 1848, Report of the Professor of Engineering, Faculty and Departmental Reports, 1843-1844, Virginia Military Institute Archives.

40. 30 January 1842, Board of Trustee Minutes, 11 January 1845–October 1844, Special Collections, James Graham Leyburn Library, Washington and Lee University, 172–173.

41. Ibid., 173.

42. Ibid., 173–174. Emphasis in original.

43. 1845 Board of Visitors Report to Governor, Board of Visitors Minutes, vol. 2, 1839–1853, Virginia Military Institute Archives, 158.

44. Prof. J. T. L. Preston, 13 June 1844, Report of the Professor of Languages [and] of the Progress of the Classes Under His Instruction, Faculty and Departmental Reports, 1843-1844, Virginia Military Institute Archives.

45. Smith, *Introductory Address*, 11.

46. Board of Visitors of the Virginia Military Institute, *Regulations of the Virginia Military Institute at Lexington* (Richmond, VA: Shepherd & Colin, 1839), 5.

47. 30 January 1842, Board of Trustees Minutes, 11 January, 1815–October 1844, Special Collections, James Graham Leyburn Library, Washington and Lee University, 170–171.

48. 1845 Board of Visitors Report to Governor, Board of Visitors Minutes, vol. 2, 1839–1853, Virginia Military Institute Archives, 158.

49. Register of the Officers and Cadets of the Virginia Military Institute, Lexington, VA, 1843, 1844, 1845, 1846, Publications Catalog, 1840-1864, Virginia Military Institute Archives; Francis H. Smith, 1845, Superintendent's Report, Superintendent's Annual Reports to the Board of Visitors, Virginia Military Institute Archives, 7.

50. F. H. Smith, 1842, Superintendent's Report, Superintendent's Annual Reports to the Board of Visitors, Virginia Military Institute Archives, 10.

51. Smith, *Introductory Address*, 11.

52. Pappas, *To the Point*, 77.

53. Smith, *Introductory Address*, 11.

54. Register of the Officers and Cadets of the Virginia Military Institute, Lexington, VA, July 1843 and July 1846, Publications Catalog, 1840–1864, Virginia Military Institute Archives.

55. F. H. Smith to Claudius Crozet, 11 November 1841, Superintendent's Report,

Superintendent's Annual Reports to the Board of Visitors, Virginia Military Institute Archives, 2.

56. Register of the Officers and Cadets of the Virginia Military Institute, Lexington, VA, July 1843, Publications Catalog, 1840–1864, Virginia Military Institute Archives.

57. Ibid.

58. Francis H. Smith, 1845, Superintendent's Report, Superintendent's Annual Reports to the Board of Visitors, Virginia Military Institute Archives, 6–7.

59. Keith Hoskin, "Textbooks and the Mathematisation of American Reality: The Role of Charles Davies and the US Military Academy at West Point," *Paradigm* 13 (1994): 25; Kidwell, Ackerberg-Hastings, and Roberts, *Tools of American Mathematics Teaching*, 18–19, 52.

60. Francis H. Smith, *An Elementary Treatise on Algebra: Prepared for the Use of the Cadets of the Virginia Military Institute, and Adapted to the Present State of Mathematical Instruction in the Schools, Academies, and Colleges, of the United States* (Philadelphia: Thomas, Cowperthwait & Co., 1850).

61. Ibid.

62. A. M. Legendre, *Elements of Geometry and Trigonometry; With Notes*, trans. David Brewster, rev. James Ryan (New York: N. & J. White; Collins & Hannay; Collins & Co.; James Ryan, 1832).

63. Register of the Officers and Cadets of the Virginia Military Institute, Lexington, VA, July 1850, Publications Catalog, 1840–1864, Virginia Military Institute Archives.

64. M. P. Crosland, "Biot, Jean-Baptiste," in *Dictionary of Scientific Biography*, vol. 2, edited by Charles Coulston Gillispie (New York: Charles Scribner's Sons, 1970), 133–137.

65. Francis H. Smith, *An Elementary Treatise on Analytical Geometry: Translated from the French of J. B. Biot, for the use of the Cadets of the Virginia Military Institute at Lexington, Va.: And Adapted to the Present State of Mathematical Instruction in the Colleges of the United States*, rev. ed. (Philadelphia: Thomas, Cowperthwait & Co., 1846).

66. F. H. Smith, III, "Old Spex of the VMI," Francis H. Smith, Superintendent, 1839–1889, Virginia Military Institute Archives, 209, 212.

67. Bruno Belhoste and Konstantinos Chatzis, "From Technical Corps to Technocratic Power: French State Engineers and Their Professional and Cultural Universe in the First Half of the 19th Century," *History and Technology* 23, no. 3 (2007): 217.

68. Pappas, *To the Point*, 105.

69. Charles Davies, *Elements of Descriptive Geometry, with Their Application to*

Spherical Trigonometry, Spherical Projections, and Warped Surfaces (Philadelphia: H. C. Carey and I. Lea, 1826), iii–iv.

70. Thomas H. Williamson, 20 June 1845, Report of the Instructor of Tactics and Teacher of Drawing, Faculty and Departmental Reports, 1843–1844, Virginia Military Institute Archives.

71. Konstantinos Chatzis, "Theory and Practice in the Education of French Engineers from the Middle of the 18th Century to the Present," *Archives internationales d'histoire des sciences* 60, no. 164 (2010): 43–78.

72. Roger L. Geiger, "The Rise and Fall of Useful Knowledge: Higher Education for Science, Agriculture, and the Mechanic Arts, 1850–1875," in *The American College in the Nineteenth Century*, ed. Roger L. Geiger (Nashville, TN: Vanderbilt University Press, 2000), 154.

73. Francis H. Smith, 1845, Superintendent's Report, Superintendent's Annual Reports to the Board of Visitors, Virginia Military Institute Archives, 6.

74. Francis H. Smith, 1842, Superintendent's Report, Superintendent's Annual Reports to the Board of Visitors, Virginia Military Institute Archives, 7–8.

75. Ibid., 5.

76. J.-L. Boucharlat, *Éléments de mécanique*, 3rd ed. (Paris: Bachelier, Imprimeur-Librarie de L'École Polytechnique, 1840).

77. William Gilham, 20 June 1847, Report of the Professor of Physical Sciences, Instructor of Tactics, and Commandant of Cadets, Faculty and Departmental Reports, 1843–1844, Virginia Military Institute Archives; William H. C. Bartlett, *An Elementary Treatise on Optics, Designed for the Use of the Cadets of the Unites States Military Academy* (New York: Wiley and Putnam, 1839).

78. William Gilham, 20 June 1847, Report of the Professor of Physical Sciences, Instructor of Tactics, and Commandant of Cadets, Faculty and Departmental Reports, 1843–1844, Virginia Military Institute Archives.

79. Eda Kranakis, *Constructing a Bridge: An Exploration of Engineering Culture, Design and Research in Nineteenth-Century France and America* (Cambridge, MA: MIT Press, 1997), 221.

80. Geiger, "Rise and Fall," 154–155.

81. Register of the Officers and Cadets of the Virginia Military Institute, Lexington, VA, July 1851, Publications Catalog, 1840–1864, Virginia Military Institute Archives.

82. Charles Davies, *Elements of Surveying, and Navigation, with Descriptions of the Instruments and the Necessary Tables*, rev. ed. (New York: A. S. Barnes & Co., 154).

83. Antoine Picon, *French Architects and Engineers in the Age of Enlightenment*, trans. Martin Thom (Cambridge: Cambridge University Press, 1992), 153–155, 217, 224–225.

84. Register of the Officers and Cadets of the Virginia Military Institute, Lexington, VA, July 1843, July 1845, Publications Catalog, 1840–1864, Virginia Military Institute Archives.

85. Francis H. Smith, 1841, Superintendent's Report, Superintendent's Annual Reports to the Board of Visitors, Virginia Military Institute Archives, 2. Emphasis in original.

86. Charles Davies, *A Treatise on Shades and Shadows, and Linear Perspective*, 2nd ed. (New York: Wiley & Putnam, Collins, Keese & Co., 1838), iii–iv.

87. Ibid., 138–148.

88. See Cadet Architectural Drawings, Virginia Military Institute Archives.

89. Marvin J. Anderson, "The Architectural Education of Nineteenth-Century American Engineers: Dennis Hart Mahan at West Point," *Journal of the Society of Architectural Historians* 67, no. 2 (2008): 222–247.

90. Thomas H. Williamson, *An Elementary Course of Architecture and Civil Engineering, Compiled from the Most Approved Authors for the Use of the Cadets of the Virginia Military Institute* (Lexington, VA: Samuel Gillock, 1850).

91. Anderson, "Architectural Education," 230, 234.

92. Picon, *French Architects and Engineers*, 99–110, 135.

93. Anderson, "Architectural Education," 222, 234.

94. Williamson, *Elementary Course of Architecture*.

95. Thomas H. Williamson, 21 June 1848, Report of the Professor of Engineering, Faculty and Departmental Reports, 1843–1844, Virginia Military Institute Archives.

96. Jeffrey A. Cohen, "Building a Discipline: Early Institutional Settings for Architectural Education in Philadelphia, 1804–1890," *Journal of the Society of Architectural Historians* 53, no. 2 (1994): 139–140; Mary N. Woods, *From Craft to Profession: The Practice of Architecture in Nineteenth-Century America* (Berkeley: University of California Press, 1999), 4, 6, 7, 11–12, 16, 58, 60–63.

97. Anderson, "Architectural Education"; Cohen, "Building a Discipline," 140; Arthur Clason Weatherhead, "The History of Collegiate Education in Architecture in the United States" (PhD diss., Columbia University, 1941), 8–9, 24–25.

98. Dennis H. Mahan, *An Elementary Course of Civil Engineering: For the Use of Cadets of the United States' Military Academy*, 6th ed. (New York: John Wiley, 1864).

99. Dennis H. Mahan, *A Complete Treatise on Field Fortification, with the General Outline of the Principles Regulating the Arrangement, the Attack, and the Defence of Permanent Works* (New York: Wiley & Long, 1836).

100. Davies, *Elements of Surveying*.

101. Williamson, *Elementary Course of Architecture*.

102. Mahan, *Elementary Course of Civil Engineering*, iv, 12–13, 80, 83–84, 92.

103. Ibid., 383.

104. Ibid., 140.

105. Mahan, *Complete Treatise on Field Fortification*, 9.

106. Ibid.

107. Artz, *Development of Technical Education*, 234–235; Bruno Belhoste, "The École Polytechnique and Mathematics in Nineteenth-Century France," in *Changing Images in Mathematics: From the French Revolution to the New Millennium*, ed. Umberto Bottazzini and Amy Dahan Dalmedico (London: Routledge, 2001), 22–26; Stephen Crawford, "The Making of the French Engineer," in *Engineering Labour: Technical Workers in Comparative Perspective*, ed. Peter Meiksins and Chris Smith (New York: Verso, 1996), 104–106; Picon, *French Architects and Engineers*, 132, 135, 229, 338; Antoine Picon, "The Engineer as Judge: Engineering Analysis and Political Economy in Eighteenth Century France," *Engineering Studies* 1, no. 1 (2009): 30–31.

108. Col. J. T. L. Preston, Historical Sketch of the Establishment and Organization of the Virginia Military Institute, Prepared at the Request of the Board of Visitors, 4 July 1889, MS 240 (facsimile), Virginia Military Institute Archives, 19.

109. Geiger, "Rise and Fall," 154–155; Jennifer R. Green, *Military Education and the Emerging Middle Class in the Old South* (New York: Cambridge University Press, 2008), 134.

110. Green, *Military Education*, 1, 132–134, 136, 142–143.

111. Ibid., 163.

CHAPTER FIVE

1. 11 November 1841, Superintendent's Report, Superintendent's Annual Reports to the Board of Visitors, Virginia Military Institute Archives, 2.

2. Ken Alder, "French Engineers Become Professionals; or, How Meritocracy Made Knowledge Objective," in *The Sciences in Enlightened Europe*, ed. William Clark, Jan Golinski, and Simon Schaffer (Chicago: University of Chicago Press, 1999), 124.

3. Matthew Wisnioski, *Engineers for Change: Competing Visions of Technology in 1960s America* (Cambridge, MA: MIT Press, 2012), 95.

4. Francis H. Smith, *Introductory Address to the Corps of Cadets of the Virginia Military Institute, on the Resumption of Academic Duties, September 2nd, 1856* (Richmond, VA: MacFarlane & Fergusson, 1856), 22; for the cadet graduating from the École Polytechnique, see Alfred Landon Rives in *The 2000 Register*

of *Former Cadets of the Virginia Military Institute* (Lexington, VA: VMI Alumni Association, 2001).

5. Board of Visitors of the Virginia Military Institute, *Regulations of the Virginia Military Institute at Lexington* (Richmond, VA: Shepherd & Colin, 1839), 5, 34; Board of Visitors of the Virginia Military Institute, *Regulations of the Virginia Military Institute at Lexington* (New York: John Wiley, 1848), 9; the Board of Visitors did not use the terms *state* and *pay* cadets until 1841; see 9 July 1841, Board of Visitor Minutes, vol. 2, 1839–1853, Virginia Military Institute Archives.

6. 12 September 1839, 20 June 1840, Board of Visitor Minutes, vol. 2, 1839–1853, Virginia Military Institute Archives.

7. Rod Andrew Jr., *Long Gray Lines: The Southern Military School Tradition, 1839–1915* (Chapel Hill: University of North Carolina Press, 2001), 16.

8. 6 January 1845, Superintendent's 1845 Semi-Annular Report Superintendent's Annual Reports to the Board of Visitors, Virginia Military Institute Archives.

9. 6 January 1845, Superintendent's 1845 Semi-Annular Report Superintendent's Annual Reports to the Board of Visitors, Virginia Military Institute Archives.

10. 4 July 1848, 1848 Report to Governor, Board of Visitor Minutes, vol. 1, 1839 May–1844, Virginia Military Institute Archives.

11. Board of Visitors of the Virginia Military Institute, *Regulations of the Virginia Military Institute at Lexington* (New York: John Wiley, 1848), 9.

12. Carl F. Kaestle, *Pillars of the Republic: Common Schools and American Society, 1780–1860* (New York: Hill and Wang, 1983), 24, 75, 80–82, 100, 106–107, 194–200.

13. Introduction, 1849, Superintendent's Semi-Annual Report, Semi-Annual Reports of the Virginia Military Institute, Virginia Military Institute Archives, 2.

14. 1850, Superintendent's Report, Report of the Board of Visitors of the Virginia Military Institute, Virginia Military Institute Archives, 10–11.

15. Jennifer Green, *Military Education and the Emerging Middle Class in the Old South* (New York: Cambridge University Press, 2008), 184.

16. Francis H. Smith, *The Virginia Military Institute: Its Building and Rebuilding* (Lynchburg, VA: J. P. Bell Company, 1912), 79–80.

17. Smith, *Virginia Military Institute*, 77–78.

18. 1846 Report to Governor, Board of Visitor Minutes, vol. 1, 1839 May–1844, Virginia Military Institute Archives, 153.

19. 17 June 1844, Campbell Governor David 1844 011, Superintendent (Francis H. Smith) Correspondence, Incoming, Numbered Letter Series, 1839–1844, Virginia Military Institute Archives.

20. 4 July 1848, 1848 Report to Governor, Board of Visitor Minutes, vol. 1, 1839 May–1844, Virginia Military Institute Archives, 224.

21. A. Partridge, "Mr. Partridge's Letter to Col. Dorman, Jan. 6, 1836," *Lexington Gazette*, February 12, 1836, 1–2.

22. 19 January 1839, folder 82, box 222, Virginia General Assembly Legislative Petitions, Rockbridge County, 3 February 1834–1864, Library of Virginia, Richmond, VA.

23. Daniel Hovey Calhoun, *The American Civil Engineer: Origins and Conflict* (Cambridge, MA: Technology Press, 1960), 31.

24. Rockbridge, "To the Friends of Internal Improvements in Western Virginia," *Lexington Gazette*, March 21, 1844; "Internal Improvements," *Lexington Gazette*, March 6, 1845; "Internal Improvements, and Education," *Lexington Gazette*, April 10, 1845; "To the People of Eastern Virginia," *Lexington Gazette*, April 16, 1846.

25. Rockbridge, "To the Friends of Internal Improvements in Western Virginia," *Lexington Gazette*, March 21, 1844, 1.

26. "Internal Improvements, and Education," *Lexington Gazette*, April 10, 1845, 2.

27. Robert P. Sutton, *Revolution to Secession: Constitution Making in the Old Dominion* (Charlottesville: University Press of Virginia, 1989), 109–110.

28. Ibid., 113, 134–135.

29. Claudius Crozet, *Outline of the Improvements in the State of Virginia* (Philadelphia: C. Sherman, 1848), 4–5; Robert F. Hunter and Edwin L. Dooley, Jr., *Claudius Crozet: French Engineer in America, 1790–1864* (Charlottesville: University Press of Virginia, 1989), 133.

30. 1850, Superintendent's Report, Report of the Board of Visitors of the Virginia Military Institute, Virginia Military Institute Archives, 10.

31. 25 June 1851, Superintendent's Report, Report of the Board of Visitors of the Virginia Military Institute Archives, 7–8.

32. *2000 Register*.

33. Green, *Military Education*, 163.

34. *2000 Register*.

35. Smith, *Introductory Address*, 22; For the cadet graduating from the École Polytechnique, see Alfred Landon Rives in *2000 Register*.

36. *2000 Register*.

37. Green, *Military Education*, 145, 159.

38. *2000 Register*; Smith, *Introductory Address*, 12–13.

39. 22 June 1854, Superintendent's Report, Report of the Board of Visitors of the Virginia Military Institute Archives, 30.

40. Gary Lee Downey and Juan C. Lucena, "Knowledge and Professional Identity

in Engineering: Code-Switching and the Metrics of Progress," *History and Technology* 20, no. 4 (December 2004); 401–402; Gary Lee Downey, "Low Cost, Mass Use: American Engineers and the Metrics of Progress," *History and Technology* 23, no. 3 (September 2007): 294.

41. Philip St. George Cocke to Francis H. Smith, 28 May 1850, 048, Superintendent (Francis H. Smith) Correspondence, Incoming Numbered Letters Series (1849–1850), Virginia Military Institute Archives.

42. 25 June 1851, Superintendent's Report, Report of the Board of Visitors of the Virginia Military Institute, Virginia Military Institute Archives.

43. Philip St. George Cocke to General W. H. Richardson, 19 November 1850, letter 050 Superintendent (Francis H. Smith) Correspondence, Incoming Numbered Letters Series (1849–1850), Virginia Military Institute Archives.

44. Merritt Roe Smith, "Technological Determinism in American Culture," in *Does Technology Drive History? The Dilemma of Technological Determinism*, ed. Merritt Roe Smith and Leo Marx (Cambridge, MA: MIT Press, 1994), 7.

45. Smith, "Technological Determinism," 13; Ruth Oldenziel, *Making Technology Masculine: Men, Women and Modern Machines in America, 1870–1945* (Amsterdam: Amsterdam University Press, 1999), 14, 23 43–44.

46. Smith, "Technological Determinism," 9.

47. Frederick Merk and Lois Bannister Merk, *Manifest Destiny and Mission in American History: A Reinterpretation* (1963; Cambridge, MA: Harvard University Press, 1995), xvi, 29, 33, 261, 262, 265.

48. Thomas R. Hietala, *Manifest Design: American Exceptionalism and Empire*, rev. ed. (Ithaca, NY: Cornell University Press, 2003), xiii, xvii.

49. Adam Dahl, *Empire of the People: Settler Colonialism and the Foundations of Modern Democratic Thought* (Lawrence: University Press of Kansas, 2018), 102–103.

50. Merk and Merk, *Manifest Destiny*, 24, 29; Dahl, *Empire of the People*, 101.

51. Reginald Horsman, *Race and Manifest Destiny: The Origins of American Racial Anglo-Saxonism* (Cambridge, MA: Harvard University Press, 1981), 4, 62.

52. Ibid., 162–163, 167, 174.

53. Ibid., 32–33, 38.

54. Ibid., 236; Daniel Walker Howe, *The Political Culture of the American Whigs* (Chicago: University of Chicago Press, 1979), 21; Harry L. Watson, *Liberty and Power: The Politics of Jacksonian America* (New York: Noonday Press, 1990), 242, 245.

55. Horsman, *Race and Manifest Destiny*, 167, 182, 238.

56. Jennings C. Wise, *The Military History of the Virginia Military Institute from 1839–1865* (Lynchburg, VA: J. P. Bell Company, 1915), 62.

57. 18 June 1850, Superintendent's Report, Report of the Board of Visitors of the Virginia Military Institute, Virginia Military Institute Archives, 10.

58. Thermopylae refers to the 480 BC battle in which a force led by Spartans, outnumbered twenty to one, held off the superior Persian force at the mountain pass of Thermopylae for three days and inflicted seven times as many casualties as they received before being defeated. See the *Histories* of Herodotus. Francis H. Smith to Philip St. Geo. Cocke Esqr., 25 March 1847, 313 1844 Feb 10–1848 Dec 30 Superintendent (Francis H. Smith) Correspondence, Outgoing Letter Book, Virginia Military Institute Archives.

59. Claudius Crozet to Francis H. Smith, 26 September 1846, 022 Superintendent (Francis H. Smith) Correspondence, Incoming Numbered Letters Series (1845–1846), Virginia Military Institute Archives; Couper, *Claudius Crozet*, 111, 120.

60. Downey and Lucena, "Knowledge and Professional Identity," 412.

CHAPTER SIX

1. Cives, "The Lexington Arsenal-No. II," *Lexington Gazette*, September 4, 1835, 1.

2. 4 July 1846, Board of Visitor Minutes, vol. 2, 1839–1853, Virginia Military Institute Archives.

3. 6 January 1845, Superintendent's Semi-Annual Report, Superintendent's Annual Reports to the Board of Visitors, Virginia Military Institute Archives, 10.

4. Jennifer Green, *Military Education and the Emerging Middle Class in the Old South* (New York: Cambridge University Press, 2008), 168.

5. Ibid., 43–44; Board of Visitors at the Virginia Military Institute, *Regulations of the Virginia Military Institute at Lexington* (New York: John Wiley, 1848).

6. Green, *Military Education*, 19–20; Jonathan Daniel Wells, *The Origins of the Southern Middle Class, 1800–1861* (Chapel Hill: University of North Carolina Press, 2004), 6, 8, 11–12, 67, 156. Quotation from Wells.

7. Francis H. Smith, *Introductory Address to the Corps of Cadets of the Virginia Military Institute, on the Resumption of Academic Duties, September 2nd, 1856* (Richmond, VA: MacFarlane & Fergusson, 1856), 39.

8. Green, *Military Education*, 52–53.

9. "Lexington Institutions," *Lexington Gazette*, October 5, 1843, 2. Reprinted from the *Richmond Compiler*.

10. 6 January 1845, Superintendent's 1845 Semi-Annular Report, Superintendent's Annual Reports to the Board of Visitors, Virginia Military Institute Archives, 8.

11. David Hackett Fischer, *Albion's Seed: Four British Folkways in America* (New York: Oxford University Press, 1989), 365–368, 385–389, 398–405, 410–418, 615, 628–629, 754–758, 777–782; Edmund S. Morgan, *American Slavery, American Freedom: The Ordeal of Colonial Virginia* (New York: Norton, 1975), 65–69, 84; Colin Woodard, *American Nations: A History of the Eleven Rival Regional Cultures of North America* (New York: Penguin, 2012), 55–56, 102, 104–105.

12. Pierre Bourdieu, *Masculine Domination*, trans. Richard Nice (Stanford, CA: Stanford University Press, 2001), 22–28.

13. 6 January 1845, Superintendent's 1845 Semi-Annular Report, Superintendent's Annual Reports to the Board of Visitors, Virginia Military Institute Archives, 10. Emphasis added.

14. Board of Visitors of the Virginia Military Institute, *Regulations of the Virginia Military Institute at Lexington* (Richmond, VA: Shepherd & Colin, 1839), 4–5.

15. John Thompson Jr. to Samuel McDowell Reid, June 1841, George Coleman File, Cadet Applications & Letters of Recommendation, 1839–1864, Virginia Military Institute Archives.

16. William Browne, M.D., 18 June 1841, Lawson Botts File, Cadet Applications & Letters of Recommendation, 1839–1864, Virginia Military Institute Archives.

17. Nathaniel H. [illegible], 16 June 1846, William R. Terry File, Cadet Applications & Letters of Recommendation, 1839–1864, Virginia Military Institute Archives.

18. Board of Visitors of the Virginia Military Institute, *Regulations of the Virginia Military Institute at Lexington* (Richmond, VA: Shepherd & Colin, 1839), 19, 28; Colonel William Couper, *One Hundred Years at V.M.I.*, 4 vols. (Richmond, VA: Garrett and Massie, 1959), 1:81.

19. Board of Visitors of the Virginia Military Institute, *Regulations of the Virginia Military Institute at Lexington* (Richmond, VA: Shepherd & Colin, 1839), 14; Henry A. Wise, *Drawing Out the Man: The VMI Story* (Charlottesville: University Press of Virginia, 1978), 26.

20. Couper, *One Hundred Years*, 1:83.

21. Board of Visitors of the Virginia Military Institute, *Regulations of the Virginia Military Institute at Lexington* (Richmond, VA: Shepherd & Colin, 1839), 9, 16, 18, 20; 12 September 1839, Board of Visitor Minutes, vol. 2, 1839–1853, Virginia Military Institute Archives.

22. Board of Visitors of the Virginia Military Institute, *Regulations of the Virginia Military Institute at Lexington* (Richmond, VA: Shepherd & Colin, 1839), 20–21.

23. Smith, *Introductory Address*, 8.

24. Board of Visitors of the Virginia Military Institute, *Regulations of the Virginia Military Institute at Lexington* (Richmond, VA: Shepherd & Colin, 1839), 13–14; Board of Visitors of the Virginia Military Institute, *Regulations of the Virginia*

Military Institute at Lexington (New York: John Wiley, 1848), 24; Register of the Officers and Cadets of the U.S. Military Academy, June 1839, Official Register of the Officers and Cadets (1818 to 1966), United States Military Academy Special Collections and Archives, West Point, New York, 20.

25. "Semi-Annual Report of the Superintendent of the Virginia Military Institute, Together with Accompanying Documents," Doc. No. 28, *Journal of the House of Delegates of the Commonwealth of Virginia* (1845), 6.

26. Francis H. Smith, *College Reform* (Philadelphia: Thomas, Cowperthwait & Co., 1851), 36.

27. Cives, "The Lexington Arsenal-No. II," *Lexington Gazette*, September 4, 1835, 1.

28. Smith, *Introductory Address*, 8. Emphasis in original.

29. Smith, *College Reform*, 38–40. Emphasis in original.

30. 15 June 1847, Report on Police by Williamson, Board of Visitor Minutes, vol. 1, 1839 May–1844, Virginia Military Institute Archives, 194; for Smith's and Williamson's attendance at West Point, see United States Military Academy, *Register of the Officers and Cadets of the U.S. Military Academy, June, 1831*.

31. Green, *Military Education*, 92.

32. Charles Royster, *The Destructive War: William Tecumseh Sherman, Stonewall Jackson, and the Americans* (New York: Vintage, 1993), 61–62.

33. Francis H. Smith, *The Regulations of Military Instructions, Applied to the Conduct of Common Schools* (New York: John Wiley, 1849), 28–29.

34. John B. Boles, "Evangelical Protestantism in the Old South: From Religious Dissent to Cultural Dominance" in *Religion in the South: Essays*, ed. Charles Reagan Wilson (Jackson: University Press of Mississippi, 1985), 25; Christine Leigh Heyrman, *Southern Cross: The Beginnings of the Bible Belt* (New York: Knopf, 1997), 5; Donald G. Mathews, *Religion in the Old South* (Chicago: University of Chicago Press, 1977), xv, 38.

35. Boles, "Evangelical Protestantism," 27; Heyrman, *Southern Cross*, 6–7, 8; Mathews, *Religion*, 13, 19, 42, 89.

36. Boles, "Evangelical Protestantism," 15–17, 25–26, 29; Heyrman, *Southern Cross*, 4; Mathews, *Religion*, xvii, 9, 20, 38.

37. 6 January 1845, Superintendent's 1845 Semi-Annular Report, Superintendent's Annual Reports to the Board of Visitors, Virginia Military Institute Archives, 7; Francis H. Smith, *The Virginia Military Institute: Its Building and Rebuilding* (Lynchburg, VA: J. P. Bell Company, 1912), 95.

38. Smith, *Regulations of Military Instructions*, 29.

39. Couper, *One Hundred Years*, 1:96.

40. 4 July 1848, "1848 Report to Governor," Board of Visitor Minutes, vol. 1, 1839 May–1844, Virginia Military Institute Archives, 249–250.

41. 4 July 1848, "1848 Report to Governor," Board of Visitor Minutes, vol. 1, 1839 May–1844, Virginia Military Institute Archives, 249–250.

42. Board of Visitors of the Virginia Military Institute, *Regulations of the Virginia Military Institute at Lexington* (Richmond, VA: Shepherd & Colin, 1839), 15–17, 21.

43. Mathews, *Religion*, xv, 38.

44. Jennifer R. Green, "'Stout Chaps Who Can Bear the Distress': Young Men in Antebellum Military Academies," in *Southern Manhood: Perspectives on Masculinity in the Old South*, ed. Craig Thompson Friend and Lorri Glover (Athens: University of Georgia Press, 2004), 184–185; *The 2000 Register of Former Cadets of the Virginia Military Institute* (Lexington, VA: VMI Alumni Association, 2001).

45. Clyde Griffen, "Reconstructing Masculinity from the Evangelical Revival to the Waning of Progressivism: A Speculative Synthesis," in *Meanings for Manhood: Constructions of Masculinity in Victorian America*, ed. Mark C. Carnes and Clyde Griffen (Chicago: University of Chicago Press, 1990), 185; E. Anthony Rotundo, *American Manhood: Transformations in Masculinity from the Revolution to the Modern Era* (New York: Basic Books, 1993), 18–22; Michael Kimmel, *Manhood in America: A Cultural History* (New York: Free Press, 1996), 44–45, 70–78; Dana D. Nelson, *National Manhood: Capitalist Citizenship and the Imagined Fraternity of White Men* (Durham, NC: Duke University Press, 1998), 6–7, 11–14; Amy S. Greenberg, *Manifest Manhood and the Antebellum American Empire* (New York: Cambridge University Press, 2005), 8–14; Lorri Glover, *Southern Sons: Becoming Men in the New Nation* (Baltimore: Johns Hopkins University Press, 2007), esp. 41.

46. Green, *Military Education*, 60, 98–101, 113–121.

47. Green, "'Stout Chaps,'" 175–176. Stephanie McCurry describes yeomen's masculinity of mastery over others in South Carolina. However, these lowland yeomen were more likely to own slaves, as many as ten, than the yeomen of the backcountry of Virginia. See Stephanie McCurry, *Master of Small Worlds: Yeomen Households, Gender Relations, and the Political Culture of the Antebellum South Carolina Low Country* (New York: Oxford University Press, 1995), 50, 85–91, 218.

48. Fischer, *Albion's Seed*, 629, 668, 765–771; Woodard, *American Nations*, 102, 104–105.

49. 6 January 1845, Superintendent's Semi-Annual Report, Superintendent's Annual Reports to the Board of Visitors, Virginia Military Institute Archives. Emphasis in original.

50. Col. J. T. L. Preston, Historical Sketch of the Establishment and Organization of the Virginia Military Institute, Prepared at the Request of the Board of

Visitors, 4 July 1889, MS 240 (facsimile), Virginia Military Institute Archives, 20.

51. Green, "'Stout Chaps,'" 179–181.

52. 21 November 1839, Report of the Board of Visitors to the Governor, Virginia Military Institute Archives.

53. Col. J. T. L. Preston, Historical Sketch of the Establishment and Organization of the Virginia Military Institute, Prepared at the Request of the Board of Visitors, 4 July 1889, MS 240 (facsimile), Virginia Military Institute Archives, 20–21. Emphasis in original.

54. 4 July 1848, 1848 Report to Governor, Board of Visitor Minutes, vol. 1, 1839 May–1844, Virginia Military Institute Archives.

55. Green, *Military Education*, 60, 75, 80.

56. Ibid., 76, 85, 98–101, 113, 117.

57. Green, *Military Education*, 76, 81, 98, 101, 121, 142–143.

CHAPTER SEVEN

1. William A. Link, *Roots of Secession: Slavery and Politics in Antebellum Virginia* (Chapel Hill: University of North Carolina Press, 2003), 18.

2. F. N. Boney, *John Letcher of Virginia: The Story of Virginia's Civil War Governor* (Tuscaloosa, University of Alabama Press, 1966), 37–38; Link, *Roots of Secession*, 11.

3. Boney, *John Letcher of Virginia*, 37–38; Robert P. Sutton, *Revolution to Secession: Constitution Making in the Old Dominion* (Charlottesville: University Press of Virginia, 1989), 122, 124–130, 132–139; Colonel William Couper, *One Hundred Years at V.M.I.*, 4 vols. (Richmond, VA: Garrett and Massie, 1939), 1:258; Link, *Roots of Secession*, 18, 29–30, 37.

4. Link, *Roots of Secession*, 9–10, 35.

5. Ibid., 63–66.

6. Ibid., 7, 10, 77–79, 107–108, 113, 122–124, 140, 144–145, 159–161; E. M. Morrison, 9 May 1930, Slavery—VMI Reference File, Virginia Military Institute Archives.

7. Link, *Roots of Secession*, 159–161, 163–164, 168.

8. Ibid., 184–185, 189, 192, 195–197.

9. Henry T. Shanks, *The Secession Movement in Virginia, 1847–1861* (1934; reprint, New York: AMS Press, 1971), 116; Link, *Roots of Secession*, 195–201, 208, 210–211.

10. Link, *Roots of Secession*, 213, 217–220, 235, 248–249.

11. Shanks, *Secession Movement in Virginia*, 116; Link, *Roots of Secession*, 224–228, 240, 242.

12. Sutton, *Revolution to Secession*, 140–144, 146–147, 149–150; Link, *Roots of Secession*, 244, 252.

13. Couper, *One Hundred Years*, 1:228.

14. Quoted in ibid., 235.

15. Doc. No. 11, 1856 Annual Report of the Superintendent, Report of the Board of Visitors of the Virginia Military Institute Archives, 4. Emphasis in original.

16. E. M. Morrison, 9 May 1930, Slavery—VMI Reference File, Virginia Military Institute Archives.

17. 1846 Report to Governor, Board of Visitor Minutes, vol. 1, 1839 May–1844, Virginia Military Institute Archives, 153; Edwin L. Dooley Jr., "Francis H. Smith and the Secession Crisis of 1860–1861: The Letters of VMI Superintendent Francis H. Smith," Virginia Military Institute Archives, 4, http://digitalcollections.vmi.edu/digital/collection/p15821coll14/id/552.

18. Henry A. Wise, *Drawing Out the Man: The VMI Story* (Charlottesville: University Press of Virginia, 1978), 28.

19. Couper, *One Hundred Years*, 2:24–25, 42.

20. Wise, *Drawing Out the Man*, 34; Randolph P. Shaffner, *The Father of Virginia Military Institute: A Biography of Colonel J.T.L. Preston, CSA* (Jefferson, NC: McFarland & Company, 2014), 128, 131.

21. Edwin L. Dooley Jr., ed., "Francis H. Smith and the Secession Crisis of 1860–1861: The Letters of VMI Superintendent Francis H. Smith," Virginia Military Institute Archives, 16, http://digitalcollections.vmi.edu/digital/collection/p15821coll14/id/552.

22. Shaffner, *Father of Virginia Military Institute*, 132, 189–194.

23. Edwin L. Dooley Jr., ed., "Francis H. Smith and the Secession Crisis of 1860–1861: The Letters of VMI Superintendent Francis H. Smith," Virginia Military Institute Archives, 5, 6, 9, 16, 32, 42–43, http://digitalcollections.vmi.edu/digital/collection/p15821coll14/id/552.

24. Ibid.

25. Wise, *Drawing Out the Man*, 34–48; Rod Andrew Jr., *Long Gray Lines: The Southern Military School Tradition, 1839–1915* (Chapel Hill: University of North Carolina Press, 2001), 27, 31.

26. Andrew, *Long Gray Lines*, 36–38, 47, 62.

Bibliography

PRIMARY SOURCES

Manuscript Collections

Library of Virginia
    Executive Papers
    Virginia General Assembly Legislative Petitions, Rockbridge County
United States Military Academy, Special Collections and Archives
    Annual Report of the Board of Visitors, 1833
    Official Register of the Officers and Cadets, 1818 to 1966
Virginia Military Institute, Virginia Military Institute Archives
    Board of Visitor Minutes, vol. 1, 1839–1844
    Board of Visitor Minutes, vol. 2, 1839–1853
    Cadet Applications & Letters of Recommendation, 1839–1864
    Cadet Architectural Drawings
    Faculty and Departmental Reports, 1843–1844
    Manuscript Collection
    Preston-Smith Letters
    Publications Catalog, 1840–1864
    Register of the Officers and Cadets, 1843–1851
    Reports of the Board of Visitors to the Governor
    Superintendent (Francis H. Smith) Correspondence
    Superintendent's Annual Reports to the Board of Visitors
Washington and Lee University, James Graham Leyburn Library
    Board of Trustees Minutes
    Franklin Society and Library Company Papers

Government Publications

Acts of the General Assembly of Virginia, 1835–1839.

Board of Visitors of the Virginia Military Institute. *Regulations of the Virginia Military Institute at Lexington*. Richmond, VA: Shepherd & Colin, 1839.

Board of Visitors of the Virginia Military Institute. *Regulations of the Virginia Military Institute at Lexington*. New York: John Wiley, 1848.

General Assembly of Virginia. *The Code of Virginia: With the Declaration of Independence and Constitution of the United States and the Declaration of Rights and Constitution of Virginia*. Richmond, VA: William F. Ritchie, 1849.

General Assembly of Virginia, Earl G. Swem, and John W. Williams. *A Register of the General Assembly of Virginia, 1776–1918, and of the Constitutional Convention*. Richmond, VA: Commonwealth of Virginia, 1918.

Hening, William Waller. *The Statutes at Large: Being a Collection of all the Laws of Virginia, from the First Session of the Legislature, in the Year 1619*. Vol. 12. Richmond, Virginia, 1823.

Journal of the House of Delegates of the Commonwealth of Virginia, 1835–1845.

Proceedings and Debates of the Virginia State Convention of 1829–1830. Richmond, VA: Samuel Shepherd, 1830.

Newspapers

Lexington Gazette (Lexington, Virginia)
Valley Star (Lexington, Virginia)

Published Primary Sources

Bartlett, William H. C. *An Elementary Treatise on Optics, Designed for the Use of the Cadets of the United States Military Academy*. New York: Wiley and Putnam, 1839.

Boucharlat, J.-L. *Éléments de calcul différentiel et de calcul intégral*. 4th ed. Paris: Bachelier, 1830.

Boucharlat, J.-L. *Éléments de mécanique*. 3rd ed. Paris: Bachelier, Imprimeur-Libraire de L'École Polytechnique, 1840.

Davies, Charles. *Elements of Descriptive Geometry, with Their Application to Spherical Trigonometry, Spherical Projections, and Warped Surfaces*. Philadelphia: H. C. Carey and I. Lea, 1826.

Davies, Charles. *Elements of Surveying, and Navigation, with Descriptions of the*

Instruments and the Necessary Tables. Rev. ed. New York: A. S. Barnes & Co., 1854.

Davies, Charles. *A Treatise on Shades and Shadows, and Linear Perspective.* 2nd ed. New York: Wiley & Putnam, Collins, Keese & Co., 1838.

Crozet, Claudius. *Outline of the Improvements in the State of Virginia.* Philadelphia: C. Sherman, 1848.

Eaton, Amos. *Prodromus of a Practical Treatise on the Mathematical Arts.* Troy, NY: Elias Gates, 1838.

Legendre, A. M. *Elements of Geometry and Trigonometry; With Notes.* Translated by David Brewster. Revised by James Ryan. New York: N. & J. White; Collins & Hannay; Collins & Co.; James Ryan, 1832.

Mahan, D. H. *A Complete Treatise on Field Fortification, with the General Outlines of the Principles Regulating the Arrangement, the Attack, and the Defence of Permanent Works.* New York: Wiley & Long, 1836.

Mahan, D. H. *An Elementary Course of Civil Engineering: For the Use of Cadets of the United States' Military Academy.* 6th ed. New York: John Wiley, 1864.

Rensselaer Institute. *Rensselaer Institute.* Troy, NY: Prescott & Wilson, 1847.

Rensselaer Polytechnic Institute. *Forty-Fifth Annual Register of the Rensselaer Polytechnic Institute, 1868–1869.* Troy, NY: William H. Young, 1868.

Smith, Francis H. *College Reform.* Philadelphia: Thomas, Cowperthwait & Co., 1851.

Smith, Francis H. *An Elementary Treatise on Algebra: Prepared for the Use of the Cadets of the Virginia Military Institute, and Adapted to the Present State of Mathematical Instruction in the Schools, Academies, and Colleges, of the United States.* Philadelphia: Thomas, Cowperthwait & Co., 1850.

Smith, Francis H. *An Elementary Treatise on Analytical Geometry: Translated from the French of J. B. Biot, for the use of the Cadets of the Virginia Military Institute at Lexington, Va.: and Adapted to the Present State of Mathematical Instruction in the Colleges of the United States.* Rev ed. Philadelphia: Thomas, Cowperthwait & Co., 1846.

Smith, Francis H. *Introductory Address to the Corps of Cadets of the Virginia Military Institute, on the Resumption of Academic Duties, September 2nd, 1856.* Richmond, VA: MacFarlane & Fergusson, 1856.

Smith, Francis H. *The Regulations of Military Instructions, Applied to the Conduct of Common Schools.* New York: John Wiley, 1849.

Smith, Francis H. *The Virginia Military Institute: Its Building and Rebuilding.* Lynchburg, VA: J. P. Bell Company, 1912.

Williamson, Major Thomas H. *An Elementary Course of Architecture and Civil Engineering, Compiled from the Most Approved Authors for the Use of the Cadets of the Virginia Military Institute.* Lexington, VA: Samuel Gillock, 1850.

SECONDARY SOURCES

Alder, Ken. "French Engineers Become Professionals; or, How Meritocracy Made Knowledge Objective." In *The Sciences in Enlightened Europe*, edited by William Clark, Jan Golinski, and Simon Schaffer, 94-125. Chicago: University of Chicago Press, 1999.

Anderson, Marvin J. "The Architectural Education of Nineteenth-Century American Engineers: Dennis Hart Mahan at West Point." *Journal of the Society of Architectural Historians* 67, no. 2 (2008): 222-247.

Andrew, Rod, Jr. *Long Gray Lines: The Southern Military School Tradition, 1839-1915*. Chapel Hill: University of North Carolina Press, 2001.

Antoniou, Yiannis, Michalis Assimakopoulos, and Konstantinos Chatzis, eds. "National Identities of Engineers." Special issue, *History and Technology* 23, no. 3 (2007).

Artz, Frederick B. *The Development of Technical Education in France, 1500-1850*. Cambridge, MA: MIT Press, 1966.

Belhoste, Bruno. "The École Polytechnique and Mathematics in Nineteenth-Century France." In *Changing Images in Mathematics: From the French Revolution to the New Millennium*, edited by Umberto Bottazzini and Amy Dahan Dalmedico, 15-30. London: Routledge, 2001.

Belhoste, Bruno, and Konstantinos Chatzis. "From Technical Corps to Technocratic Power: French State Engineers and Their Professional and Cultural Universe in the First Half of the 19th Century." *History and Technology* 23, no. 3 (2007): 209-225.

Bix, Amy Sue. *Girls Coming to Tech! A History of American Engineering Education for Women*. Cambridge, MA: MIT Press, 2013.

Bledstein, Burton J. *The Culture of Professionalism: The Middle Class and the Development of Higher Education in America*. New York: Norton, 1976.

Bloch, Ruth H. "The Gendered Meanings of Virtue in Revolutionary America." *Signs* 13, no. 1 (1987): 37-58.

Boles, John B. "Evangelical Protestantism in the Old South: From Religious Dissent to Cultural Dominance." In *Religion in the South: Essays*, edited by Charles Reagan Wilson, 13-34. Jackson: University Press of Mississippi, 1985.

Boney, F. N. *John Letcher of Virginia: The Story of Virginia's Civil War Governor*. Tuscaloosa: University of Alabama Press, 1966.

Bourdieu, Pierre. *Masculine Domination*. Translated by Richard Nice. Stanford, CA: Stanford University Press, 2001.

Brinkley, John Luster. *On This Hill: A Narrative History of Hampden-Sydney College, 1774-1994*. Hampden-Sydney, VA: Hampden-Sydney College, 1994.

Brod, Harry, and Michael Kaufman, eds. *Theorizing Masculinities*. Thousand Oaks, CA: Sage Publications, 1994.

Brodie, Laura Fairchild. *Breaking Out: VMI and the Coming of Women*. New York: Vintage, 2000.

Brown, John K. "Design Plans, Working Drawings, National Styles: Engineering Practice in Great Britain and the United States, 1775–1945." *Technology and Culture* 41, no. 2 (2000): 195–238.

Bruce, Philip Alexander. *History of the University of Virginia, 1819–1919*. 5 vols. New York: Macmillan Company, 1920.

Burack, Cynthia, and Suzanne E. Franks. "Telling Stories about Engineering: Group Dynamics and Resistance to Diversity." *NWSA Journal* 16, no. 1 (2004): 79–95.

Calhoun, Daniel Hovey. *The American Civil Engineer: Origins and Conflict*. Cambridge, MA: Technology Press, 1960.

Calvert, Monte A. *The Mechanical Engineer in America, 1830–1910: Professional Cultures in Conflict*. Baltimore: Johns Hopkins University Press, 1967.

Carrigan, Tim, Bob Connell, and John Lee. "Toward a New Sociology of Masculinity." In *The Masculinity Studies Reader*, edited by Rachel Adams and David Savran, 99–118. Malden, MA: Blackwell Publishers, 2002.

Cech, Erin A., and Tom J. Waidzunas. "Navigating the Heteronormativity of Engineering: The Experiences of Lesbian, Gay, and Bisexual Students." *Engineering Studies* 3, no. 1 (2011): 1–24.

Chatzis, Konstantinos. "Introduction: The National Identities of Engineers." *History and Technology* 23, no. 3 (September 2007): 193–196.

Chatzis, Konstantinos. "Theory and Practice in the Education of French Engineers from the Middle of the 18th Century to the Present." *Archives internationales d'histoire des sciences* 60, no. 164 (2010): 43–78.

Cohen, Jeffrey A. "Building a Discipline: Early Institutional Settings for Architectural Education in Philadelphia, 1804–1890." *Journal of the Society of Architectural Historians* 53, no. 2 (1994): 139–183.

Cohen, Michael David. *Reconstructing the Campus: Higher Education and the American Civil War*. Charlottesville: University of Virginia Press, 2012.

Cohen, Philip. "More Women Are Doctors and Lawyers Than Ever—but Progress Is Stalling." *The Atlantic*, December 11, 2012. http://www.theatlantic.com/sexes/archive/2012/12/more-women-are-doctors-and-lawyers-than-ever-but-progress-is-stalling/266115/.

Couper, William. *Claudius Crozet: Soldier-Scholar-Educator-Engineer (1789–1864)*. Charlottesville, VA: The Historical Publishing Company, 1936.

Couper, William. *One Hundred Years at V.M.I.* 4 vols. Richmond, VA: Garrett and Massie, 1939.

Crawford, Stephen. "The Making of the French Engineer." In *Engineering Labour: Technical Workers in Comparative Perspective*, edited by Peter Meiksins and Chris Smith, 98–131. New York: Verso, 1996.

Crenshaw, Ollinger. *General Lee's College: The Rise and Growth of Washington and Lee University.* New York: Random House, 1969.

Cress, Lawrence Delbert. *Citizens in Arms: The Army and the Militia in American Society to the War of 1812.* Chapel Hill: University of North Carolina Press, 1982.

Crosland, M. P. "Biot, Jean-Baptiste." In *Dictionary of Scientific Biography*, volume 2, edited by Charles Coulston Gillispie, 133–140. New York: Charles Scribner's Sons, 1970.

Dahl, Adam. *Empire of the People: Settler Colonialism and the Foundations of Modern Democratic Thought.* Lawrence: University Press of Kansas, 2018.

DeBow, J. D. B. *The Seventh Census of the United States: 1850.* Washington, DC: Robert Armstrong, 1853.

Downey, Gary Lee. "Low Cost, Mass Use: American Engineers and the Metrics of Progress." *History and Technology* 23, no. 3 (September 2007): 289–308.

Downey, Gary Lee, and Juan C. Lucena. "Knowledge and Professional Identity in Engineering: Code-Switching and the Metrics of Progress." *History and Technology* 20, no. 4 (December 2004): 393–420.

Dreicer, Gregory K. "Building Bridges and Boundaries: The Lattice and the Tube, 1820–1860." *Technology and Culture* 51, no. 1 (2010): 126–163.

Edwards, R. A. R. *Words Made Flesh: Nineteenth-Century Deaf Education and the Growth of Deaf Culture.* New York: New York University Press, 2012.

Falcone, Alissa, Scott Gabriel Knowles, Jonson Miller, Tiago Saraiva, and Amy E. Slaton. "Continuous Reinvention: A History of Engineering Education at Drexel University." In *Building Drexel: The University and Its City, 1891–2016*, edited by Richardson Dilworth and Scott Gabriel Knowles, 39–66. Philadelphia: Temple University Press, 2017.

Faulkner, Wendy. "Doing Gender in Engineering Workplace Cultures. I. Observations from the Field." *Engineering Studies* 1, no. 1 (2009): 3–18.

Faulkner, Wendy. "Doing Gender in Engineering Workplace Cultures. II. Gender In/authenticity and the In/visibility Paradox." *Engineering Studies* 1, no. 3 (2009): 169–189.

Fischer, David Hackett. *Albion's Seed: Four British Folkways in America.* New York: Oxford University Press, 1989.

Frehill, Lisa M. "The Gendered Construction of the Engineering Profession in the United States, 1893–1920." *Men and Masculinities* 6, no. 4 (April 2004): 383–403.

Friend, Craig Thompson, and Lorri Glover, eds. *Southern Manhood: Perspectives on Masculinity in the Old South*. Athens: University of Georgia Press, 2004.

Geiger, Roger L. "The Rise and Fall of Useful Knowledge: Higher Education for Science, Agriculture, and the Mechanic Arts, 1850–1875." In *The American College in the Nineteenth Century*, edited by Roger L. Geiger, 153–168. Nashville, TN: Vanderbilt University Press, 2000.

Glover, Lorri. *Southern Sons: Becoming Men in the New Nation*. Baltimore: Johns Hopkins University Press, 2007.

Gossett, Thomas F. *Race: The History of an Idea in America*. 2nd ed. New York: Oxford University Press, 1997.

Gouévitch, Irina, and Peter Jones, eds. "Theme Issue: Becoming an Engineer in Eighteenth-Century Europe: The Construction of a Professional Identity." Special issue, *Engineering Studies* 3, no. 3 (2011): 149–253.

Green, Jennifer R. *Military Education and the Emerging Middle Class in the Old South*. New York: Cambridge University Press, 2008.

Green, Jennifer R. "'Practical Progress Is the Watchword': Military Education and the Expansion of Opportunity in the Old South." *Journal of the Historical Society* 5, no. 3 (Fall 2005): 363–390.

Green, Jennifer R. "'Stout Chaps Who Can Bear the Distress': Young Men in Antebellum Military Academies." In *Southern Manhood: Perspectives on Masculinity in the Old South*, edited by Craig Thompson Friend and Lorri Glover, 174–195. Athens: University of Georgia Press, 2004.

Greenberg, Amy S. *Manifest Manhood and the Antebellum American Empire*. New York: Cambridge University Press, 2005.

Griffen, Clyde. "Reconstructing Masculinity from the Evangelical Revival to the Waning of Progressivism: A Speculative Synthesis." In *Meanings for Manhood: Constructions of Masculinity in Victorian America*, edited by Mark C. Carnes and Clyde Griffen, 183–204. Chicago: University of Chicago Press, 1990.

Grzanka, Patrick R. "The (Intersectional) Self and Society." In *Intersectionality: A Foundations and Frontiers Reader*, edited by Patrick R. Grzanka, 67–72. Boulder, CO: Westview Press, 2014.

Hacker, Sally L. "Mathematization of Engineering: Limits on Women and the Field." In *Machina Ex Dea: Feminist Perspectives on Technology*, edited by Joan Rothschild, 38–58. New York: Pergamon Press, 1983.

Hall, Aaron. "Slaves of the State: Infrastructure and Governance through Slavery in the Antebellum South." *Journal of American History* 106, no. 1 (June 2019): 19–46.

Hannaford, Ivan. *Race: The History of an Idea in the West*. Washington, DC: Woodrow Wilson Center Press, 1996.

Heyrman, Christine Leigh. *Southern Cross: The Beginnings of the Bible Belt*. New York: Knopf, 1997.

Hicks, Marie. *Programmed Inequality: How Britain Discarded Women Technologists and Lost Its Edge in Computing*. Cambridge, MA: MIT Press, 2017.

Hietala, Thomas R. *Manifest Design: American Exceptionalism and Empire*. Rev. ed. Ithaca, NY: Cornell University Press, 2003.

Hoganson, Kristin L. *Fighting for American Manhood: How Gender Politics Provoked the Spanish-American and Philippine-American Wars*. New Haven, CT: Yale University Press, 1998.

hooks, bell. *We Real Cool: Black Men and Masculinity*. New York: Routledge, 2004.

Horsman, Reginald. *Race and Manifest Destiny: The Origins of American Racial Anglo-Saxonism*. Cambridge, MA: Harvard University Press, 1981.

Hoskin, Keith. "Textbooks and the Mathematisation of American Reality: The Role of Charles Davies and the US Military Academy at West Point." *Paradigm* 13 (1994): 11–41.

Howe, Daniel Walker. *The Political Culture of the American Whigs*. Chicago: University of Chicago Press, 1979.

Hunter, Robert F. "Turnpike Construction in Antebellum Virginia." In *The Engineer in America: A Historical Anthology from* Technology and Culture, edited by Terry S. Reynolds, 43–68. Chicago: University of Chicago Press, 1991.

Hunter, Robert F., and Edwin L. Dooley Jr. *Claudius Crozet: French Engineer in America, 1790–1864*. Charlottesville: University Press of Virginia, 1989.

Isaac, Rhys. *The Transformation of Virginia: 1740–1790*. Chapel Hill: University of North Carolina Press, 1982.

Jacobson, Matthew Frye. *Whiteness of a Different Color: European Immigrants and the Alchemy of Race*. Cambridge, MA: Harvard University Press, 1998.

Jeffords, Susan. *The Remasculinization of America: Gender and the Vietnam War*. Bloomington: Indiana University Press, 1989.

Kaestle, Carl F. *Pillars of the Republic: Common Schools and American Society, 1780–1860*. New York: Hill and Wang, 1983.

Kann, Mark E. *The Gendering of American Politics: Founding Mothers, Founding Fathers, and Political Patriarchy*. Westport, CT: Praeger, 1999.

Keyssar, Alexander. *The Right to Vote: The Contested History of Democracy in the United States*. With a new afterword. New York: Basic Books, 2000.

Kidwell, Peggy Aldrich, Amy Ackerberg-Hastings, and David Lindsay Roberts. *Tools of American Mathematics Teaching, 1800–2000*. Baltimore: Johns Hopkins University Press, 2008.

Kimmel, Michael. *Manhood in America: A Cultural History*. New York: Free Press, 1996.

Kranakis, Eda. *Constructing a Bridge: An Exploration of Engineering Culture, Design, and Research in Nineteenth-Century France and America*. Cambridge, MA: MIT Press, 1997.

Kranzberg, Melvin, ed. *Technological Education—Technological Style*. San Francisco: San Francisco Press, 1986.

Larson, John Lauritz. *Internal Improvement: National Public Works and the Promise of Popular Government in the Early United States*. Chapel Hill: University of North Carolina Press, 2001.

Link, William A. *Roots of Secession: Slavery and Politics in Antebellum Virginia*. Chapel Hill: University of North Carolina Press, 2003.

Mahon, John K. *History of the Militia and the National Guard*. New York: Macmillan, 1983.

Masur, Louis P. "Nat Turner and Sectional Crisis." In *Nat Turner: A Slave Rebellion in History and Memory*, edited by Kenneth S. Greenberg, 148–161. New York: Oxford University Press, 2003.

Mathews, Donald G. *Religion in the Old South*. Chicago: University of Chicago Press, 1977.

McCurry, Stephanie. *Master of Small Worlds: Yeomen Households, Gender Relations, and the Political Culture of the Antebellum South Carolina Low Country*. New York: Oxford University Press, 1995.

Meiksins, Peter. "Engineers in the United States: A House Divided." In *Engineering Labour: Technical Workers in Comparative Perspective*, edited by Peter Meiksins and Chris Smith, 61–97. New York: Verso, 1996.

Meiksins, Peter, and Chris Smith, eds. *Engineering Labour: Technical Workers in Comparative Perspective*. New York: Verso, 1996.

Merk, Frederick, and Lois Bannister Merk. *Manifest Destiny and Mission in American History: A Reinterpretation*. 1963. Reprint, Cambridge, MA: Harvard University Press, 1995.

Miller, Jonson. "Pathways and Purposes of the 'French Tradition' of Engineering in Antebellum America: The Case of the Virginia Military Institute." *Engineering Studies* 5, no. 2 (2013): 117–136.

Millett, Allan R., Peter Maslowski, and William B. Feis. *For the Common Defense: A Military History of the United States from 1607 to 2012*. Rev. ed. New York: Free Press, 2012.

Morgan, Edmund S. *American Slavery, American Freedom: The Ordeal of Colonial Virginia*. New York: Norton, 1975.

Morrison, James L., Jr. *"The Best School in the World": West Point, the Pre-Civil War Years, 1833–1866*. Kent, OH: Kent State University Press, 1986.

Morton, Oren F. *A History of Rockbridge County, Virginia*. Staunton, VA: McClure, 1920.

Mullins, Jeffrey A. "'In the Sweat of Thy Brow': Education, Manual Labor, and the Market Revolution." In *Cultural Change and the Market Revolution in America, 1789–1860*, edited by Scott C. Martin, 143–180. New York: Rowman & Littlefield, 2005.

Nason, Henry B., ed. *Biographical Record of the Officers and Graduates of the Rensselaer Polytechnic Institute, 1824–1886*. Troy, NY: William H. Young, 1887.

National Action Council for Minorities in Engineering. *2011 NACME Data Book: A Comprehensive Analysis of the "New" American Dilemma*. White Plains, NY: NACME, 2011.

National Action Council for Minorities in Engineering. *2013 NACME Data Book: A Comprehensive Analysis of the "New" American Dilemma*. White Plains, NY: NACME, 2013.

National Center for Education Statistics. "Degrees Conferred by Sex and Race." https://nces.ed.gov/fastfacts/display.asp?id=72.

Nelson, Dana D. *National Manhood: Capitalist Citizenship and the Imagined Fraternity of White Men*. Durham, NC: Duke University Press, 1998.

Noble, Stuart G. *A History of American Education*. Rev. ed. Westport, CT: Greenwood Press, 1970.

Oldenziel, Ruth. *Making Technology Masculine: Men, Women and Modern Machines in America, 1870–1945*. Amsterdam: Amsterdam University Press, 1999.

Pappas, George S. *To the Point: The United States Military Academy, 1802–1902*. Westport, CT: Praeger, 1993.

Pawley, Alice L. "What Counts as 'Engineering': Toward a Redefinition." In *Engineering and Social Justice: In the University and Beyond*, edited by Caroline Baille, Alice L. Pawley, and Donna Riley, 59–85. West Lafayette, IN: Purdue University Press, 2012.

Picon, Antoine. "The Engineer as Judge: Engineering Analysis and Political Economy in Eighteenth Century France." *Engineering Studies* 1, no. 1 (2009): 19–34.

Picon, Antoine. *French Architects and Engineers in the Age of Enlightenment*. Translated by Martin Thom. Cambridge: Cambridge University Press, 1992.

Picon, Antoine. "Technological Traditions and National Identities: A Comparison between France and Great Britain During the XIXth Century." In *Science, Technology, and the 19th Century State*, edited by Efthymios Nicolaidis and Konstantinos Chatzis, 13–21. Athens, Greece: Institute for Neohellenic Research/National Hellenic Research Foundation, 2000.

Pierson, George Wilson. *A Yale Book of Numbers: Historical Statistics of the College and University, 1701–1976*. New Haven, CT: Yale University Press, 1983.

Pugh, David G. *Sons of Liberty: The Masculine Mind in Nineteenth Century America*. Westport, CT: Greenwood Press, 1983.

Rae, John B. "Engineers Are People." *Technology and Culture* 16, no. 3 (July 1975): 404–418.

Reynolds, Terry S. "The Education of Engineers in America before the Morrill Act of 1862." *History of Education Quarterly* 32, no. 4 (1992): 459–482.

Reynolds, Terry S. "The Engineer in 19th-Century America." In *The Engineer in America: A Historical Anthology from* Technology and Culture, edited by Terry S. Reynolds, 7–26. Chicago: University of Chicago Press, 1991.

Rickets, Palmer C. *Introduction to Extracts from the Report of Director B. Franklin Greene Upon the Reorganization of the Institute*. Troy, NY: Rensselaer Polytechnic Institute, 1931.

Riley, Donna. *Engineering and Social Justice: Synthesis Lectures on Engineers, Technology, and Society*. San Rafael, CA: Morgan and Claypool, 2008.

Roediger, David R. *The Wages of Whiteness: Race and the Making of the American Working Class*. Rev. ed. New York: Verso, 1999.

Rosser, Sue V. "Using POWRE to ADVANCE: Institutional Barriers Identified by Women Scientists and Engineers." *NWSA Journal* 16, no. 1 (2004): 50–78.

Rothman, David J. *The Discovery of the Asylum: Social Order and Disorder in the New Republic*. Boston: Little, Brown, 1971.

Rotundo, E. Anthony. *American Manhood: Transformations in Masculinity from the Revolution to the Modern Era*. New York: Basic Books, 1993.

Royster, Charles. *The Destructive War: William Tecumseh Sherman, Stonewall Jackson, and the Americans*. New York: Vintage, 1993.

Rudolph, Frederick. *The American College and University: A History*. 1962. Reprint, with an introductory essay and supplemental bibliography by John R. Thelin. Athens: University of Georgia Press, 1990.

Sellers, Charles. *The Market Revolution: Jacksonian America, 1815–1846*. New York: Oxford University Press, 1991.

Shade, William G. *Democratizing the Old Dominion: Virginia and the Second Party System, 1824–1861*. Charlottesville: University Press of Virginia, 1996.

Shaffner, Randolph P. *The Father of Virginia Military Institute: A Biography of Colonel J.T.L. Preston, CSA*. Jefferson, NC: McFarland & Company, 2014.

Shalhope, Robert E. "Republicanism and Early American Historiography." *The William and Mary Quarterly* 39, no. 2 (1982): 334–356.

Shanks, Henry T. *The Secession Movement in Virginia, 1847–1861*. 1934. Reprint, New York: AMS Press, 1971.

Sheriff, Carol. *The Artificial River: The Erie Canal and the Paradox of Progress, 1817–1862.* New York: Hill and Wang, 1996.

Shields, Stephanie A. "Gender: An Intersectional Perspective." *Sex Roles* 59, nos. 5–6 (September 2008): 301–311.

Singh, Nikhil Pal. *Black Is a Country: Race and the Unfinished Struggle for Democracy.* Cambridge, MA: Harvard University Press, 2004.

Slaton, Amy E. *Race, Rigor, and Selectivity in U.S. Engineering: The History of an Occupational Color Line.* Cambridge, MA: Harvard University Press, 2010.

Smith, Merritt Roe. "Technological Determinism in American Culture." In *Does Technology Drive History? The Dilemma of Technological Determinism,* edited by Merritt Roe Smith and Leo Marx, 1–35. Cambridge, MA: MIT Press, 1994.

Snider, William D. *Light on the Hill: A History of the University of North Carolina at Chapel Hill.* Chapel Hill: University of North Carolina Press, 1992.

Spring, Joel. *The American School: From the Puritans to the Trump Era.* 10th ed. New York: Routledge, 2018.

Sutton, Robert P. *Revolution to Secession: Constitution Making in the Old Dominion.* Charlottesville: University Press of Virginia, 1989.

Tonso, Karen L. *On the Outskirts of Engineering: Learning Identity, Gender, and Power via Engineering Practice.* Rotterdam: Sense Publishers, 2007.

Turner, Charles W. "The Franklin Society, 1800–1891." *The Virginia Magazine of History and Biography* 66 (October 1958): 432–447.

The 2000 Register of Former Cadets of the Virginia Military Institute. Lexington, VA: VMI Alumni Association, 2001.

United States Census Bureau. "STEM Occupations by Sex, Race, and Hispanic Origin: 2012–2016 ACS 5-Year." https://www.census.gov/data/tables/time-series/demo/industry-occupation/stem.html.

Watson, Harry L. *Liberty and Power: The Politics of Jacksonian America.* New York: Noonday Press, 1990.

Wells, Jonathan Daniel. *The Origins of the Southern Middle Class, 1800–1861.* Chapel Hill: University of North Carolina Press, 2004.

Wertenbaker, Thomas Jefferson. *Princeton, 1746–1896.* Princeton, NJ: Princeton University Press, 1946.

Wiegman, Robyn. *American Anatomies: Theorizing Race and Gender.* Durham, NC: Duke University Press, 1995.

Williams, Heather Andrea. *Self-Taught: African American Education in Slavery and Freedom.* Chapel Hill: University of North Carolina Press, 2005.

Wineman, Bradford. "J.T.L. Preston and the Origins of the Virginia Military Institute, 1834–1842." *The Virginia Magazine of History and Biography* 114, no. 2 (2006): 226–261.

Wise, Henry A. *Drawing Out the Man: The VMI Story*. Charlottesville: University Press of Virginia, 1978.

Wise, Jennings C. *The Military History of the Virginia Military Institute from 1839–1865*. Lynchburg, VA: J. P. Bell Company, 1915.

Wisnioski, Matthew. *Engineers for Change: Competing Visions of Technology in 1960s America*. Cambridge, MA: MIT Press, 2012.

Wood, Gordon, S. *The Radicalism of the American Revolution*. New York: Vintage Books, 1991.

Woodard, Colin. *American Nations: A History of the Eleven Rival Regional Cultures of North America*. New York: Penguin, 2012.

Woods, Mary N. *From Craft to Profession: The Practice of Architecture in Nineteenth-Century America*. Berkeley: University of California Press, 1999.

UNPUBLISHED DISSERTATIONS

Baker, Dean Paul. "The Partridge Connection: Alden Partridge and Southern Military Education." PhD diss., University of North Carolina at Chapel Hill, 1986.

Weatherhead, Arthur Clason. "The History of Collegiate Education in Architecture in the United States." PhD diss., Columbia University, 1941.

Acknowledgments

Like every historian, I am indebted to the librarians, archivists, and their staff who are not only competent and patient but who actually take pleasure in helping us interlopers grub up precious historical materials. My thanks to the staffs of the American Philosophical Society; the Hagley Museum and Library, especially Chris Baer for guiding me through the numerous maps and cards on Virginia's antebellum infrastructure projects; the Historical Society of Pennsylvania; the Library Company of Philadelphia, especially Connie King; the Tennessee State Library and Archives; the University of Pennsylvania Libraries; Vanderbilt University's Special Collections and University Archives, especially Teresa Gray; the Virginia Museum of History and Culture; the Virginia Military Institute Library and Archives, especially Diane Jacob, Mary-Laura Kludy, and Megan Newman; the Virginia State Archives and Libraries; the Virginia Tech Library and Special Collections; and the Washington and Lee University Archives and Special Collections.

Many colleagues, some former teachers or dissertation committee members, aided me along the way and made this work possible. My thanks to Dan Breslau, Gary Downey, and Ann Laberge who helped get this project started. Gary has offered continued aid and guidance long since. Marian Mollin taught me how to be a historian. Many colleagues, friends, and teachers at Virginia Tech offered advice, criticism, encouragement, and insight, including Donna Augustine, Chris Clement, Saul Halfon, Brent Jesiek, Jane Lehr, Anita Puckett, Jody Roberts, and participants in the Research in Engineering Studies group. Likewise, I have received much help from colleagues at Drexel University, including Scott Knowles, Jonathan Seitz, and Amy Slaton. Scott found me invaluable time for writing and additional research. Amy and also my partner Jo Freehand kept me going by reminding me of the value of the project when I doubted that it was worth continuing. Amy read chapters and revealed insights that I hadn't even realized were in the manuscript. Jo read several drafts and helped me improve my argument. I thank the staff and anonymous reviewers of *Engineering Studies*, whose comments greatly improved chapter 4, as well as Lever Press editor Beth Bouloukos, production manager Amanda Karby, the extraordinary copy editor Alja Kooistra, and anonymous reviewers of this book's manuscript for criticizing, finding value in, and improving it.

A 2005–2006 Virginia Tech College of Liberal Arts and Human Sciences Graduate Endowed Scholarship helped me start the project. A Consortium for History of Science, Technology and Medicine 2014–2015 Research Fellowship helped me finish it. I thank both institutions for their support.

CPSIA information can be obtained
at www.ICGtesting.com
Printed in the USA
BVHW040654280820
587506BV00008B/92